The Economics of Tourism and Sustainable Development

THE FONDAZIONE ENI ENRICO MATTEI (FEEM) SERIES ON ECONOMICS AND THE ENVIRONMENT

Series Editor: Carlo Carraro, *University of Venice, Venice and Research Director, Fondazione Eni Enrico Mattei (FEEM), Milan, Italy*

Editorial Board

Kenneth J. Arrow, *Department of Economics, Stanford University, Stanford, California, USA*

William J. Baumol, *CV Starr Center for Applied Economics, New York University, New York City, USA*

Partha Dasgupta, *Cambridge University, Cambridge, UK*

Karl-Göran Mäler, *The Beijer International Institute of Ecological Economics, The Royal Swedish Academy of Sciences, Stockholm, Sweden*

Ignazio Musu, *University of Venice, Venice, Italy*

Henry Tulkens, *Center for Operations Research and Econometrics (CORE), Université Catholique de Louvain, Louvain-la-Neuve, Belgium*

The Fondazione Eni Enrico Mattei (FEEM) was established in 1989 as a non-profit, non-partisan research institution. It carries out high-profile research in the fields of economic development, energy and the environment, thanks to an international network of researchers who contribute to disseminate knowledge through seminars, congresses and publications. The main objective of the Fondazione is to foster interactions among academic, industrial and public policy spheres in an effort to find solutions to environmental problems. Over the years it has thus become a major European institution for research on sustainable development and the privileged interlocutor of a number of leading national and international policy institutions.

The Fondazione Eni Enrico Mattei (FEEM) Series on Economics and the Environment publishes leading-edge research findings providing an authoritative and up-to-date source of information in all aspects of sustainable development. FEEM research outputs are the results of a sound and acknowledged cooperation between its internal staff and a worldwide network of outstanding researchers and practitioners. A Scientific Advisory Board of distinguished academics ensures the quality of the publications.

This series serves as an outlet for the main results of FEEM's research programmes in the areas of economics, energy and the environment.

Titles in the series include:

Game Practice and the Environment
Edited by Carlo Carraro and Vito Fragnelli

Analysing Strategic Environment Assessment
Towards Better Decision-Making
Edited by Pietro Caratti, Holger Dalkmann and Rodrigo Jiliberto

Trade and Environment
Theory and Policy in the Context of EU Enlargement and Economic Transition
Edited by John W. Maxwell and Rafael Reuveny

Green Accounting in Europe
A Comparative Study, Volume 2
Edited by Anil Markandya and Marialuisa Tamborra

The Economics of Tourism and Sustainable Development
Edited by Alessandro Lanza, Anil Markandya and Francesco Pigliaru

The Economics of Tourism and Sustainable Development

Edited by

Alessandro Lanza

Director, Fondazione Eni Enrico Mattei (FEEM), Milan, Italy

Anil Markandya

Fondazione Eni Enrico Mattei (FEEM), Milan, Italy and Professor of Economics, University of Bath, UK

Francesco Pigliaru

Professor of Economics, University of Cagliari and CRENoS, Italy

THE FONDAZIONE ENI ENRICO MATTEI (FEEM) SERIES ON ECONOMICS AND THE ENVIRONMENT

Edward Elgar
Cheltenham, UK • Northampton, MA, USA

Published by
Edward Elgar Publishing Limited
Glensanda House
Montpellier Parade
Cheltenham
Glos GL50 1UA
UK

Edward Elgar Publishing, Inc.
136 West Street
Suite 202
Northampton
Massachusetts 01060
USA

A catalogue record for this book
is available from the British Library

ISBN 1 84542 401 8

Printed and bound in Great Britain by MPG Books Ltd, Bodmin, Cornwall

Contents

Contributors

Andrea Bigano, Fondazione Eni Enrico Mattei, Italy

Valentina Bosetti, University of Milan-Bicocca and Fondazione Eni Enrico Mattei, Italy

Rinaldo Brau, University of Cagliari and CRENoS, Sardinia, Italy

Mariaester Cassinelli, University of Milan-Bicocca and Fondazione Eni Enrico Mattei, Italy

Felix Chan, School of Economics and Commerce, University of Western Australia

Cesare Costantino, Istat – Environmental Accounting Unit, Italy

Maja Fredotovic, Faculty of Economics, University of Split, Croatia

Carlos Mario Gómez Gómez, University of Alcalá de Henares, Spain

Alessandra Goria, Fondazione Eni Enrico Mattei, Italy

Jacqueline Hamilton, Hamburg University, Germany

Suhejla Hoti, School of Economics and Commerce, University of Western Australia

Javier Lozano Ibáñez, University of the Balearic Islands, Spain

Alessandro Lanza, Fondazione Eni Enrico Mattei, Italy

Anil Markandya, Fondazione Eni Enrico Mattei, Italy and University of Bath, UK

Michael McAleer, School of Economics and Commerce, University of Western Australia

Sanae Morimoto, Department of Economics, Okayama Shoka University, Japan

Jean-Jacques Nowak, University of Lille, France

Javier Rey-Maquieira Palmer, University of the Balearic Islands, Spain

Suzette Pedroso, World Bank, Washington, DC, USA

Francesco Pigliaru, University of Cagliari and CRENoS, Sardinia, Italy

Daria Povh, PAP-RAC, Split, Croatia

Giovanni Ruta, World Bank, Washington, DC, USA

Mondher Sahli, University of Wellington, New Zealand

Pasquale Sgro, Johns Hopkins University, Bologna, Italy

Riaz Shareef, School of Economics and Commerce, University of Western Australia

Tim Taylor, Department of Economics and International Development, University of Bath, UK

Richard S.J. Tol, Hamburg University, Germany

Angelica Tudini, Istat – Environmental Accounting Unit, Italy

Introduction

Alessandro Lanza, Anil Markandya and Francesco Pigliaru

Tourism is big business and getting bigger. In the 20 years from 1980 to 2000 global tourism receipts increased at an annual rate of nearly 8 per cent, much faster than the rate of world economic growth of around 3 per cent. In 2000, income from tourism combined with passenger transport totaled more than $575 billion, making this sector the world number one export earner, ahead of automotive production, chemicals, petroleum and food (UNEP web site[1]). So it is no surprise that people are paying attention to tourism when they debate how the world can move to a more sustainable pattern of development.

Given the increasing importance of the sector, an enormous literature has emerged on the three pillars of sustainable development – environmental, cultural and economic – and on how tourism impacts on them and how these aspects of tourism can be enhanced. In this active and somewhat crowded field, what is the purpose of introducing yet another book? In spite of all that has been produced, we would argue that we do offer something special. Unlike much of the literature that has primarily an environment and sociological perspective, our effort is firmly grounded in economics – its theory and applications. Economics here is made to be the servant of policy in the field of tourism. But economics has increasingly become a technical subject and its methods and results are not easy for the policy maker to comprehend. In this book, we try to present some important economics results, and relate them to the policy debate. If we are successful, our approach offers the prescriptions for moving tourism, and economic development generally, closer to a sustainable ideal, with a firm analytical anchor. This is important if we are to be taken seriously by important decision makers in governments – in ministries of economy and finance, for example.

SUSTAINABLE TOURISM: A MACROECONOMIC PERSPECTIVE

What are these tools of economic analysis, and how do they relate to tourism? The first is the 'macroeconomics tool box'. This allows us to study the growth performance of countries and understand the sources of growth. There is, of course, great controversy on this topic, especially on what are the main drivers for growth (see, for example, Easterly, 2002). Physical capital, human capital, population control, good governance and good policies have all been given prominence in the growth debate. Fashions change and presently institutional reforms for good policies are probably the most popular explanation. Of course, no one factor is sufficient and all the above are, to some extent or another, necessary. For this book, we are interested in the role of export-led sectoral growth – that is, leading the growth process by rapid increases in the output of a sector that is not constrained by domestic demand. The sector in question is of course the tourism sector. The chapter by Brau, Lanza and Pigliaru (Chapter 1) shows that 'tourism countries' have achieved a higher rate of growth than other sub-groups. Given that tourism has been a fast-growing sector, is this simply a 'good luck' phenomenon, or is it the result of deliberate good policies? The chapter analyses the performance of these economies, and finds that tourism explains a part of the growth independently of other factors, such as investment and openness (that is, 'good' policies). Moreover, the governments in these countries did not have to promote tourism to the extent that they did. That was a choice – and it turns out to have been a good one. Finally the chapter shows that while being a small economy can be bad for growth, this effect can be mitigated by increasing the role of tourism in that economy.

Like any important piece of research, this chapter opens up a number of areas for further study. What is the 'right' amount of emphasis for governments to put on tourism to achieve the highest level of sustainable growth? Does this process need detailed direction from the government or is it one that is best driven by market factors? Answers to the second question definitely point to a *dirigiste* role for the government, and these are provided by some of the other chapters in the volume. Before discussing these we turn to a number of others that use the macroeconomic tool kit.

One macro level issue is how tourism affects the use of land. As we build more golf courses and hotel complexes and so on, we take land away from agriculture and we encroach on the natural environment, which may be the reason the tourists came in the first place. Thus the shift of land to tourism, which will promote growth as shown in the chapter by Brau et al. (Chapter 1), may be taken too far and, without some constraints, the process may overreach itself, resulting in lower real incomes for the population.

The chapter by Palmer, Ibáñez and Gómez (Chapter 3) analyses these trade-offs. Not surprisingly, they show that it does not pay society to expand tourism to the point where the private marginal benefit is zero – the classic externality argument that market production is too high for a good with negative externalities. The chapter further shows that, to attain the maximum sustainable long run level of well-being for local people, it is desirable to limit tourism below its private marginal benefit even when the price of tourism services rises continuously relative to the price of other uses to which the land can be put. The implications from a growth point of view are important – an economy cannot depend on expanding tourism to be the engine of growth for ever. Of course, it may take quite a long time to reach that limit, especially if we allow for the possibility of expanding tourism by improving quality rather than increasing volume (an option not allowed for in the model).

That there should be limits to the level of free market tourism development is not surprising given the extent to which this sector is associated with externalities and market failures of various kinds. But, even in the absence of such effects, a tourism boom may not increase welfare. The reason is due to trade effects. The chapter by Nowak, Sahli and Sgro (Chapter 4) argues that a tourism boom can cause a decline in welfare. This can arise if the shift out of the manufacturing sector and into the services sector (needed to fuel the tourism boom) generates welfare losses in manufacturing which offset the gains in welfare due to the increase in the price of non-traded goods. In their model this is likely to happen if the tourism sector is more labor intensive than the agricultural traded sector, which is, of course, an empirical question. But the labor intensity of tourism is not fixed; it is possible to develop tourism that is more 'land intensive'. Furthermore, where tourism needs to be labor intensive, it may be possible to import workers. Nevertheless, the chapter provides a warning: take care of the economy-wide effects of tourism when developing a policy of expansion of the sector.

To all but the most convinced free marketers the need for some state involvement in regulating the tourism sector is clear. But any regulation requires good data, especially statistical data, and this is the responsibility of the government. The chapter by Costantino and Tudini (Chapter 5) contributes to the discussion by showing what is needed to develop an accounting framework for ecologically sustainable tourism. A start for developing a full set of sectoral accounts for tourism is the preparation of 'satellite accounts', which are not fully integrated into the system of national accounts but are based on the same principles as the main accounts. Initially we need to know how much tourism demands from other sectors in the economy, how much it demands of goods imported from abroad, and how much it generates in the form of net financial flows to the government. For this, the convention sectors of the economy have to be mapped into the 'tourism sectors'. All this provides the important building blocks for a detailed economic analysis of tourism. Following on from that, we would like to be able to measure the environmental impacts of tourism more accurately. Once the tourism sectors have been defined, the environmental burdens can be measured. None of this is straightforward and it does require political will on the part of government to carry out the work. Fortunately, we are seeing progress in these areas although we are not there yet.

FORECASTING NUMBERS OF VISITORS

Good economic accounts data relating to tourism, which is clearly important, needs to be complemented by good data on the demand for tourism within the country. Visitor numbers can be notoriously volatile, especially in the face of natural disasters, or threats (real and imagined) of terrorism. The chapter by Chan, Hoti, McAleer and Shareef (Chapter 2) provides a relatively robust model for forecasting the impact and duration of shocks in terms of visitor numbers for small island economies. This is important not only for the private sector, but also for policy makers, who need to promote activities that can take up the slack in the economy in the event of a sharp fall in tourism.

For investment and planning purposes, governments and private investors need to know what the long-term trends in tourism flows are likely to be and one of the most important factors that is emerging in determining the flows of tourists is climate change. The chapter by Bigano, Goria, Hamilton and Tol (Chapter 6) reviews the studies of the impact of climate change on tourist destinations, based on the experience of the recent past, when we have seen some unusually hot summers and mild winters. The data show that people tend to go in greater numbers to summer destinations when these destinations become warmer and in fewer numbers to winter destinations when they become milder, making winter sports less attractive. This is pretty much what one would expect, although the attractions of higher temperatures must wane at some point. The literature suggests that the optimal temperature in the destination country is around 21°C, which is useful information for those planning to invest in tourism development in warm climes. The chapter also reports on the impact of climate on domestic tourism flows in Italy, and finds that warmer summers do increase such tourism significantly. Extreme weather events also deter tourists, more so for short breaks when visitors have not committed to the trip a long time in advance. There is no doubt that such considerations must play an increasing role in determining where developments in tourism will take place, and in adapting tourism to a changing climate through measures that make the experience less vulnerable to extreme events.

MICROECONOMIC PERSPECTIVES FOR SUSTAINABLE TOURISM

At the microeconomic level, questions about sustainable tourism can be asked covering at least two areas:

- What economic and other instruments do we have at our disposal to promote sustainable tourism? Is the management of tourism at the national level adequate and what measures are available to improve it?
- What is the demand for environmentally friendly tourism and do we have the right tools for estimating this demand?

This book includes two chapters covering the first set of questions and three covering the second.

On the use and availability of economic instruments, many experts have proposed the use of some kind of tourism tax to limit visitor numbers in places and at times when a free market would result in congestion and excessive environmental degradation. One only has to spend a day in Venice or Florence in August to appreciate that the experience would be better if the number of visitors could be reduced, and some sites do this simply by preventing access at critical times. But a tax or charge would do this by providing an economic disincentive, and would also raise some revenues that could be used for environmental and cultural protection of the sites. The introduction of an 'eco-charge' on tourists, however, is controversial. Local authorities are reluctant to impose it in case it causes a really serious decline in demand and national authorities can be against it on the grounds that taxation authority is vested at the national level and 'earmarked' taxes are fiscally inadvisable, as they limit the flexibility of governments to spend money where it is most needed. These issues have been debated for a long time (and not only in the context of tourism charges), so we cannot expect a quick resolution. The Balearic Islands introduced an 'eco-tax' to finance a 'Tourist Area Restoration Fund'. There has been a challenge to this tax from the central government, which was overturned and the situation is changing even as we write. There are other examples of some earmarked taxes in other countries (Bhutan, Dominica), provided in the chapter by Taylor, Fredotovic, Povh and Markandya (Chapter 7). That chapter is mainly devoted, however, to examining the political economy of another tourism tax in detail – the one introduced on the island of Hvar in Croatia. The authorities on the island have been concerned for some time by the heavy environmental burdens imposed by the tourists, and the lack of funds to address them. Hence they agreed to look at a charge that would be earmarked to reduce coastal pollution and finance the removal of litter and so on during peak tourism periods.

The study of the options involved extensive consultations with stakeholders and with the relevant authorities to ensure that such an instrument was indeed legal. A modest charge rate of €0.21 to €0.57 was recommended, based on a willingness-to-pay study of visitors, and the tax is likely to be implemented next season (2005). The lesson is that with careful consultation and detailed analysis, economic instruments can be designed to move us in the direction of sustainable tourism.

The other chapter on tourism management is the one by Bosetti, Cassinelli and Lanza (Chapter 9). They address the important problem of measuring the performance of local governments in managing tourism. A supplier of a service is efficient if he or she makes use of a combination of inputs which cannot be bettered – that is, you cannot reduce any one input without increasing at least one other input. To measure how efficient Italian municipalities are in providing a service called 'beds occupied' by tourists, the researchers measure inputs of number of beds and amount of solid waste generated and use linear programming techniques to identify the efficiency frontier. Measures of efficiency reveal substantial differences between municipalities (the worst – Portovenere – is 3.7 times less efficient than the best – Rio nel'Elba) and between regions (Emilia Romagna is nearly 15 times less efficient than Liguria). The analysis also looks at changes in efficiency between 2000 and 2001. The results are interesting and important but one is bound to ask (a) can this analysis be extended to more inputs and how would the rankings look then, and (b) what are the factors that determine efficiency? As the work progresses answers will, no doubt, be provided to these questions.

The remaining three chapters in the volume analyze the demand for environmentally friendly tourism. Ideally with sustainable tourism both the environment and the economy benefit from tourism. The chapter by Markandya, Taylor and Pedroso (Chapter 8) looks at how much the projects and programs supporting tourism at the World Bank subscribe to this principle. As one of the main institutions financing projects under the Global Environment Facility (GEF), which includes biodiversity protection as one of its areas of activity, one would imagine that a large number of Bank projects would have a tourism-related component. One finds, however, that although many projects mention tourism as one of the potential benefits of a conservation project, very few actually measure these benefits in any degree of detail. On the other side, looking at strategies for development in developing countries, there is discussion of tourism, especially in relation to transport projects but also in projects covering cultural heritage protection and health (tourism can spread diseases such as HIV/AIDS). The much-vaunted Poverty Reduction Strategy Process (PRSP), which is the main instrument for promoting pro-poor growth in a coordinated way, has given little attention so far to the contribution of sustainable tourism. To sum up, therefore, the Bank has not, so far, realized the potential of sustainable tourism in its development strategy for developing countries.

If governments spend money to protect the environment, how much of this can be recovered in terms of higher payments by tourists? The chapter by Ruta and Pedroso (Chapter 10) looks at the evidence from the Dominican Republic, where two areas are identified: one on the east coast, where the natural environment is generally still good; and the north, where there has been rapid tourism development and where the area suffers from relatively high loads of organic pollution. Using econometric methods the researchers find that hotel room rates are affected by a number of environmental variables, such as smell, municipal water connections and the existence of sewage treatment in the area. The results are not altogether conclusive, but they do point to positive private benefits to hotel owners from improvements in public goods. If these are accepted, they could form the basis for the financing of some of these improvements.

The final chapter (Chapter 11) is by Morimoto, who examines tourist preferences in Laos. By using 'choice experiment' techniques, she compares preferences between packages of sites during a visit to the country and obtains values for visits to particular sites. She then uses the results to estimate what people would pay for some new tourism options, such as a new trekking route, an artisan village and so on. These costs can provide useful information in designing tourist activities and even in setting fees for access to the sites.

Sustainable tourism is a fast-growing subject and a book such as this can only touch on some of the issues. Nevertheless, we hope that the chapters provide some important insights and stimulate readers' interest in the subject.

NOTE

1. www.uneptie.org/pc/tourism/sust-tourism/economic.htm.

REFERENCE

Easterly, W. (2002), *The Elusive Quest for Growth: Economists' Adventures and Mis-adventures in the Tropics*, Cambridge, MA: The MIT Press.

1. An investigation on the growth performance of small tourism countries[1]

Rinaldo Brau, Alessandro Lanza and Francesco Pigliaru

1. INTRODUCTION

In a recent paper, Easterly and Kraay (2000) investigate whether or not being small represents an economic disadvantage for a country. Their finding is that smaller countries are not poorer than average, nor that they grow more slowly. Similar results are also provided by Armstrong and Read (1995) and Armstrong et al. (1998). Yet reasons for being pessimistic are not difficult to find, especially in literature on endogenous growth, where scale effects often play a role in the determination of an economy's growth rate (Grossman and Helpman, 1991; Aghion and Howitt, 1998).

Likewise, countries which rely strongly on international tourism are suspected of being locked into a slow growth path. Again, endogenous growth theories tend to emphasize the virtues of high-tech sectors, whose potential for high long-run growth is regarded as more promising than that of non-high-tech service sectors such as tourism.[2] In addition, countries in which tourism is the prominent sector are often very small. So expectations about their economic performance are not high, to say the least. Nevertheless, this pessimistic perspective is challenged by a growing stream of literature on small and island countries' economic performance, where tourism is generally associated to higher than average income levels (e.g. Read, 2004 for a recent survey).

In this chapter we assess the reliability of these different views about the likely role of tourism as a growth engine by looking at the cross-country evidence. To this aim, we use Easterly and Kraay's (2000) analysis on a 1960–95 dataset on 157 countries as a benchmark against which to compare our results. We find that, in the period 1980–95, tourism specialization affects growth positively. A corollary of this finding is that being small is far from a disadvantage if tourism is a key sector of the economy. By detecting this effect, however, we find that smaller countries do not show a lower growth rate on average only because small tourism countries outperform other countries' aggregates. If one discriminates for tourism specialization, smallness turns out to be a disadvantage.

Our evidence on the positive relative performance of small tourism countries poses further interesting questions concerning the economic mechanisms that lie behind it. Is this performance either temporary or sustainable? Is it based on an increasing (perhaps unsustainable) exploitation of the environment that attracts the tourists? Is it based on a 'terms of trade effect' which makes the value of that environment increase significantly over time? In this chapter we define and discuss a number of alternative explanations, all compatible with our evidence, although we do not test them empirically, since a much more detailed cross-country dataset than the one currently available to us would be required.

The chapter is organized as follows. Section 2 is devoted to the discussion of our data and variables. In section 3 we give a descriptive picture of the relative performance of the various groups of countries. In section 4 the econometric evidence is presented. In section 5 we describe the degree of heterogeneity in growth performance within the STCs (small tourism countries) group. In section 6 we discuss various alternative explanations of our empirical results. Concluding remarks are in section 7.

2.   DATA AND MAIN DEFINITIONS

The Easterly and Kraay (2000) (E–K from now on) dataset is our starting point. However, in order to investigate the relative economic performance of countries specialized in tourism, we need cross-country data on international tourism receipts.[3] For this purpose, we use data from the 2000 edition of *World Development Indicators* by the World Bank. The first year for which data are available is 1980, and not for all the countries listed in the E–K dataset. As a consequence, the resulting dataset – the one we shall use in this chapter – is smaller in both the time and the cross-section dimensions. In particular, the period covered is 1980–95, and 143 countries instead of the original 157 are included, with the sub-set of small countries diminishing from 33 to 29.

Following E–K, we define small countries as countries with an average population of less than one million during 1960–95.[4] In our dataset, 29 countries out of a total of 143 meet this condition. As for the definition of 'tourism country', henceforth the degree of tourism specialization is defined by the ratio of international tourist receipts to GDP. In Table 1.1 we list all countries in our dataset with a degree of tourism specialization

Table 1.1   Countries with tourism specialization greater than 10 per cent

Country name	Index of tourism specialization (average 1980–95)
Jordan*,***	10.1
Singapore*	11.4
Samoa	12.6
Fiji	13.0
Jamaica*	18.4
Grenada	18.8
Cyprus	19.1
Malta	21.1
St Vincent and the Grenadines	22.2
Vanuatu**	22.9
Seychelles	25.9
Barbados	28.8
Bermuda	31.3
St Kitts and Nevis	35.0
St Lucia	40.9
Bahamas	41.2
Maldives	60.8

Notes: * Not small countries; ** 1998 data; ***1997/98 data.

greater than 10 per cent on average over the period 1980–95. Of the 17 countries that come into this category, 14 meet our adopted definition of small state (the exceptions are Jordan, Singapore and Jamaica, all with populations exceeding one million).

The remaining 15 small countries, whose degree of tourism specialization is smaller than 10 per cent, are listed in Table 1.2. Therefore, the subsample of 29 small countries in our dataset is split into two almost identical parts: 14 countries are above the 10 per cent tourism share of GDP and 15 are below it.

3.   COMPARATIVE GROWTH PERFORMANCE OF SMALL TOURISM COUNTRIES

In this section we consider the growth performance of STCs as a whole, relative to the performance of a number of well-established sub-sets of countries – namely, OECD, oil, small (as defined above), and LDCs[5] – and assess the degree of economic heterogeneity within the STCs' sub-set. Before

Table 1.2   Countries with tourism specialization smaller than 10 per cent

Country name	Index of tourism specialization (average 1980–95)
Belize	9.4
Mauritius	8.2
Gambia	7.8
Guyana	5.3
Bahrain	4.0
Solomon Islands***	3.6
Swaziland	3.4
Comoros	3.3
Botswana	2.7
Luxembourg	2.5
Cape Verde**	1.8
Iceland	1.8
Suriname	1.7
Djibouti	1.2
Gabon	0.2

Notes: ** 1998 data; ***1993/98 average.

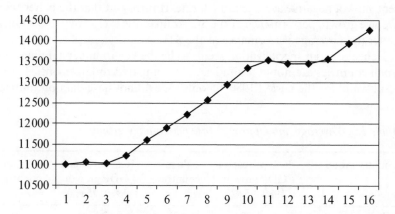

Figure 1.1   OECD, real per capita GDP in constant dollars (international prices, base year 1985)

analysing the relative growth performance of each group, let us consider for a moment the more general picture. Figure 1.1 shows the time path of per capita GDP in the OECD countries as a group. The period 1980–95 is one of relatively slow growth, due to the existence of two sub-periods of very slow or even negative growth (at the beginning of the 1980s and of the 1990s). As a result, the annual average growth rate in the OECD group is 1.8 per cent per year. The average growth rate of the whole sample is much lower than this, at 0.4 per cent per year – an outcome mainly due to the poor performance of the oil (15 countries, growing on average at −2.3 per cent per year) and the LDC groups (37 countries, growing on average at −0.5 per cent per year). This picture is in sharp contrast to what had characterized the previous two decades, when the average annual growth rate in the sample was about 2.6 per cent, and all groups were performing rather well.

The relative performances of the individual groups are summarized in Table 1.3, which shows the average growth rates for all groups in 1980–95. By considering the relative performances within the small countries group, first of all we note that the average small country (SC) grows faster than the average country in the sample, but slower than the average OECD country. Moreover, when we isolate the performance of STCs from that of the other small countries, we see that tourism specialization is clearly beneficial for growth. This is a result independent of the proportion of tourism receipts on GDP adopted in our classification of 'tourism countries', since adopting 15 per cent or 20 per cent instead of 10 per cent as the demarcation value would leave the results unaffected. Remarkably, the remaining 15 small countries with a share of tourism receipts in GDP lower than 10 per cent show a negative average growth rate. It turns out that the better than average growth performance of the SC group is due exclusively to the much better than average performance of the STCs.

Hence tourism specialization seems to be the key to understanding why small countries are not at a disadvantage compared to larger ones. Is this result valid for the period 1980–95 only? We do not have data on tourism

Table 1.3   Average annual growth rate per country group

Country group	Real per capita GDP growth 1980–95 (%)	No. of countries	Real per capita GDP growth 1960–95 (%)	No. of countries
OECD	1.79	21	2.81	21
Oil	−2.31	14	0.17	14
Small	1.13	29	1.85	26
Small tour. > 20%	2.51	10	2.29	7
Small tour. > 10%	2.53	14	2.51	11
Small < 10%	−0.18	15	1.67	15
LDCs	−0.52	37	0.22	36
All	0.45	143	1.63	140

receipts for the years 1960–79, so we cannot answer this question directly. However, by using the series reported in the E–K dataset, we can compare the performance of our groups of countries over a longer period (1960–95), but we have to bear in mind that, given the current limitation of the available data, the definition of STCs is based on the data of the second sub-period. Also, note that the sample is reduced to 140 from the original 143. What matters most from our point of view is that the number of STCs with an index of specialization more than 10 per cent also decreases, from 14 to 11.

Two other features shown on the right side of Table 1.3 are worth mentioning. First, STCs are among the fastest growing group in 1960–95 too. Second, the difference in the growth rate of SC and of STC increases significantly in the second sub-period. Again, the expansion of tourism specialization in some of the SC countries in the most recent period might be the explanation for this pattern.

4.   ECONOMETRIC EVIDENCE OF THE DETERMINANTS OF STCS' GROWTH

We now turn to the econometric analysis of the relative growth performance of STCs. We first test whether in our dataset it is possible to detect significant advantages/disadvantages for SCs and STCs. To do this, we use the full set of continental dummies used in E–K, as well as dummies for oil, OECD and LDC countries.

The picture that emerges from Table 1.4 strongly supports our findings in section 3. After controlling for continental location and other important characteristics, the above average growth performance of the SCs as a group (regression (1)) is crucially due to the performance of the tourism countries. Once the SC group is split in two using a demarcation value of 10 per cent, STCs outperform the remaining small countries (regression (2)). In regression (3) we add the LDC dummy as a further control, and in regression (4) we change the demarcation value of tourism specialization from 10 per cent to 20 per cent. The STC dummy stays significant at 1 per cent in all regressions.[6]

In Table 1.5 we test whether tourism specialization remains growth-enhancing after a number of traditional growth factors are taken into account. For instance, STCs might be on a faster growth path simply because they are poorer than average – a mechanism fully predicted by the traditional Solovian growth model. Possibilities of this type are controlled for in all regressions in Table 1.5, in which we adopt a Mankiw, Romer and Weil (1992) (M–R–W) approach to the analysis of cross-country growth differentials.[7] Regressions (2) and (3) show that the STC dummy stays

Table 1.4   Growth and STCs – I

Dependent variable: average annual real per capita GDP growth, 1980–95				
Dummies	(1)	(2)	(3)	(4)
OECD	0.0034	0.0058	0.0048	0.0036
	(0.78)	(1.41)	(1.09)	(0.77)
Oil	−0.0244	−0.0234	−0.0257	−0.0257
	(−3.46)***	(−3.29)***	(−3.73)***	(−3.73)***
SC	0.0093			
	(1.98)**			
STC>10%		0.0185	0.0191	
		(2.60)***	(2.85)***	
SC<10%		0.0014		
		(0.26)		
LDC			−0.0103	−0.0100
			(−1.89)*	(−1.91)*
STC>20%				0.0213
				(2.83)***
No. of obs.	143	143	143	143
R²	0.389	0.412	0.432	0.429

Notes:
All regressions include a full set of regional dummies as defined in E–K. Omitted dummy for country group is 'Other'.
Figures in parentheses are *t*-statistics (standard errors are White-corrected).
* Significant at 10%; ** significant at 5%; *** significant at 1%.

significant at the 1 per cent confidence level even after other growth factors, such as the initial level of per capita GDP and an index of openness, are taken into account. Adding an index of volatility does not alter this result (regressions (4) and (5)).

In regressions (6) and (7) we further test for the presence of a growth-enhancing effect of tourism. Namely, in regression (6) the index of tourism specialization is used instead of the usual STC dummy. The index is significant at the 1 per cent confidence level, and the value of its coefficient implies that an increase of 10 per cent in the ratio of tourism receipts to GDP is associated to an increase of 0.7 per cent in the annual growth rate of per capita GDP. In regression (7) we interact the index of openness with the STC>10 per cent dummy. The idea is to test whether being specialized in tourism generates a premium over the average positive effect of openness on growth. The coefficient of the new interactive variable is significant and its value is large.

An additional way to test whether factors other than tourism specialization are the source of the positive performance of STCs is to consider how

Table 1.5   Growth and STCs – II

Dependent variable: average annual real per capita GDP growth, 1980–95

Dummies and variables	(1)	(2)	(3)	(4)	(5)	(6)	(7)
OECD	0.0156	0.0187	0.0174	0.0156	0.0143	0.0186	0.0185
	(2.31)**	(3.05)***	(2.65)***	(2.46)**	(2.12)**	(3.00)***	(3.02)***
Oil	−0.0186	−0.0175	−0.0176	−0.0157	−0.0159	−0.0156	−0.0174
	(−2.99)***	(−2.80)***	(−2.82)***	(−2.57)***	(−2.59)***	(−2.48)**	(−2.79)***
LDC	−0.0149	−0.0166	−0.0162	−0.0151	−0.0147	−0.0168	−0.0160
	(−2.58)***	(−2.94)***	(−2.93)***	(−2.63)***	(−2.62)***	(−3.09)***	(−2.82)***
Ln % GDP 1980	−0.0099	−0.0100	−0.0098	−0.0096	−0.0094	−0.0095	−0.0097
	(−2.63)***	(−2.81)***	(−2.67)***	(−2.76)***	(−2.63)***	(−2.64)***	(−2.71)***
Share of trade in GDP 1980–95	0.0125	0.0092	0.0092	0.0094	0.0095	0.0064	0.0085
	(4.03)***	(2.80)***	(2.85)***	(3.18)***	(3.21)***	(1.87)*	(2.52)**
Standard dev. of growth rates 1980–95				−0.2051	−0.2060		
				(−1.28)	(−1.27)		
Average share of tourism receipts in GDP 1980–95						0.0775	
						(4.40)***	
STC>10%		0.0182		0.0172			
		(2.80)***		(2.77)***			
STC>20%			0.0204		0.0193		
			(2.79)***		(2.71)***		
Share of trade* STC>10%							0.0159
							(3.50)***
No. of obs.	141	141	141	141	141	141	141
R²	0.431	0.469	0.466	0.482	0.478	0.487	0.475

Notes:
All regressions include a full set of regional dummies as defined in E–K.
Omitted dummy for country group is 'Other'.
Figures in parentheses are *t*-statistics (standard errors are White-corrected).
* Significant at 10%; ** significant at 5%; *** significant at 1%.

15

Table 1.6   Growth determinants and STCs

Dummies	(1) Log real per-c. GDP, average 1980–95	(2) Log inv. as a share of GDP, aver. 1980–95	(3) Share of trade in GDP, aver. 1980–95	(4) Standard dev. of GDP growth, 1980–95
OECD	1.3853	0.2410	−0.1315	−0.0139***
	(10.67)***	(2.09)**	(−1.25)	(−4.79)
Oil	0.7623	0.2715	0.1368	0.0111
	(3.98)***	(1.64)*	(1.46)	(2.47)**
STC >10%	0.4487	0.2816	0.5393	−0.003
	(2.20)**	(2.29)**	(5.27)***	(−1.00)
SC< 10%	0.3261	0.4424	0.5492	0.0069
	(1.91)*	(3.51)	(5.15)***	(1.68)*
No. of obs.	143	138	141	143
R^2	0.711	0.413	0.245	0.279

Notes:
All regressions include a full set of regional dummies as defined in E–K.
Omitted dummy for country group is 'Other'.
Figures in parentheses are *t*-statistics (standard errors are White-corrected).
* Significant at 10%; ** significant at 5%; *** significant at 1%.

different STCs are from other small and larger countries in terms of a number of growth determinants. In Table 1.6 we see that the reason why STCs are growing faster *is not*:

(i)   that they are poorer than other small countries (regression (1): they are not, given that the latter show a lower coefficient. Moreover, the average per capita GDP of STCs in the period amounted to $3986 (1985 international dollars), as compared to a sample mean of $2798);
(ii)   that they have particularly high saving/investment propensities (regression (2): other small countries save/invest more than STCs);
(iii) that they are particularly open to trade (regression (3): they are very open to trade, but not more than the other small, low-growth countries in the sample).

In addition to this, regression (4) shows that STCs are less subject to volatility in their growth rates than the other SCs and the oil countries.

Result (i) is in line with preceding analyses, where it is shown that small countries in general do not register significant lower-than-average income levels, and that tourism specialization is associated to higher GNP per capita values (cf. Easterly and Kraay, 2000; Armstrong et al., 1998;

Armstrong and Read, 1995, 2000). On the other hand, this kind of finding rules out absolute convergence as a major source of high growth rates in STCs.

On the whole, this further evidence confirms the results shown in our previous tables. The positive performance of STCs relative to that of the other groups is not significantly accounted for by the traditional growth factors of the M–R–W type models. Tourism specialization appears to be an independent determinant.

5. STCS' GROWTH AND HETEROGENEITY

Let us now consider the heterogeneity of the countries included in the STC 'club' in terms of their growth performance. Eleven of the 14 STCs grow faster than the average in the sample (above 0.4 per cent per year);[8] eight of them show high growth performances (above 2.0 per cent per year); three perform worse than average: Bermuda, the Bahamas and Vanuatu. The last seems to represent a unique case. It is the only initially very poor STC to experience no growth. The other two bad performers are the richest in the group: in 1980 a resident in Bermuda (the Bahamas) was 9 (7.5) times richer than a resident in Vanuatu. Moreover, Vanuatu has also seen its index of tourism specialization falling during the period under analysis.

To get an idea of the relative magnitude of the dispersion of growth rates across STCs, in Table 1.7 we compare the standard deviation of the growth rates of the various groups of countries. The standard deviation of STCs is higher than that of OECD countries, and is slightly lower than that of all the other groups and of the whole sample.

Although explaining the observed dispersion in the growth rates of STCs is an interesting issue, it is well beyond the scope of the present chapter. Among other things, a satisfactory answer should model, and test

Table 1.7   Comparison of standard deviation of growth rates

Countries	S.D. growth
OECD	0.008
Oil	0.031
SC	0.023
STC 10%	0.019
LDCs	0.022
All	0.024

empirically, the widely different patterns of tourism development adopted by countries with a comparative advantage in this sector.[9]

Here we only address a simpler and preliminary empirical question – namely, whether countries within the STC group are becoming more or less homogeneous over time in terms of their growth rates and – perhaps – per capita GDP levels. A standard way of evaluating the pattern over time of a cross-country index of dispersion is the so-called σ-convergence analysis. Figure 1.2(a) shows the pattern of the coefficient of variation (per cent) within the STC group from 1980 to 1995.[10] σ-convergence was clearly at work between 1980 and 1990, a period in which the coefficient of variation decreased from 9.1 per cent to 8.0 per cent. However, since 1990 it has remained constant around this latter value.[11] Again, this pattern differs sharply from the one characterizing the group of 15 non-tourism small countries (Figure 1.2(b)), whose level of the index of inequality is higher

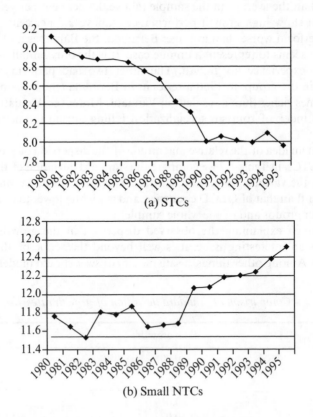

(a) STCs

(b) Small NTCs

Figure 1.2   σ-convergence, 1980–95, coefficient of variation, logs of per capita income

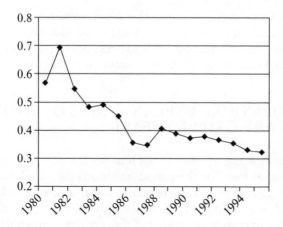

Figure 1.3   σ-convergence, 1980–95, standard deviation, logs of tourism receipts per arrival

(11.8 per cent in 1980) and, more importantly, there is a marked tendency for inequality to increase over time (12.5 per cent in 1995).

At this stage, it would be helpful to complement the above analysis by testing for the presence of β-convergence across the STCs. However, we have too few cross-section observations (14) for a reliable estimate of a standard cross-country growth regression.

Keeping this shortcoming in mind, we report that an OLS (ordinary least squares) regression between growth rates and the logs of the 1980 level of per capita GDP generates a negative (as expected) coefficient equal to –0.0111, significant at the 10 per cent level ($R^2 = 0.189$). Adding a dummy to control for Vanuatu, we obtain a coefficient equal to –0.0115, significant at the 1 per cent level ($R^2 = 0.467$).

It is also interesting to report that, underlying the observed per capita GDP convergence, some convergence also seems to be at work in tourism receipts per arrival. This is shown in Figure 1.3.

On the whole, the evidence discussed in this section gives some support to the idea that a significant part of the observed heterogeneity within the STC group might be based on a rather simple explanation. Within this 'club', the dispersion of per capita GDP tends to decrease, with poorer countries growing faster than richer ones. At this stage of our research, we do not know how robust this finding is, nor whether an absolute or conditional process of convergence is at work – if any. In 1985, the Maldives had a per capita GDP equal to 10 per cent of that of the Bahamas; a decade later, the Maldives had doubled that initial relative value. Are they converging to the high per capita GDP of the Bahamas? Are most of the STCs converging to that level? If, on the other hand, convergence is conditional rather than absolute, is the type of tourism development adopted in a country a relevant conditioning factor? These questions are important, and future research should pay them the attention they deserve.

6.   THEORETICAL EXPLANATIONS OF WHY THE STCS ARE GROWING FAST

The previous evidence has shown that tourism can be a growth-enhancing specialization, at least for the period under analysis. Understanding the mechanisms behind this phenomenon is important, especially from the viewpoint of economic policy. Taken at face value, our results seem to justify a rather optimistic perception of the economic consequences of specializing in tourism. However, is the above-described performance an episode or are we dealing with something of a more persistent nature?

Various interpretations are possible at this stage. Here we discuss explicitly two different mechanisms that could generate the above-described performance, and suggest what type of additional data would be required to identify their empirical relevance.

A simple analytical setting within which the two hypotheses can be defined and compared is offered by Lanza and Pigliaru in a series of papers (1994, 2000a,b). In these papers Lucas's (1988) two-sector endogenous growth model is shown to be simple and detailed enough for the analytical evaluation of the effects of tourism specialization.

Consider a world formed of a continuum of small countries characterized by a two-sector economy (M for manufacturing, T for tourism) and total labour endowment L, in which the engine of growth – the accumulation of human capital – takes the exclusive form of learning-by-doing, so that pure competition prevails. While physical production in the manufacturing sector is determined by human capital only through its productivity effects on the labour force (L_M) in the sector, production of T requires an additional input, a natural resource whose fixed endowment is $\bar{R}$. This association with natural resources implies that each worker in the tourism sector must be endowed with (at least) a minimum quantity $\underline{\rho}$ in order to make production of T feasible.

The association between L_T and $\bar{R}$ also plays a role in determining the comparative advantage of individual countries. Countries with a small $\bar{R}$ face constraints in the number of workers they can allocate to sector T; no constraint exists in countries with larger $\bar{R}$. Given the mechanisms governing the determination of the relative price in autarchy, countries with larger $L_T(\bar{R})$ will tend to develop a comparative advantage in T, while the opposite is true for countries with smaller $L_T(\bar{R})$.[12] Notice that, as far as small countries have higher than average $\bar{R}/L$, this result would be compatible with the stylized fact that T countries are generally small.[13]

In each sector the potential for learning-by-doing is defined by a constant, λ_i. In our case, manufacturing is the 'high-technology' sector, so that $\lambda_M > \lambda_T$. Given that international trade will force all countries to specialize completely according to their comparative advantage, the (physical) growth rate of a country is consequently equal to

$$\frac{\dot{y}_i}{y_i} = \lambda_i, \text{ with } i=T,M. \tag{1.1}$$

However, international trade also affects the terms of trade ($p \equiv p_T/p_M$). In particular, with Cobb–Douglas preferences, p moves in favour of the slow-growing good exactly counterbalancing the growth differential between the two countries, so that in the long run we should expect STCs to grow at the same rate as industrialized countries.[14]

This holds by keeping the utilization of the natural resource constant. Consider now a T country in which, at a certain point in time, not all $\bar{R}$ is used, so that $\rho < \bar{\rho}$, where $\bar{\rho} \equiv \bar{R}/L$ is the upper limit of natural resource per worker in the event of complete specialization in T. If in this country the rate of utilization of its natural endowment increases, then its growth rate in terms of the manufacturing good is equal to

$$\dot{y}_T/y_T + \dot{p}/p + \dot{\rho}/\rho. \tag{1.2}$$

However, this growth rate can only be observed in the short term. In the long run, $\dot{\rho}/\rho$ tends to zero as the upper bound $\bar{\rho}$ is approached. Consequently, in the long run tourism specialization is neutral for growth (unless the cases of σ greater/smaller than 1 are considered).

This simple analytical setting can be used to define alternative explanations of why STCs have grown faster.

The Pessimistic Interpretation

International preferences are Cobb–Douglas (or CES with $\sigma > 1$), so that the terms of trade effect cannot outweigh the productivity differential. In this case, other things being constant, the index of tourism specialization should play no role in our regressions (a negative role with $\sigma > 1$). If that is the case, a way to reconcile theory with our evidence is that, perhaps, the rate of utilization of the natural endowment in STCs has increased significantly during the period under analysis ($\dot{\rho}/\rho > 0$), so that

$$\dot{y}_T/y_T + \dot{p}/p + \dot{\rho}/\rho > \dot{y}_M/y_M \geq \dot{y}_T/y_T + \dot{p}/p. \tag{1.3}$$

Clearly, with this additional term, the growth rate of a T country can be greater than $\dot{y}_M/y_M$, the growth rate of the average M country. However, this performance can only be observed in the short term. In the long run, $\dot{\rho}/\rho$ tends to zero as the upper limit $\bar{\rho}$ is approached. In this setting, in the long run the T countries should not outperform the M countries.

The Optimistic Interpretation

The second interpretation relies on a 'terms of trade effect'. In other words, tourism is not harmful for growth if the prevailing international terms of trade move fast enough to more than offset the gap in sectoral productivity growth. If this happens, the sum $\dot{y}_T/y_T + \dot{p}/p$ would be persistently greater than $\dot{y}_M/y_M$.[15] Adding non-homothetic preferences with T as the luxury good would yield further analytical support to the possibility that the terms of trade move fast enough in favour of the T good[16] and, consequently, to an optimistic interpretation of our current evidence. In both cases we have:

$$\dot{y}_T/y_T + \dot{p}/p + \dot{\rho}/\rho > \dot{y}_T/y_T + \dot{p}/p > \dot{y}_M/y_M. \qquad (1.4)$$

To sum up, we have 'productivity pessimism' and 'terms of trade optimism'. A growth episode based on a fast supply expansion in the T sector might temporarily hide the growth-neutral or even damaging nature of tourism specialization. On the other hand, consumer preferences might be such that tourism specialization (or some types of tourism specialization) is highly valued in the international marketplace. This second mechanism – not crucially based on output expansion – tends to make sustainability of tourism-based development easier to achieve.

An important task for future research is to identify the relative importance of the various types of growth-enhancing mechanisms associated with tourism specialization, in order to assess their economic (and environmental) sustainability. Cross-country data on the dynamics of the terms of trade between tourism services and a composite other good are required, as well as data on the natural resource endowment and indexes of the latter's degree of exploitation for tourism purposes.

7.   CONCLUSIONS

Is specialization in tourism a good option for those less developed countries and regions in which development through industrialization is not easy due to the existence of persistent gaps in technology levels?

To answer this question, in this chapter we have compared the relative growth performance of 14 'tourism countries' from a sample of 143 countries, observed during the 1980–95 period. We have seen that the STCs grew significantly faster than all the other sub-groups considered in our analysis (OECD, oil, LDC, small). Moreover, we have shown that the reason why they grow faster is not that they are poorer than average, that they have particularly high saving/investment propensities or that they are very open to trade.

In other words, our findings point to the fact that the positive performance of STCs is not significantly accounted for by the traditional growth factors of the Mankiw, Romer and Weil type of models. Tourism specialization appears to be an independent determinant of growth performance.

A corollary of our results is that the role played by the tourism sector should not be ignored by the debate about whether smallness is harmful for growth. Half of the 30 countries classified as microstate in this literature are heavily dependent on tourism. Once this distinction is adopted, it is easy to see that the STCs perform much better than the remaining small countries. In our findings, smallness *per se* can be bad for growth, while the opposite is true when smallness is combined with tourism specialization.

Additional questions which can constitute scope for future research are related to these results. In particular, an aspect which remains unresolved in our chapter is that of the very long-run consequences of specializing in tourism, which could not match the rather optimistic perception that emerges from a first browsing of our results. As a matter of fact, various interpretations are possible at this stage. In section 6, we have discussed two alternative mechanisms that would be compatible with our empirical evidence. The first is based on a 'terms of trade effect' which would allow STCs to enjoy sustainable fast growth in the long run. The second implies a far less optimistic scenario: STCs can achieve fast growth for a period by accelerating the exploitation of the environment to which tourists are attracted. The long-run scenario might be very different, especially if the dynamics of sectoral productivities are in favour of high-tech industries, as suggested by much of the current endogenous growth literature. Identifying the relative strength of these mechanisms in explaining the positive performance of the STCs is an important task which is left for future stages of our research, given that a much more detailed cross-country dataset than the one currently available to us would be required.

NOTES

1. In previous stages of our research, we benefited from the comments and suggestions of Guido Candela, Roberto Cellini, Anil Markandya, Thea Sinclair, Clem Tisdell, Giovanni Urga and the participants to the conference held in Cagliari. Special thanks

for helpful suggestions go to Luca De Benedictis. Excellent research assistance by Fabio Manca is gratefully acknowledged. Financial support from Interreg IIIc is gratefully acknowledged by Francesco Pigliaru.
2. On the growth perspectives of tourism countries see Copeland (1991), Hazari and Sgro (1995), Lanza and Pigliaru (1994, 2000a,b).
3. International tourism receipts are defined as expenditures by international inbound visitors, including payments to national carriers for international transport. Data are in current US dollars. For more information, see *WDI*, Table 6.14.
4. This is of course an *ad hoc* threshold. More on this issue in Srinivasan (1986) and Armstrong and Read (1998).
5. Countries in each group are listed in the Appendix. With the exception of LDCs, the groups in our chapter coincide with those used in Easterly and Kraay (2000).
6. The same result is obtained when the three 'non-small' tourism countries (Jamaica, Jordan and Singapore) are added to the STC dummy regressions (4), (5) (as for regression (6) only small countries have an index of tourism specialization greater than 20 per cent).
7. Human capital – a crucial variable in M–R–W – is not included in our regressions because data on six of our STCs are not available.
8. The annual growth rates of real per capita GDP (average 1980–95) in STCs are as follows: Samoa 0.6 per cent, Fiji 0.9 per cent, Grenada 3.8 per cent, Cyprus 4.3 per cent, Malta 4.1 per cent, St Vincent and the Grenadines 3.7 per cent, Vanuatu −0.1 per cent, Seychelles 2.4 per cent, Barbados 0.5 per cent, Bermuda 0.2 per cent, St Kitts and Nevis 3.9 per cent, St Lucia 3.8 per cent, the Bahamas −0.1 per cent, Maldives 4.9 per cent.
9. For instance, as we argue in section 5, a rapid and intense use of the environment could generate a high but declining growth rate; *vice versa*, a less intense use of the environment could generate growth benefits in the longer run rather than the short term. Moreover, destination countries could display some differences in the quality of the tourist services offered, whether in the form of more luxury accommodation or better preserved natural resources, which could match different paths of international demand growth.
10. We use the coefficient of variation instead of the standard deviation to control for the rather different averages in per capita income across the various groups of countries.
11. In 1980 the same index was equal to 12.8 per cent for the whole sample and to 4.0 per cent for the OECD countries.
12. The details of the role played by R in generating the comparative advantage depends on the demand elasticity of substitution. See Lanza and Pigliaru (2000b).
13. More on this in Lanza and Pigliaru (2000b).
14. In the more general case of CES preferences, the rate of change of p is equal to $(\lambda_M - \lambda_T)\sigma^{-1}$, where σ is the elasticity of substitution, so that the terms of trade effect will outweigh the productivity differential when σ is smaller than unity (see Lanza and Pigliaru, 1994, 2000a,b).
15. In terms of the model to which we have referred in this section, $\sigma<1$ is sufficient for this result to hold. For evidence favourable to this hypothesis, see Brau (1995), Lanza (1997) and Lanza et al. (2003).
16. See also Pigliaru (2002).

REFERENCES

Aghion P. and Howitt, P. (1998), *Endogenous Growth Theory*, Cambridge, MA: The MIT Press.

Armstrong, H.W. and Read, R. (1995), 'Western European micro-states and EU Autonomous Regions: the advantages of size and sovereignty', *World Development*, **23**, 1229–45.

Armstrong, H.W. and Read, R. (1998), 'Trade and growth in small states: the impact of global trade liberalisation', *World Economy*, **21**, 563–85.

Armstrong, H.W. and Read, R. (2000), 'Comparing the economic performance of dependent territories and sovereign micro-states', *Economic Development and Cultural Change*, **48**, 285–306.

Armstrong, H.W., de Kervenoael, R.J., Li, X. and Read, R. (1998), 'A comparison of the economic performance of different micro-states and between micro-states and larger countries', *World Development*, **26**, 639–56.

Brau, R. (1995), *Analisi econometrica della domanda turistica in Europa*, Contributi di Ricerca CRENoS, 95/2.

Copeland, B.R. (1991), 'Tourism, welfare and de-industrialization in a small open economy', *Economica*, **58**, 515–29.

Easterly, W. and Kraay, A. (2000), 'Small states, small problems? Income, growth and volatility in small states', *World Development*, **28**, 2013–27.

Grossman, G. and Helpman, E. (1991), *Innovation and Growth in the Global Economy*, Cambridge, MA: The MIT Press.

Hazari, B.R. and Sgro, P.M. (1995), 'Tourism and growth in a dynamic model of trade', *Journal of International Trade & Economic Development*, **4**, 243–52.

Lanza, A. (1997), 'Is tourism harmful to economic growth?', *Statistica*, **57**, 421–33.

Lanza, A. and Pigliaru, F. (1994), 'The tourism sector in the open economy', *Rivista Internazionale di Scienze Economiche e Commerciali*, **41**, 15–28.

Lanza, A. and Pigliaru, F. (2000a), 'Tourism and economic growth: does country's size matter?', *Rivista Internazionale di Scienze Economiche e Commerciali*, **47**, 77–85.

Lanza, A. and Pigliaru, F. (2000b), 'Why are tourism countries small and fast-growing?', in A. Fossati and G. Panella (eds), *Tourism and Sustainable Economic Development*, Dordrecht: Kluwer, pp. 57–69.

Lanza, A., Temple, P. and Urga, G. (2003), 'The implications of tourism specialization in the long term: an econometric analysis for 13 OECD economies', *Tourism Management*, **24**(3), 315–21.

Lucas, R. (1988), 'On the mechanics of economic development', *Journal of Monetary Economics*, **22**, 3–42.

Mankiw, N.G., Romer, D. and Weil, D.N. (1992), 'A contribution to the empirics of economic growth', *Quarterly Journal of Economics*, **107**, 408–37.

Pigliaru, F. (2002), 'Turismo, crescita e qualità ambientale', in R. Paci and S. Usai (eds), *L'ultima spiaggia*, Cagliari: CUEC.

Read, R. (2004), 'The implications of increasing globalization and regionalism for the economic growth of small island states', *World Development*, **32**, 365–78.

Srinivasan, T.N. (1986), 'The costs and benefits of being a small remote island land-locked or ministate economy', *World Bank Research Observer*, **1**, 205–18.

APPENDIX: DATA SOURCES

The Easterly–Kraay (E–K) 'Small States Dataset'

This dataset consists of 157 countries for which at least ten years of annual data on per capita GDP adjusted for differences in purchasing power parity are available. Among these countries 33 are defined as small countries having an average population during 1960–95 of less than one million. Other variables include:

(a)   Regional dummies (country selection from the World Bank World Tables (WB))
(b)   Real GDP per capita measured in 1985 international dollars.

For a more exhaustive description on data sources see p. 2027 of E–K (2000).

The dataset used in this chapter
The dataset consists of 143 countries for which data on tourist receipts and at least ten years of annual data on per capita GDP adjusted for differences in purchasing power parity are available. The main source of data for our dataset is the 'macro6-2001' file of the Global Development Network Growth Database from the World Bank: (http://www.worldbank.org/research/growth/GDNdata.htm).

Variables

1.   Real per capita GDP levels (international prices, base year 1985): *Source*: Global Development Network Growth Database (for 1980–95) and Easterly and Kraay (2000) dataset (1960–95).
2.   Real per capita GDP growth rate: logs of first available year and last year as below:

$$Ln\left(\frac{GDP_{t1}}{GDP_{t0}}\right)\Big/T$$

This variable has been computed for 1960–95 and 1980–95.
3.   Average tourism specialization:

$$\left(\frac{\text{International tourism receipts}}{\text{GDP at market prices}}\right)$$

Source for both series: World Bank *Development Indicators*, current US$.

4. Average share of trade:

$$\left(\frac{\text{Imports } + \text{exports}}{\text{GDP at market prices}} \right)$$

Source for both series: World Bank *Development Indicators*, current US$.

5. Average investments to GDP: *Source*: Global Development Network Growth Database.
6. Average standard deviation of growth rate: growth rates of (2).

A set of different dummies has also been considered:

(a) According to population
     Twenty-nine are small countries (average population during 1960–95 < 1 million).
(b) According to tourism specialization
     Ten are tourism countries with a specialization > = 20 per cent. (For a complete definition of specialization see below.)
     Thirteen are tourism countries with a specialization > = 15 per cent.
     Seventeen are tourism countries with a specialization > = 10 per cent.
     Three countries among this group are not small (Jamaica, Singapore and Jordan).
(c) According to tourism specialization and population
     Nineteen are small not tourism (specialization < = 20 per cent).
     Seventeen are small not tourism (specialization < = 15 per cent).
     Fifteen are small not tourism (specialization < = 10 per cent).
(d) Other relevant dummies
     Thirty-seven less developed countries (of these, six small not tourism and two small tourism).
     Twenty-one OECD.
     Fourteen oil.

The different subsets of countries are listed in Table 1A.1.

Table 1A.1

	OECD	Oil	Small	LDC
1	Australia	Algeria	Bahamas, The	Angola
2	Austria	Angola	Bahrain	Bangladesh
3	Belgium	Bahrain	Barbados	Benin
4	Canada	Congo, Rep.	Belize	Burkina Faso
5	Denmark	Gabon	Bermuda	Burundi
6	Finland	Iran, Islamic Rep.	Botswana	Cape Verde
7	France	Iraq	Cape Verde	Central African Republic
8	Iceland	Kuwait	Comoros	Chad
9	Ireland	Nigeria	Cyprus	Comoros
10	Italy	Oman	Djibouti	Congo, Dem. Rep.
11	Japan	Saudi Arabia	Fiji	Djibouti
12	Luxembourg	Trinidad and Tobago	Gabon	Ethiopia
13	Netherlands	United Arab Emirates	Gambia	Gambia
14	New Zealand	Venezuela	Grenada	Guinea
15	Norway		Guyana	Haiti
16	Portugal		Iceland	Lao PDR
17	Spain		Luxembourg	Lesotho
18	Sweden		Maldives	Liberia
19	Switzerland		Malta	Madagascar
20	United Kingdom		Mauritius	Malawi
21	United States		Samoa	Maldives
22			Seychelles	Mali
23			Solomon Islands	Mauritania
24			St Kitts and Nevis	Nepal

25	Niger
26	Rwanda
27	Samoa
28	Sierra Leone
29	Solomon Islands
30	Somalia
31	Sudan
32	Tanzania
33	Togo
34	Uganda
35	Vanuatu
36	Yemen, Rep.
37	Zambia

St Lucia
St Vincent and Grenadines
Suriname
Swaziland
Vanuatu

2. Forecasting international tourism demand and uncertainty for Barbados, Cyprus and Fiji

Felix Chan, Suhejla Hoti, Michael McAleer and Riaz Shareef

1. INTRODUCTION

Volatility in monthly international tourist arrivals is the squared deviation from the mean monthly international tourist arrivals, and is widely used as a measure of risk or uncertainty. Monthly international tourist arrivals to each of the three Small Island Tourism Economies (SITEs) analysed in this chapter, namely Barbados, Cyprus and Fiji, exhibit distinct patterns and positive trends. However, monthly international tourist arrivals for some SITEs have increased rapidly for extended periods, and stabilized thereafter. Most importantly, there have been increasing variations in monthly international tourist arrivals in SITEs for extended periods, with subsequently dampened variations. Such fluctuating variations in monthly international tourist arrivals, which vary over time, are regarded as the conditional volatility in tourist arrivals, and can be modelled using financial econometric time series techniques.

Fluctuating variations, or conditional volatility, in international monthly tourist arrivals are typically associated with unanticipated events. There are time-varying effects related to SITEs, such as natural disasters, ethnic conflicts, crime, the threat of terrorism, and business cycles in tourist source countries, among many others, which can cause variations in monthly international tourist arrivals. Owing to the nature of these events, recovery from variations in tourist arrivals from unanticipated events may take longer for some countries than for others. These time-varying effects may not necessarily exist within SITEs, and hence may be intrinsic to the tourist source countries.

In this chapter, we show how the generalized autoregressive conditional heteroscedasticity (GARCH) model can be used to measure the conditional volatility in monthly international tourist arrivals to three SITEs. It is, for example, possible to measure the extent to which the 1991 Gulf War influenced variations in monthly international tourist arrivals to Cyprus, and to what extent the *coups d'état* of 1987 and 2000 affected subsequent monthly international tourist arrivals to Fiji.

An awareness of the conditional volatility inherent in monthly international tourist arrivals and techniques for modelling such volatility are vital for a critical analysis of SITEs, which depend heavily on tourism for their macroeconomic stability. The information that can be ascertained from these models about the volatility in monthly international tourist arrivals is crucial for policy makers in the public and private sectors, as such information would enable them to instigate policies regarding income, bilateral exchange rates, employment, government revenue and so forth. Such information is also crucial for decision-makers in the private sector, as it would enable them to alter their marketing and management operations according to fluctuations in volatility.

The GARCH model is well established in the financial economics and econometrics literature. After the development by Engle (1982) and Bollerslev (1986), extensive theoretical developments regarding the structural and statistical properties of the model have evolved (for derivations of the regularity conditions and asymptotic properties of a wide variety of univariate GARCH models, see Ling and McAleer, 2002a, 2002b, 2003). Wide-ranging applications of the GARCH model include economic and financial time series data, such as share prices and returns, stock market indexes and returns, intellectual property (especially patents), and country risk ratings and returns, among others. Such widespread analysis has led to the GARCH model being at the forefront of estimating conditional volatility in economic and financial time series.

In this chapter we extend the concept of conditional volatility and the GARCH model to estimate and forecast monthly international tourist arrivals data. The GARCH model is applied to monthly international tourist arrivals in three SITEs, which rely overwhelmingly on tourism as a primary source of export revenue. Such research would be expected to make a significant contribution to the existing tourism research literature, as tourism research on the volatility of monthly international tourist arrivals would appear to be non-existent. The GARCH model is appealing because both the conditional mean, which is used to capture the trends and growth rates in international tourism arrivals, and the conditional variance, which is used to capture deviations from the mean monthly international tourist arrivals, are estimated simultaneously. Consequently, the parameter estimates of both the conditional mean and the conditional variance can be obtained jointly for purposes of statistical inference, and also lead to more precise forecast confidence intervals.

This chapter shows how variations of the GARCH model can be used to forecast international tourism demand and uncertainty by modelling the conditional volatility in monthly international tourist arrivals to Barbados, Cyprus and Fiji. The sample periods for these three SITEs are as follows: Barbados, January 1973 to December 2002 (Barbados Tourism Authority); Cyprus, January 1976 to December 2002 (Cyprus Tourism Organization and Statistics Service of Cyprus); and Fiji, January 1968 to December 2002 (Fiji Islands Bureau of Statistics). In the case of Cyprus, monthly tourist arrivals data were not available for 1995, so the mean monthly tourist arrivals for 1993, 1994, 1996 and 1997 were used to construct the data for 1995 in estimating the trends and volatilities in international tourist arrivals.

The main contributions of this chapter are as follows. First, the importance of conditional volatility in monthly international tourist arrivals is examined and modelled, and the macroeconomic implications for SITEs are appraised. Second, the conditional volatilities are estimated and an economic interpretation is provided. Third, the conditional volatilities are used in obtaining more precise forecast confidence intervals. In achieving these objectives, we examine the existing literature on the impact of tourism in small island economies in relation to their gross domestic product, balance of payments, employment and foreign direct investment, among other factors.

As positive and negative shocks in international tourism arrivals may have different effects on tourism demand volatility, it is also useful to examine two asymmetric models of conditional volatility. For this reason, two popular univariate models of conditional volatility, namely the asymmetric GJR model of Glosten et al. (1992) and the exponential GARCH (or EGARCH) model of Nelson (1991), are estimated and discussed. Some concluding remarks on the outcome of this research are also provided.

2.   SMALL ISLAND TOURISM ECONOMIES

A small island tourism economy (SITE) can best be defined by examining its three main properties, which are its (relatively) small size, its nature as an island, and its reliance on tourism receipts. These three aspects of SITEs will be discussed in greater detail below.

2.1   Small Size

There have been numerous attempts made to conceptualize the size of an economy, yet there has been little agreement to date. The notion of size first emerged in economics of international trade, where the small country is the price taker and the large country is the price maker with respect to both imports and to export prices in world markets. Armstrong and Read (2002) argue that this concept of size is flawed because it tends to focus on the inclusion of larger countries and exclusion of smaller countries.

Size is a relative rather than absolute concept. In the literature, the size of an economy is referenced with quantifiable variables, so that population, GDP and land area are the most widely used. Some examples emphasizing size that are worth mentioning are in Kuznets (1960), where a country with a population of 10 million or less is regarded as small. By this measure, the World Bank's World Development Indicators (WDI) 2002 data show there are 130 small economies. Robinson (1960) uses a population threshold of 10 to 15 million to distinguish a small economy. Population is often used because it is convenient and provides information about the size of the domestic market and labour force (Armstrong and Read, 2002). It is quite clear that there is a debate in the literature as to the definition of what constitutes a 'small' country.

While there have been variations in the levels of arbitrarily chosen population thresholds, it is not explicitly stated in the literature why a particular threshold is used. The choice of economies analysed in this chapter is not based on a particular population or a GDP threshold. As Shareef (2003a) explains, some SITEs such as the Dominican Republic, Haiti, Jamaica and Mauritius have populations above 1 million, and yet share numerous features of being small. In circumstances where a population, GDP or a land-area threshold is chosen, undesirable outcomes are inevitable because countries can overshoot it and continue to feature characteristics of being 'small'.

Armstrong and Read (1995) probably best explain the size of an economy by employing the concept of suboptimality in a macroeconomic framework. The basis for determining size in this approach is by incorporating the interaction of production and trade, while a necessary condition of minimum efficient scale (MES), or the level of output of goods and services at which production is feasible, is upheld for the economy. In the case of small economies, the scale of national output is established by the MES, the shape of the average cost curve below the MES, and transport costs. The advantage of this concept of size is that it provides a more precise understanding of the implications of being a small economy.

This chapter examines three SITEs for which monthly international tourist arrivals data are available. In Table 2.1, the common size measures show that these three SITES account for more than 1.8 million people. Their populations range in size for a mini-economy like Barbados, with a population of 260 000, and Cyprus and Fiji, which have populations of around 700 000. All of these economies are former British colonies which

Table 2.1   Common size measures of SITEs

SITEs	Mean 1980–2000		2000		Surface area (km²)
	Pop. (m)	GDP per capita (US$)	Pop. (m)	GDP per capita (US$)	
Barbados	0.26	7 100	0.27	8 300	430
Cyprus	0.69	10 000	0.76	14 100	9 240
Fiji	0.73	2 300	0.81	2 400	18 270
Mean	0.56	6 467	0.61	8 267	9 313

Source: World Bank (2002).

gained independence during the latter half of the last century. All of these SITEs have relatively large per capita GDP figures. These SITEs are in three geographic regions of the world, with one of them in the Caribbean, one in the Pacific Ocean and one in the Mediterranean.

2.2   Island Economies

'Not all free-standing land masses are islands' and 'an island is not a piece of land completely surrounded by water' (Dommen, 1980, p. 932). This conclusion was reached through comparing and matching economic, social and political indicators, and not because of the geological nature of land formations of the countries chosen. Nevertheless, the SITEs analysed in this chapter are sovereign island economies because of their geophysical nature. Most of them are archipelagic, have risen from the ocean through volcanic activity, and lie along the weaker parts of the earth's crust. Tourists typically reach these countries by air, and freight is usually carried by sea.

These island economies are consistently threatened by natural disasters as well as the effects of environmental damage and have inherited the world's most delicate ecosystems. In Briguglio (1995) it is argued that all islands are insular but not situated in remote areas of the globe, while insularity and remoteness give rise to transport and communications problems. Moreover, Armstrong and Read (2002, p. 438) reiterate that 'both internal and external communication and trade may be very costly and have implications for their internal political and social cohesiveness as well as competitiveness'. These SITEs are in regions of the world where they are frequently faced with unsympathetic climatic conditions, which usually affect all economic activity and the population.

2.3   Reliance on Tourism

In all of these SITEs, tourism is the mainstay of the economy and earnings from it account for a significant proportion of the value-added in their national product. The fundamental aim of tourism development in SITEs is to increase foreign exchange earnings to finance imports. Due to their limited natural resource base, these SITEs have an overwhelming reliance on service industries (including value-added in wholesale and retail trade (including hotels and restaurants), transport, government, financial, professional and personal services such as education, health care and real estate services), of which tourism accounts for the highest proportion in foreign exchange earnings. During the period 1980 to 2000, the average earnings from tourism as a proportion of gross export earnings accounted for 51 per cent in Barbados, 37 per cent in Cyprus and 25 per cent in Fiji (World Bank, 2002). In economic planning, tourism has a predominant emphasis in SITEs where the climate is well suited for tourism development and the islands are strategically located.

A large proportion of tourism earnings leave the economy instantaneously to finance imports to sustain the tourism industry. As given in the Commonwealth Secretariat/World Bank Joint Task Force on Small States (2000), imports to service the tourism industry mostly comprise non-indigenous goods. For instance, meat and dairy products feature heavily in the Caribbean. Due to its scarcity in some SITEs, labour is also imported for employment in tourism and results in substantial foreign exchange outflows.

The tourism establishment in SITEs mostly consists of cooperative developments isolated from the core economy. Hence the desired effects to the economy are sometimes limited. Tourism requires careful planning in order to maintain sustainability and to limit environmental damage. While tourism has contributed to economic development in many SITEs, it needs to be managed responsibly in order to secure its long-term sustainability. Further discussions of the above characteristic features of SITEs are given in Shareef (2003a).

2.4   Implications of Uncertainty in Tourism Arrivals in SITEs

The volatility of the GDP growth rate is defined as the square of the deviation from its mean. In SITEs, the volatility of GDP growth rate tends to be very high. In Shareef (2003a), the volatility of the real GDP growth rates for 20 SITEs is given. The lowest mean volatility of real GDP growth rate was recorded for Malta in the Mediterranean for the period 1980–2002, while St Lucia in the Caribbean recorded the highest mean volatility of 56.9 for the same period.

The Commonwealth Secretariat/World Bank Joint Task Force on Small States (2000) reports that the high volatility in the GDP growth rate recorded among SITEs is due to three main reasons. First, SITEs are more susceptible to changes in the international market conditions since they are highly open to the rest of the world and because of their narrow productive base. Moreover, SITEs produce a limited range of uncompetitive exports, they operate under the same rules and regulations as other countries, and have fewer options to hedge against any losses. Finally, SITEs are frequently affected by natural disasters, which adversely affect all the sectors in their economies. The significance of the above varies significantly among SITEs as smallness is associated with relatively high levels of specialization in production and trade.

Armstrong and Read (1998) explain that the most prominent feature of SITEs is their narrow productive base and the small domestic market. Therefore there is less motivation for SITEs to diversify industry when the domestic market is small. It is quite common in SITEs to have one dominant economic activity such that, when it starts to decline, another dominant economic activity replaces it rather than the economy becoming more diversified. In the last 15 years or so, earnings from manufactured exports have declined while income from tourism has increased substantially.

In Briguglio (1995), vulnerability is defined as the exposure to exogenous shocks over which the affected country has little or no control, and low resilience to withstand and recover from these shocks. SITEs are less likely to be resilient to these shocks, given the narrow economic structures and limited resources. Furthermore, Briguglio (1995) explains that vulnerability can exist in the form of economic, strategic and environmental factors. Economic vulnerability examines the narrow productive base, the susceptibility of the economy to external shocks, and the high incidence of natural disasters. Strategic vulnerability accounts for the political vulnerability to their colonial history, as well as their larger neighbours. Environmental vulnerability explains the intensity of the fragility of the delicate ecosystems of SITEs.

Although SITEs produce a narrow range of goods, they consume a broader range through international trade. As a result, the ratio of trade to GDP is relatively high among SITEs. Generally, SITEs hold a much greater stake in world markets because of the smaller proportion of world trade that they hold and are bound by the same rules and regulations (see Commonwealth Secretariat/World Bank Joint Task Force on Small States, 2000). SITEs do not necessarily receive preferential treatment, except for a few former British colonies with regard to banana exports. Therefore the terms of trade of SITEs do not exhibit irregular changes when compared with other larger developing countries. SITEs rely on import tariff receipts as a major source of government revenue and any measure to liberalize trade could hamper crucial development expenditures and result in unsustainable government debt in SITEs.

International foreign capital inflow is essential for SITEs to smooth out consumption over the long run. This is to compensate for adverse shocks to domestic production particularly due to unfavourable climatic conditions in SITEs. SITEs depend heavily on foreign aid to finance development (see Commonwealth Secretariat/World Bank Joint Task Force on Small States, 2000). Aid flows have dropped sharply during the last decade of the twentieth century, due to the collapse of communism in Europe. Aid from donor countries has been diverted towards former Soviet allies. SITEs have experienced a dramatic decline in per capita aid of around US$145 in 1990 to less than US$100 per capita in 2000 (World Bank, 2002). Liou and Ding (2002) argue that in allocating development aid, attention could be given to the specific attributes of small states, so that their economic development is more effective and manageable. SITEs have very limited access to commercial borrowings because they are perceived to suffer from frequent natural disasters or for other reasons are considered to be high risk.

SITEs have relatively low levels of indebtedness, but they have difficulties in borrowing on commercial terms. As discussed in Shareef (2003b), insufficient and unreliable information on SITEs and low country risk ratings are major impediments to borrowing. The cost of borrowing for SITEs is relatively high due to the difficulty in prosecuting illegal activities, which makes enforcing contracts very costly for investors. Hence it becomes more difficult for SITEs to integrate into the international financial system. Foreign direct investment not only links SITEs to the developed world, but it brings in entrepreneurship and expertise in creating efficiency and improving management control in the private sector. Moreover, this would also bring in state-of-the-art technology and increase market opportunities for local firms.

Most SITEs have high per capita GDP compared to the larger developing countries, but poverty continues to be an unabated challenge. With the increase in per capita GDP one would expect poverty levels to decline. But according to the Commonwealth Secretariat/World Bank Joint Task Force on Small States (2000), there are a number of small economies that have higher poverty rates than reflected in their per capita incomes, particularly in SITEs because they are archipelagos. In SITEs, a large proportion of economic activity is held in the capital, while the isolated communities remain poor. Due to the unequal distribution of income in SITEs, poverty becomes prevalent. Because of the high volatility of GDP coupled with the SITEs' capacity to withhold adverse shocks to national output, income inequality and hardship is further intensified.

These vulnerability factors make the economic management of SITEs difficult and sensitive to the information delivered about changes in the key flows of resources into and out of the economy. For countries that are dominated by tourism, one of the most important factors is the variability in international tourist arrivals. It is critical, therefore, that policy makers in these countries have the most accurate estimate of tourist arrivals, and preferably as far in advance as possible, so that appropriate actions can be taken. Policy areas where data on fluctuations in international tourist arrivals have the greatest impact include the following:

1. *Fiscal policy*
    Tourism taxes and other tourism-related income, such as service charges, make direct contributions to government revenue. Any adverse effects on tourist arrivals would affect fiscal policy adversely, and economic development would also be hampered. Therefore, tourism has a direct effect on sustainable development, and hence on the optimal management of development expenditures.
2. *Balance of payments*
    An adverse effect on tourism numbers will lead to a decline in the overall balance, so that foreign exchange reserves will also decline. This could lead to an exchange rate devaluation, which will make imports more expensive. Such an outcome is crucial to the management of foreign reserves in SITEs, which rely heavily on imports.
3. *Employment in the tourism sector*
    As tourism is one of the most important sectors in the economies in SITEs, any shocks that affect the patterns of tourism will affect the sustainability of employment.
4. *Tourism in SITEs has substantial multiplier effects*
    Although the agricultural sector in SITEs is typically insignificant, the output of the agriculture sector can be fully absorbed by the tourism sector. Therefore, sustainable tourism can have positive effects on other sectors. Moreover, the construction sector depends highly on the tourism sector for upgrading tourism infrastructure and developing new construction projects. With an increase in the number of international tourists worldwide, tourist destinations need to increase their capacity significantly.

Therefore, due to the nature of SITEs and the implications of being a SITE, as described above, it is clear that tourism sustainability is necessary for SITEs to sustain their economic development. Consequently, it is imperative that forecasts of inbound international tourism demand to these SITEs are obtained accurately.

3. INTERNATIONAL TOURIST ARRIVALS COMPOSITION IN SITES

International tourist arrivals from 11 major tourist source countries represent a significant proportion of the total international tourist arrivals to SITEs. Among these 11 tourist source countries are the world's richest seven countries, the G7. The other four countries, namely Switzerland, Sweden, Australia and New Zealand, are also among the highest per capita income countries in the world.

With respect to the three SITEs examined in this chapter, the 11 tourist source countries are geographically situated with varying distances. These tourist source countries have diverse social and economic cultures, and they account for a high percentage of the composition of international tourist arrivals in all the SITEs. For Barbados and Cyprus, international tourist arrivals accounted for six of the 11 source markets, while Fiji welcomed tourists from seven of these 11 sources.

In the three SITEs, the dominant tourist source countries are the USA, the UK and Germany. Additionally, these three tourist source countries correspond to substantial mean percentages across many SITEs. Although the USA is the world's largest and richest economy, its prominence in international tourist arrivals is notable only in Barbados, followed by Fiji. The UK tourists feature more evenly among the three economies compared with US tourists. UK tourists are the most widely travelled among the 11 tourism markets, arguably because of the British colonial heritage attached to these SITEs. In general, European tourists seem to travel more to island destinations compared with US and Canadian tourists. German tourists have smaller magnitudes than their UK counterparts. The Germans are followed by French and Italian tourists, who travel more to the Indian Ocean SITEs, namely the Maldives and Seychelles, as compared with their Mediterranean and Caribbean counterparts. Canadian, Swiss, Swedish and Japanese tourist arrivals appear among three SITEs, with varying visitor profiles. Canadians tend to travel to the Caribbean and the Pacific, Swiss and Swedish tourists are present among all the regions except the Pacific, while Japanese tourists appear in the Indian Ocean and Pacific Ocean SITEs. Australian and New Zealand tourists travel substantially to SITEs in the Pacific region, but their arrivals are relatively small among the other SITEs.

4. DATA

This chapter models the conditional volatility of international tourist arrivals in three SITEs, and also provides forecasts of international tourist arrivals. For these SITEs, the frequency of the data is monthly, and the samples are as follows: Barbados, January 1973 to December 2002; Cyprus, January 1976 to December 2002; and Fiji, January 1968 to December 2002.

Figure 2.1 presents the trends and volatilities of monthly international tourist arrivals to Barbados, Cyprus and Fiji. Each of the three international

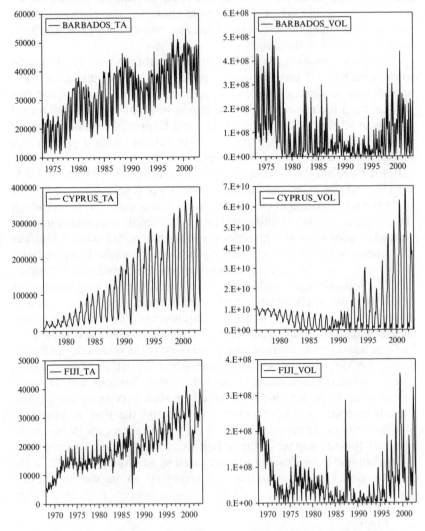

Note: TA and VOL refer to monthly tourist arrivals and associated volatility (squared deviation of each observation from their respective sample mean), respectively.

Figure 2.1   Monthly international tourist arrivals and volatility

tourist arrival series exhibits distinct seasonal patterns and positive trends. For Barbados, there are some cyclical effects, which coincide with the business cycles in the US economy. These business cycles are the boom period in the latter half of the 1970s, the slump due to the second oil price shock of 1979, and the recession in the early 1990s. In Cyprus, the only visible change in monthly international tourist arrivals is the outlier of the 1991 Gulf War. For Fiji, the *coups* of 1987 and 2000 are quite noticeable.

The volatility of the deseasonalized and detrended monthly tourist arrivals can be calculated from the square of the estimated residuals using non-linear least squares. As presented in Figure 2.2, the most visible cases of volatility clusterings of monthly international tourism demand are Barbados and Cyprus. In Barbados, international tourist arrivals have been highly volatile owing to the economic cycles in the US economy. The volatility of the international tourist arrivals to Cyprus increased substantially after the 1979 oil price shock. For Fiji, the volatility is low over the sample, with two volatility peaks associated with the *coups d'état* of 1987 and 2000.

The volatility of the growth rate of deseasonalized monthly international tourist arrivals can be calculated from the square of the estimated residuals using non-linear least squares (the data and figures are available on request). For Barbados, there is clear evidence of volatility clustering during the early 1970s and in the mid-1980s, after which there is little evidence of volatility clustering. Volatility clustering is visible for Cyprus in the mid-1970s. The volatility structure of Fiji resembles that of a financial time series, with volatility clustering not so profound, except for outliers, which signify the *coups d'état* of 1987 and 2000.

Overall, the volatility in monthly international tourist arrivals to the three SITEs shows similar behavioural patterns, but there are visible differences in the magnitudes of the calculated volatility, particularly for Barbados and Fiji. This is plausible for monthly international tourist arrivals to these SITEs, so there would seem to be a strong case for estimating both symmetric and asymmetric conditional volatility models.

5.   UNIVARIATE MODELS OF TOURISM DEMAND

This section discusses alternative models of the volatility of international tourist arrivals using the autoregressive conditional heteroscedasticity (ARCH) model proposed by Engle (1982), as well as subsequent developments in Bollerslev (1986), Bollerslev et al. (1992), Bollerslev et al. (1994), and Li et al. (2002), among others. The most widely used variation for symmetric shocks is the generalized ARCH (GARCH) model of Bollerslev

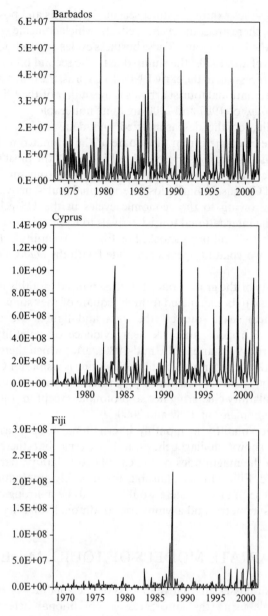

Note: The sample volatility, v_t, for each of the three series is calculated as $v_t = (y_t - E(y_t|\Im_{t-1}))^2 = \varepsilon_t^2$. The mean specification for each of the three series is given in Tables 2.3–2.5.

Figure 2.2   Volatility of tourist arrivals to Barbados, Cyprus and Fiji

(1986). In the presence of asymmetric behaviour between positive and negative shocks, the GJR model of Glosten et al. (1992) and the EGARCH model of Nelson (1991) are also widely used. Ling and McAleer (2002a, 2002b, 2003) have made further theoretical advances in both the univariate and multivariate frameworks.

5.1 Symmetric GARCH(1,1)

The uncertainty or risk (h_t) in the ARMA(1,1)–GARCH(1,1) model for monthly international tourist arrivals is given in Table 2.2, and the unconditional shocks for monthly international tourist arrivals are given by ε_t^2, where $\omega > 0$, $\alpha \geq 0$ and $\beta \geq 0$ are sufficient conditions to ensure that the conditional variance $h_t > 0$. The ARCH (or α) effect captures the short-run persistence of shocks to international tourist arrivals, while the GARCH (or β) effect measures the contribution of shocks to long-run persistence of shocks, $\alpha + \beta$. The parameters are typically estimated by maximum likelihood to obtain quasi-maximum likelihood estimators (QMLEs) in the absence of normality of the standardized shocks, η_t.

It has been shown by Ling and McAleer (2003) that the QMLE of GARCH (p,q) is consistent if the second moment is finite. The well-known

Table 2.2   GARCH(1,1), GJR(1,1) and EGARCH(1,1) conditional volatility models

Model specification	Sufficient conditions for $h_t > 0$	Regularity conditions
Symmetric specification ARMA–GARCH(1,1): $\varepsilon_t = \eta_t \sqrt{h_t}, \quad \eta_t \sim iid\,(0,1)$ $h_t = \omega + \alpha\varepsilon_{t-1}^2 + \beta h_{t-1}$	$\omega > 0$ $\alpha \geq 0$ $\beta \geq 0$	Log-moment: $E[\log(\alpha\eta_t^2 + \beta)] < 0$ Second moment: $\alpha + \beta < 1$
Asymmetric specifications $\varepsilon_t = \eta_t \sqrt{h_t}, \quad \eta_t \sim iid\,(0,1)$		
(1) ARMA–GJR(1,1): $h_t = \omega + (\alpha + \gamma I(\eta_{t-1}))\varepsilon_{t-1}^2 + \beta h_{t-1}$ $I(\eta_t) = \begin{cases} 1, & \eta_t < 0 \\ 0, & \eta_t \geq 0 \end{cases}$	$\omega > 0$ $\alpha \geq 0$ $\alpha + \gamma \geq 0$ $\beta \geq 0$	Log-moment: $E[(\log((\alpha + \gamma I(\eta_t))\eta_t^2 + \beta)] < 0$ Second moment: $\alpha + \beta + \gamma/2 < 1$
(2) ARMA–EGARCH(1,1): $\log h_t = \omega + \alpha\lvert\eta_{t-1}\rvert + \gamma\eta_{t-1}$ $\quad + \beta\log h_{t-1}$	Not necessary	$\lvert\beta\rvert < 1$

necessary and sufficient condition for the existence of the second moment of ε_t for GARCH(1,1) is $\alpha + \beta < 1$, which is also sufficient for consistency of the QMLE. Jeantheau (1998) showed that the weaker log-moment condition is sufficient for consistency of the QMLE for the univariate GARCH (p,q) model. Hence a sufficient condition for the QMLE of GARCH(1,1) to be consistent and asymptotically normal is given by the log-moment condition (see Table 2.2). McAleer et al. (2003) argue that this conclusion is not straightforward to check in practice as it involves the expectation of an unknown random variable and unknown parameters. Moreover, the second moment condition is far more straightforward to check in practice, although it is a stronger condition.

5.2   Asymmetric GJR(1,1) and EGARCH(1,1)

The effects of positive shocks on the conditional variance h_t are assumed to be the same as negative shocks in the symmetric GARCH model. Asymmetric behaviour is captured in the GJR model, as defined in Table 2.2, where $\omega > 0$, $\alpha \geq 0$, $\alpha + \gamma \geq 0$ and $\beta \geq 0$ are sufficient conditions for $h_t > 0$, and $I(\eta_t)$ is an indicator variable (see Table 2.2). The indicator variable distinguishes between positive and negative shocks such that asymmetric effects are captured by γ, with $\gamma > 0$. In the GJR model, the asymmetric effect, γ, measures the contribution of shocks to both short-run persistence, $\alpha + \gamma/2$, and long-run persistence, $\alpha + \beta + \gamma/2$. The necessary and sufficient condition for the existence of the second moment of GJR(1,1) under symmetry of η_t is given in Table 2.2 (see Ling and McAleer, 2002b). The weaker sufficient log-moment condition for GJR(1,1) is also given in Table 2.2. McAleer et al. (2003) demonstrated that the QMLEs of the parameters are consistent and asymptotically normal if the log-normal condition is satisfied.

An alternative model to capture asymmetric behaviour in the conditional variance is the EGARCH(1,1) model of Nelson (1991). When $\beta = 0$, EGARCH(1,1) becomes EARCH(1). There are some distinct differences between EGARCH, on the one hand, and GARCH(1,1) and GJR(1,1), on the other, as follows: (i) EGARCH is a model of the logarithm of the conditional variance, which implies that no restrictions on the parameters are required to ensure $h_t > 0$; (ii) Nelson (1991) showed that $|\beta| < 1$ ensures stationarity and ergodicity for EGARCH(1,1); (iii) Shephard (1996) observed that $|\beta| < 1$ is likely to be a sufficient condition for consistency of QMLE for EGARCH(1,1); (iv) as the conditional (or standardized) shocks appear in equation (2.4), McAleer et al. (2003) observed that it is likely $|\beta| < 1$ is a sufficient condition for the existence of all moments, and hence also sufficient for asymptotic normality of the QMLE of EGARCH(1,1).

6.   EMPIRICAL ESTIMATES AND FORECASTS

This section models the monthly international tourist arrivals to Barbados, Cyprus and Fiji for the periods 1973(1)–2001(12), 1976(1)–2001(12) and 1968(1)–2001(12), respectively, using a variety of models, namely: (i) OLS constant variance (or non-time-varying volatility) model; and (ii) various time-varying conditional volatility models, namely the ARCH(1), GJR(1,0), EARCH(1), GARCH(1,1), GJR(1,1) and EGARCH(1,1) models. The GJR(1,0) model is also known as the asymmetric ARCH(1) model.

For each country, the empirical results obtained from the conditional volatility models are compared with their OLS counterparts. The conditional mean specifications for the three countries are given as follows:

$$BRB_t = \phi BRB_{t-1} + \sum_{i=1}^{2}\tau_i t^i + \sum_{i=1}^{12}\delta_i D_i + \theta\varepsilon_{t-1} + \varepsilon_t \qquad (2.1)$$

$$CYP_t = \phi CYP_{t-1} + \sum_{i=1}^{12}\delta_i D_i t + \varepsilon_t \qquad (2.2)$$

$$FJI_t = \phi FJI_{t-1} + \sum_{i=1}^{2}\tau_i t_i + \sum_{i=1}^{12}\delta_i D_i + \theta\varepsilon_{t-1} + \varepsilon_t \qquad (2.3)$$

$$t_1 = \begin{cases} t, & t = 1,\ldots,88 \\ 0, & t = 89,\ldots,T \end{cases} \qquad t_2 = \begin{cases} t, & t = 89,\ldots,T \\ 0, & t = 1,\ldots,88 \end{cases}$$

where BRB_t, CYP_t and FJI_t are the total monthly international tourist arrivals at time t for Barbados, Cyprus and Fiji, respectively; D_i (= 1 in month $i = 1, 2, \ldots, 12$, and = 0 elsewhere) denotes 12 seasonal dummy variables; and $t = 1, \ldots, T$, where $T = 347$, 311 and 407 for Barbados, Cyprus and Fiji, respectively.

Autoregressive (AR(1)) specifications were used for each country, but there was no evidence of unit roots in any of the three international tourist arrivals series. Different deterministic time trends were used for each of the three SITEs according to their respective empirical regularities. The time trend is the simplest for Cyprus, but is more complicated for Barbados and Fiji, with each of the latter having breaking trends and moving average (MA(1)) error processes.

There is a distinct seasonal pattern in each tourist arrivals series. Although there are several alternative methods for modelling seasonality, 12 seasonal dummy variables are included for simplicity in the respective tourist arrivals models. The empirical estimates are discussed only for the constant volatility linear regression model and three conditional volatility models. The three optimal time-varying conditional volatility specifications for each country, namely ARCH(1), GJR(1,0) and EGARCH(1,1) for Barbados, ARCH(1), GJR(1,0) and EARCH(1) for Cyprus, and GARCH(1,1), GJR(1,1) and EGARCH(1,1) for Fiji, are selected on the basis of the significance of their parameter estimates and on their overall forecast accuracy performance.

All the estimates are obtained using the Berndt et al. (1974) algorithm in the EViews 4 econometric software package. Virtually identical estimates were obtained using the RATS program. Several different sets of initial values have been used in each case, but do not lead to substantial differences in the estimates.

Estimates of the parameters of both the international tourist arrivals and conditional volatility models for the univariate OLS linear regression model and various univariate GARCH models for Barbados, Cyprus and Fiji are presented in Tables 2.3–2.5, respectively. Asymptotic standard errors are reported under each corresponding parameter estimate. The tourist arrivals estimates for the linear regression constant volatility model and the three time-varying conditional volatility models vary across the three countries, as well as total international tourist arrivals. There is highly significant seasonality in international tourist arrivals for each country and for each month. The lagged effects of monthly international tourist arrivals are highly significant for all three countries, and especially so for Barbados.

The constant volatility linear regression model estimated by OLS is compared with the three optimal time-varying conditional volatility models for Barbados, namely ARCH(1), GJR(1,0) and EGARCH(1,1). Asymmetric effects are not significant for GJR(1,0) but are significant for EGARCH(1,1). The contribution of shocks to long-run persistence is not significant for either ARCH(1) or GJR(1,0).

For Cyprus, the constant volatility linear regression model estimated by OLS is compared with the three optimal time-varying conditional volatility models, namely ARCH(1), GJR(1,0) and EARCH(1). Asymmetric effects are not significant for either GJR(1,0) or EGARCH(1,1). The contribution of shocks to long-run persistence is not significant for any of the three time-varying conditional volatility models.

Finally, the constant volatility linear regression model estimated by OLS is compared with the three optimal time-varying conditional volatility models for Fiji, namely GARCH(1,1), GJR(1,1) and EGARCH(1,1). Asymmetric effects are not significant for either GJR(1,0) or EGARCH(1,1). The contribution of shocks to long-run persistence is significant for each of the three time-varying conditional volatility models.

Overall, the results show that the parameter estimates for the short-run persistence of shocks to international tourist arrivals, and occasionally also the long-run persistence of shocks to international tourist arrivals,

Table 2.3   Barbados: $BRB_t = \phi BRB_{t-1} + \sum_{i=1}^{2} \tau_i t^i + \sum_{i=1}^{12} \delta_i D_i + \theta \varepsilon_{t-1} + \varepsilon_t$

Estimates	OLS	ARCH(1)	GJR(1,0)	EGARCH(1,1)
ϕ	0.919	0.924	0.923	0.906
	32.658	31.423	30.555	33.496
τ_1	7.673	7.666	7.145	7.678
	2.011	1.952	1.833	2.065
τ_2	−0.007	−0.008	−0.006	−0.005
	−0.857	−0.932	−0.741	−0.583
δ_1	−135.644	−286.987	−253.747	120.088
	−0.156	−0.316	−0.274	0.141
δ_2	2893.206	2828.579	2830.022	3261.480
	3.522	3.231	3.221	4.240
δ_3	3071.638	2747.482	2863.464	3407.770
	3.658	3.181	3.267	3.969
δ_4	−1052.647	−1059.075	−867.435	−322.568
	−1.218	−1.212	−0.963	−0.383
δ_5	−5306.594	−5472.281	−5452.205	−4950.037
	−6.629	−6.310	−6.196	−6.550
δ_6	−1488.289	−1626.663	−1705.372	−1340.453
	−2.216	−1.620	−1.739	−2.393
δ_7	12320.958	12188.295	12301.648	12457.768
	19.488	18.871	19.647	16.264
δ_8	746.181	671.204	991.355	1718.250
	0.895	0.776	1.109	2.112
δ_9	−10281.521	−10477.097	−10565.309	−10124.148
	−12.694	−12.582	−12.216	−12.900
δ_{10}	5646.661	5572.344	5679.242	5874.362
	9.273	7.300	7.571	11.462
δ_{11}	6361.296	6167.258	6163.531	6542.286
	9.409	8.514	8.491	10.517
δ_{12}	6277.338	6132.180	6172.355	6743.942
	8.174	8.241	8.173	8.775
θ	−0.501	−0.500	−0.490	−0.449
	−8.152	−7.597	−6.772	−7.306
ω		5591272.813	5553966.677	6.749
		10.396	10.526	1.544
α		0.064	0.148	−0.064
		1.028	1.347	−6.230
γ			−0.154	0.166
			−1.264	2.127
β				0.570
				2.020

Note: Asymptotic t-ratios are reported under each corresponding parameter estimate.

Table 2.4　　Cyprus: $CYP_t = \phi \, CYP_{t-1} + \sum_{i=1}^{12} \delta_i D_i t + \varepsilon_t$

Estimates	OLS	ARCH(1)	GJR(1,0)	EARCH(1)
ϕ	0.780	0.786	0.783	0.797
	21.785	22.020	34.418	23.267
δ_1	−15.235	−14.932	−11.491	−19.169
	−0.909	−1.090	−1.441	−1.484
δ_2	96.943	97.580	97.853	92.829
	6.572	8.778	12.886	8.058
δ_3	264.697	257.892	258.142	254.917
	16.907	14.573	18.354	15.304
δ_4	349.825	350.666	352.813	342.728
	16.693	12.748	16.914	13.563
δ_5	358.917	337.161	341.233	331.013
	12.623	10.723	16.120	10.839
δ_6	198.726	191.799	195.042	182.313
	5.694	5.730	20.167	5.607
δ_7	414.996	409.020	412.804	402.026
	11.981	12.187	58.172	12.568
δ_8	271.828	266.787	269.925	256.752
	6.510	6.564	32.189	6.723
δ_9	123.153	114.221	119.461	105.361
	2.902	2.848	10.215	2.732
δ_{10}	92.591	86.245	89.984	73.058
	2.443	2.457	7.909	2.212
δ_{11}	−272.852	−271.253	−267.091	−278.233
	−8.175	−8.478	−22.391	−9.131
δ_{12}	−3.533	0.459	1.374	−5.338
	−0.190	0.027	0.144	−0.324
ω		73620917.673	74523980.142	18.025
		8.246	8.033	144.143
α		0.406	0.494	0.582
		1.847	1.389	4.825
γ			−0.195	0.081
			−0.482	1.045

Note:　Asymptotic *t*-ratios are reported under each corresponding parameter estimate.

are significant. The asymmetric effects of shocks in some of the GARCH, GJR and EGARCH specifications are also significant. These results show that the OLS linear regression model with constant variance (that is, non-time-varying volatility) is not the optimal specification for modelling international tourist arrivals to Barbados, Cyprus and Fiji.

Table 2.5   *Fiji:* $FJI_t = \phi FJI_{t-1} + \sum_{i=1}^{2} \tau_i t_i + \sum_{i=1}^{12} \delta_i D_i + \theta \varepsilon_{t-1} + \varepsilon_t$

$$t_1 = \begin{cases} t, & t = 1, \ldots, 88 \\ 0, & t = 89, \ldots, T \end{cases} \quad t_2 = \begin{cases} t, & t = 89, \ldots, T \\ 0, & t = 1, \ldots, 88 \end{cases}$$

Estimates	OLS	GARCH(1,1)	GJR(1,1)	EGARCH(1,1)
ϕ	0.667	0.797	0.799	0.851
	12.328	23.132	31.714	25.255
τ_1	19.869	12.506	12.372	10.093
	5.699	5.259	6.701	4.290
τ_2	38.812	23.433	23.211	22.053
	3.863	4.207	4.930	4.007
δ_1	1044.796	200.430	218.338	156.115
	1.588	0.511	0.569	0.380
δ_2	−157.418	−774.421	−715.719	−675.495
	−0.259	−2.110	−2.204	−1.917
δ_3	3457.884	2388.051	2289.588	1394.980
	6.190	5.881	5.657	4.689
δ_4	841.667	−217.658	−203.335	−628.799
	1.377	−0.519	−0.454	−1.932
δ_5	1940.630	2318.276	2290.502	1807.135
	3.329	5.555	5.791	5.704
δ_6	1774.130	964.159	863.071	72.126
	3.012	2.284	2.073	0.214
δ_7	5172.349	4220.663	4182.181	3283.947
	8.761	11.283	11.793	8.862
δ_8	5335.148	4707.900	4665.460	4126.746
	7.659	10.452	11.442	9.885
δ_9	244.714	−1831.471	−1926.020	−2893.680
	0.310	−3.939	−5.059	−7.313
δ_{10}	2372.121	1631.019	1595.012	1017.260
	3.578	4.869	5.441	3.484
δ_{11}	1780.591	774.102	761.385	726.108
	2.706	2.246	2.467	1.940
δ_{12}	2832.173	2039.194	2048.571	1951.914
	4.447	5.904	6.357	5.967
θ	0.056	−0.251	−0.260	−0.294
	0.765	−3.803	−9.930	−3.546
ω		1499028.575	1420679.169	0.538
		5.553	4.732	1.710
α		0.453	0.394	0.382
		3.722	2.342	2.602

Table 2.5   (continued)

Estimates	OLS	GARCH(1,1)	GJR(1,1)	EGARCH(1,1)
γ			0.147	−0.101
			0.621	−1.539
β		0.295	0.307	0.946
		2.364	10.585	43.438

Note: Asymptotic *t*-ratios are reported under each corresponding parameter estimate.

Descriptive statistics of monthly international tourist arrivals and volatility are given in Table 2.6, while the graphs of the respective series are given in Figures 2.1 and 2.2. It is not surprising that the volatilities of monthly international tourist arrivals to each of the three SITEs is positively skewed.

The constant volatility OLS linear regression model and the three optimal time-varying conditional volatility models for each country are used to forecast the final 12 observations in the sample. The four criteria used to evaluate the respective forecast performance of the models for each country are as follows:

1. Root mean square error:

$$RMSE = \sqrt{\frac{\sum\limits_{\tau=T+1}^{T+m} (\hat{y}_\tau - y_\tau)^2}{m+1}}$$

2. Mean absolute error:

$$MAE = \frac{1}{(m+1)} \sum\limits_{\tau=T+1}^{T+m} |\hat{y}_\tau - y_\tau|$$

3. Mean absolute percentage error:

$$MAPE = \frac{1}{(m+1)} \sum\limits_{\tau=T+1}^{T+m} \left| \frac{\bar{y}_\tau - y_\tau}{y_\tau} \right|$$

4. Forecast standard error:

$$\sqrt{\hat{V}ar(\hat{y}_\tau - y_\tau | x_\tau)} = \hat{h}_\tau^{\frac{1}{2}} \left(1 + \frac{1}{T} + \frac{(x_\tau - \bar{x})^2}{\sum\limits_{t=1}^{T}(x_t - \bar{x})^2} \right)^{\frac{1}{2}},$$

Table 2.6   Descriptive statistics of monthly international tourist arrivals and volatility

Barbados

Statistics	y_t	v_t
Mean	31979	5982681
Median	32707	2398085
Maximum	54730	50123872
Minimum	11259	112
SD	9282	9060982
Skewness	−0.132	2.578
Kurtosis	2.421	10.415

Cyprus

Statistics	y_t	v_t
Mean	107733	1.13E+08
Median	77238	46320405
Maximum	373385	1.25E+09
Minimum	3998	2642
SD	91025	1.91E+08
Skewness	1.000	3.223
Kurtosis	3.033	14.851

Fiji

Statistics	y_t	v_t
Mean	19262	5851579
Median	18033	1438284
Maximum	41031	2.78E+08
Minimum	3974	13
SD	7524	20032580
Skewness	0.432	9.815
Kurtosis	2.746	118.693

where $y_t = E(y_t|x_t) + \varepsilon_t$, m denotes the size of the forecast horizon, T denotes the sample size used for within sample parameter estimation, and $\hat{h}_\tau$ denotes the estimated conditional variance for time τ.

The forecast results are reported in Table 2.7, with the rankings of the models by forecast standard errors for the 12 months being based on the largest number of accurate monthly forecasts. For Barbados, the optimal

Table 2.7   Forecast results for monthly international tourist arrivals

Barbados	RMSE	MAE	MAPE	FSE (ranking)
OLS	2951	2552	6.01	4
ARCH(1)	3013	2612	6.13	2
GJR(1,0)	2931	2513	5.93	3
EGARCH(1,1)	2847	2424	5.8	1

Cyprus	RMSE	MAE	MAPE	FSE (ranking)
OLS	24675	17254	9.35	2
ARCH(1)	24089	16582	9.07	4
GJR(1,0)	24475	17415	10.01	3
EARCH(1)	23842	16712	9.35	1

Fiji	RMSE	MAE	MAPE	FSE (ranking)
OLS	3404	2595	7.31	3
GARCH(1,1)	3109	2300	6.51	1
GJR(1,1)	3180	2361	6.68	2
EGARCH(1,1)	3201	2575	7.56	4

Notes:
RMSE = root mean square error.
MAE = mean absolute error.
MAPE denotes mean absolute percentage error.
FSE denotes forecast standard error.
For definitions, see text.

forecasting model overall based on the four criteria is EGARCH(1,1), followed by GJR(1,0), so that both asymmetry and the long-run persistence of shocks assist in the optimal forecasting of monthly international tourist arrivals. The optimal forecasting model for Cyprus overall based on the four criteria is EARCH(1), followed by ARCH(1), so that asymmetry, but not the long-run persistence of shocks, assists in the optimal forecasting of monthly international tourist arrivals. Finally, for Fiji, the optimal forecasting model overall based on the four criteria is GARCH(1,1), followed by GJR(1,1), so that both asymmetry and the long-run persistence of shocks assist in the optimal forecasting of monthly international tourist arrivals.

It is instructive that at least two of the three time-varying conditional volatility models are superior to the constant volatility linear regression model estimated by OLS for each of the three countries.

7. CONCLUSION

This chapter showed how several variations of the generalized autoregressive conditional heteroscedasticity (GARCH) model could be used to forecast monthly international tourism demand and uncertainty by modelling the conditional volatility in monthly international tourist arrivals to Barbados, Cyprus and Fiji. These small island tourism economies have extensive monthly observations on international tourist arrivals.

The international tourist arrivals estimates for the linear regression constant volatility model and the three time-varying conditional volatility models varied across the three countries, as well as total international tourist arrivals. There was highly significant seasonality in international tourist arrivals for each country and for each month. The lagged effects of monthly international tourist arrivals were highly significant for all three countries.

Overall, the results showed that the parameter estimates for the short- and long-run persistence of shocks to international tourist arrivals were significant, as were the asymmetric effects of shocks. These results showed that the OLS linear regression model with constant variance (that is, non-time-varying volatility) was not the optimal specification for modelling international tourist arrivals to Barbados, Cyprus and Fiji.

In terms of forecasting, both asymmetry and the long-run persistence of shocks generally assisted in the optimal forecasting of monthly international tourist arrivals. As at least two of the three time-varying conditional volatility models were superior to the constant volatility linear regression model estimated by OLS for each of the three countries, modelling conditional volatility was demonstrated as being important in establishing accurate confidence interval forecasts of monthly international tourist arrivals to Barbados, Cyprus and Fiji.

ACKNOWLEDGEMENTS

The authors wish to acknowledge the financial support of the Australian Research Council. The fourth author also wishes to thank the C.A. Vargovic Memorial Fund at the University of Western Australia.

REFERENCES

Armstrong, H.W. and Read, R. (1995), 'Western European Micro-States and Autonomous Regions: The Advantages of Size and Sovereignty', *World Development*, **23** (7), 1229–45.

Armstrong, H.W. and Read, R. (1998), 'Trade and Growth in Small States: The Impact of Global Trade Liberalisation', *World Economy*, **21** (4), 563–85.

Armstrong, H.W. and Read, R. (2002), 'The Phantom of Liberty?: Economic Growth and the Vulnerability of Small States', *Journal of International Development*, **14** (3), 435–58.

Berndt, E.K., Hall, B.H., Hall, R.E. and Hausman, J. (1974), 'Estimation and Inference in Nonlinear Structural Models', *Annals of Economic and Social Measurement*, **3**, 653–65.

Bollerslev, T. (1986), 'Generalised Autoregressive Conditional Heteroscedasticity', *Journal of Econometrics*, **31**, 307–27.

Bollerslev, T., Chou, R.Y. and Kroner, K.F. (1992), 'ARCH Modelling in Finance: A Review of the Theory and Empirical Evidence', *Journal of Econometrics*, **52**, 5–59.

Bollerslev, T., Engle, R.F. and Nelson, D.B. (1994), 'ARCH Models', in R.F Engle and D.L McFadden (eds), *Handbook of Econometrics*, **4**, Amsterdam: North Holland, pp. 2961–3038.

Briguglio, L. (1995), 'Small Island Developing States and Their Economic Vulnerabilities', *World Development*, **23** (9), 1615–32.

Commonwealth Secretariat/World Bank Joint Task Force on Small States (2000), 'Small States: Meeting Challenges in the Global Economy', London: Commonwealth Secretariat/Washington, DC: The World Bank.

Dommen, E. (1980), 'Some Distinguishing Characteristics of Island States', *World Development*, **8**, 931–43.

Engle, R.F. (1982), 'Autoregressive Conditional Heteroscedasticity with Estimates of the Variance of United Kingdom Inflation', *Econometrica*, **50**, 987–1007.

Glosten, L., Jagannathan, R. and Runkle, D. (1992), 'On the Relation Between the Expected Value and Volatility of Nominal Excess Return on Stocks', *Journal of Finance*, **46**, 1779–801.

Jeantheau, T. (1998), 'Strong Consistency of Estimators for Multivariate ARCH Models', *Econometric Theory*, **14**, 70–86.

Kuznets, S. (1960), 'Economic Growth of Small Nations', in E.A.G. Robinson (ed.), *The Economic Consequences of the Size of Nations*, London: Macmillan, pp. 14–32.

Li, W.K., Ling, S. and McAleer, M. (2002), 'Recent Theoretical Results for Time Series Models with GARCH Errors', *Journal of Economic Surveys*, **16**, 245–69. Reprinted in M. McAleer and L. Oxley (eds), *Contributions to Financial Econometrics: Theoretical and Practical Issues*, Oxford: Blackwell, 2002, pp. 9–33.

Ling, S. and McAleer, M. (2002a), 'Necessary and Sufficient Moment Conditions for GARCH(r,s) and Asymmetric Power of GARCH(r,s) Models', *Econometric Theory*, **18**, 722–29.

Ling, S. and McAleer, M. (2002b), 'Stationary and the Existence of Moments of a Family of GARCH Processes', *Journal of Econometrics*, **106**, 109–17.

Ling, S. and McAleer, M. (2003), 'Asymptotic Theory for a Vector ARMA-GARCH Model', *Econometric Theory*, **19**, 278–308.

Liou, F.M. and Ding, C.G. (2002), 'Subgrouping Small States Based on Socio-economic Characteristics', *World Development*, **30** (7), 1289–306.

McAleer, M., Chan, F. and Marinova, D. (2003), 'An Econometric Analysis of Asymmetric Volatility: Theory and Applications to Patents', to appear in *Journal of Econometrics*.

Nelson, D.B. (1991), 'Conditional Heteroscedasticity in Asset Returns: A New Approach', *Econometrica*, **59**, 347–70.

Robinson, E.A.G. (ed.) (1960), *Economic Consequences of the Size of Nations*, London: Macmillan, pp. 14–32.

Shareef, R. (2003a), 'Small Island Tourism Economies: A Bird's Eye View', in D. Post (ed.), *Proceedings of the International Conference on Modelling and Simulation: Socio-economic Systems*, **3**, Townsville, Australia, pp. 1124–29.

Shareef, R. (2003b), 'Small Island Tourism Economies: A Snapshot of Country Risk Ratings', in D. Post (ed.), *Proceedings of the International Conference on Modelling and Simulation: Socio-economic Systems*, **3**, Townsville, Australia, pp. 1142–47.

Shephard, N. (1996), 'Statistical Aspects of ARCH and Stochastic Volatility', in O.E. Barndorff-Nielsen, D.R. Cox and D.V. Hinkley (eds), *Statistical Models in Econometrics, Finance and Other Fields*, London: Chapman & Hall, pp. 1–67.

World Bank (2002), 'World Development Indicators', CD-ROM.

3. Land, environmental externalities and tourism development*

Javier Rey-Maquieira Palmer, Javier Lozano Ibáñez and Carlos Mario Gómez Gómez

1. INTRODUCTION

Nowadays there is wide consensus that there are limits to a tourism development based on quantitative growth. Obviously, the availability of a fixed amount of land in a tourism resort puts an ultimate limit on its carrying capacity. However, it is reasonable to assume that before the full occupation of land by tourism facilities other limiting factors will operate. Thus the continuous growth in the number of tourists and the associated urban development, especially in small tourism destinations, can give rise to costs in the form of congestion of public goods and loss of cultural, natural and environmental resources. These costs are not only borne by the residents but may also negatively affect the tourism attractiveness of the destination, the willingness to pay for tourism services provided in the tourism resort and thus a fall in the returns to investment in the tourism sector.

In this chapter we develop a two-sector dynamic general equilibrium model of a small open economy where tourism development is characterized as a process of reallocation of land in fixed supply from low productivity activities (agriculture, forestry and so on) to its use in the building of tourism facilities. This change in the use of land goes along with investment aimed at the building of accommodation and recreational facilities. Land in the traditional sector, besides being a direct production factor in this sector, contains the cultural, natural and environmental resources of the economy. These resources are not only valued by the residents but also have a positive effect on the tourism attractiveness of the resort and on the willingness to pay to visit the tourism destination. We therefore make explicit one of the characteristics of tourism development, i.e. the urbanization of land. The model allows for discussion about the limits of the quantitative tourism development in terms of three relevant factors: dependence of tourism with respect to cultural, natural and environmental assets available in fixed supply, the positive valuation of these assets by the residents and relative productivity of tourism with respect to other alternative sectors.

Despite the costs of tourism expansion, in the model tourism development is associated with improvements in the standard of living for the residents that are ultimately determined by two factors: sectoral change and investment opportunities associated with the tourism sector on the one hand and improvements in the price of tourism relative to manufactures on the other hand. While the latter has already been put forward by Lanza and Pigliaru (1994), this is to our knowledge the first chapter to consider in a dynamic general equilibrium setting the reallocation of factors from low productivity sectors to the tourism sector as a possible explanation for the fast growth of the economies that specialize in tourism.

The rest of the chapter is organized as follows. Section 2 discusses the model. Section 3 shows the optimal solution. In section 4 we obtain the behavior of the economy when the costs of tourism development are external to the decision makers. Section 5 compares the optimal and decentralized solution with the green golden rule in order to discuss several issues regarding long-term environmental degradation. Section 6 considers the case when the price of tourism relative to manufactures grows exogenously, driven by international factors, and compares the dynamics of land allocation in the optimal and decentralized solution. Finally, section 7 concludes.

2. THE MODEL

2.1 Production

We consider a region with a limited space that we normalize to one. Land has two alternative productive uses. On the one hand, it can be used in a traditional sector (agriculture, farming, forestry). On the other hand, it can be combined with physical capital to obtain tourism facilities for accommodation and recreational purposes. We denote the first type of land L_T and the second L_{NT}.

In the economy there are three sectors. First, production in the traditional sector depends on land devoted to this purpose, with decreasing returns and the following production function:

$$Y_{NT} = g(L_{NT})$$

or, given that L_T is the complementary of L_{NT}:

$$Y_{NT} = f(L_T), \tag{3.1}$$

where $f(L_T)$ and df/dL_T are continuous functions in the interval $L_T \in [0,1]$ with the following properties:

$$Y_{NT} = 0 \quad \text{when} \quad L_T = 1$$

$$\frac{dY_{NT}}{dL_{NT}} > 0, \frac{d^2 Y_{NT}}{dL_{NT}^2} < 0, \quad \lim_{L_{NT} \to 0^+} \frac{dY_{NT}}{dL_{NT}} = \infty$$

$$\frac{dY_{NT}}{dL_T} < 0, \frac{d^2 Y_{NT}}{dL_T^2} < 0, \quad \lim_{L_T \to 1^-} \frac{dY_{NT}}{dL_T} = -\infty$$

Second, a construction sector builds tourism facilities for accommodation and recreational purposes using land and investment in physical capital. For simplicity, we consider that both production factors are combined in fixed proportions to obtain units of accommodation capacity according to the following expression:

$$\dot{T} = \min(\eta \dot{L}_T, \varphi I), \tag{3.2}$$

where $\dot{T}$ are new units of accommodation capacity that are built in each moment of time. $\dot{L}_T$ and I are the amount of land and investment needed for providing the tourism facilities associated with those units of accommodation capacity, while η and φ are fixed parameters.

Given (3.2), efficiency requires that:

$$\dot{T} = \eta \dot{L}_T = \varphi I$$

and therefore:

$$\dot{L}_T = \frac{\varphi}{\eta} I \tag{3.3}$$

$$T(\tau) = \int_0^\tau \dot{T}(t)dt = \int_0^\tau \eta \dot{L}_T(t)dt = \eta L_T(\tau), \tag{3.4}$$

where in (3.4) we have assumed that $T(t=0) = L_T(t=0) = 0$.

Expression (3.3) shows the relationship between investment and land in the provision of tourism facilities, where η/φ measures the investment per unit of land. According to expression (3.4), accommodation capacity is proportional to the land devoted to tourism facilities.

Finally, a tourism sector supplies accommodation and recreational services using tourism facilities. Output of the tourism sector is measured by the number of night stays per unit of time. Assuming that night stays is a fixed multiple ϑ of the accommodation capacity, output of the tourism sector is a linear function of the land occupied by tourism facilities:

$$Y_T = AL_T, \quad A = \vartheta\eta. \tag{3.5}$$

Notice that A is the upper limit to the output of the tourism sector, that is, if $L_T = 1$, then $Y_T = A$. Therefore, this parameter can be interpreted as a measure of physical carrying capacity. The number of the night stays is a fraction of this carrying capacity determined by the fraction of the space devoted to tourism facilities.

2.2   Trade Flows

We are interested in a situation where tourism services are provided to foreigners. We assume that the economy sells the whole production of both sectors in exchange for an homogeneous good, manufactures, that is produced abroad. This imported good is used for consumption and investment and it is the numeraire. Moreover, for simplicity we assume that the economy cannot lend or borrow from abroad. Given these assumptions, the goods market clearing condition implies:

$$TR + NTR = C + I \tag{3.6}$$
$$TR = P_T Y_T$$
$$NTR = P_{NT} Y_{NT},$$

where TR and NTR stand for tourism and non-tourism revenues and P_T and P_{NT} are the prices of tourism and non-tourism production relative to manufactures, while C is aggregate consumption.

2.3   Hypothesis about Prices of Final Goods and Tourism Revenues Function

We assume that P_{NT} is fixed, that is the economy is small in the international market of this product. Without loss of generality we normalize this price to one.

Regarding the price of the tourism services, our crucial assumption is that the price of the night stay depends on the satisfaction of the tourists that visit the resort. The satisfaction of a visitor depends on many variables: some are specific to the tourism firm that provides for lodging and recreational services and some are common to the whole tourism resort. The model includes two of the first kind of characteristics that could be determinants of the satisfaction of visitors, namely capital and land per unit of accommodation capacity. However, these ratios are considered exogenous and therefore play a secondary role in the model. Our interest lies in those characteristics that are common to the tourism resort and, specifically, in landscape and cultural and environmental assets. Regarding this, we assume two hypotheses: first, loss of landscape and cultural and environmental assets reduces the satisfaction of the tourists that visit the resort; and second, these intangibles can be approximated by the allocation of land between its alternative uses. Basically we are assuming that the economy is endowed with natural and cultural assets with tourism attractiveness and these assets are intrinsically linked with that fraction of land devoted to traditional activities. With this assumption we follow works by Rubio and Goetz (1998) and Pisa (2003) where the undeveloped fraction of land is used as a proxy for environmental quality.

Formally our reasoning runs as follows. We define a utility function that measures the satisfaction per night stay of a tourist that visits the resort:

$$U_T^i = U_T^i(\omega^i, \Omega),$$

where U_T^i is satisfaction of a tourist that receives services from firm i, ω^i is a vector of those characteristics specific to that tourism firm and Ω measures characteristics that are common to the whole tourism resort (landscape, cultural and environmental assets, congestion). Given the restrictions imposed to the production sector, all the tourism firms are identical and therefore we can drop the index i. Let us now define P_U as the price a tourist is willing to pay for a unit of satisfaction obtained in the resort. We consider that this price is exogenously determined in the international market and it is a price relative to manufactures. Given this, we can obtain an expression for the price for tourism services in the resort:

$$P_T = P_U U_T(\omega, \Omega),$$

where P_T is the price paid per night stay. This function could be interpreted in the following way. In the international economy there is a continuum of tourism markets differentiated by their quality and the price paid for the tourism services. In each of them the suppliers are price-takers but they can move along the quality ladder either due to their own decisions or due to changes in the characteristics of the tourism resort where they are located. If we consider that the allocation of land is a good approximation of Ω, then:

$$P_T = P(L_{NT}), \; P'(L_{NT}) > 0$$

or, alternatively,[1]

$$P_T = P(L_T), \; P'(L_T) < 0,$$

where we have dropped the vector ω since it is constant through time and we have normalized P_U to one.

In the literature we can find several works that justify the hypothesis that the tourism price depends on the allocation of land. First, applying the contingent valuation methodology, works such as Drake (1992), Pruckner (1995) or Drake (1999) show that the willingness to pay for the landscape associated with agricultural land can be large. On this base, López et al. (1994) and Brunstad et al. (1999) consider the hypothesis that this willingness to pay is a function of the amount of land devoted to agricultural activities. Second, in the tourism field Fleischer and Tsur (2000), applying the travel cost method, show that tourists give a positive valuation to agricultural landscape that is of a large magnitude in comparison with the agricultural production value. Huybers and Bennett (2000) also measure the willingness to pay of tourists for better environmental conditions and lower congestion in the tourism resorts they visit.

Given (3.5) and the function for the price of a night stay, tourism revenues are:

$$TR = AL_T P(L_T).$$

We consider that this function is continuous and twice differentiable in the interval $L_T \in [0,1]$.

The occupation of the land by tourism facilities has two opposite effects on tourism revenues: on the one hand, a positive quantity effect given the positive relationship between night stays and land occupied by tourism facilities and, on the other hand, a negative effect on price due to the loss of intangible assets with tourism attractiveness. The relative strength of both effects determines the behavior of tourism revenues along a process of tourism development. Regarding this, we can consider two interesting scenarios.

In the first, the quantity effect dominates the price effect, that is:

$$\frac{dTR}{dL_T} > 0 \ \forall L_T \in [0,1]$$

This is the case if the elasticity of the price with respect to L_T is below one $\forall L_T \in [0,1]$

In a second interesting scenario the elasticity of the tourism price is increasing with L_T in such a way that:

$$\frac{dTR}{dL_T} > 0 \quad \text{if} \ L_T \in [0, \hat{L}_T)$$

$$\frac{dTR}{dL_T} < 0 \quad \text{if} \ L_T \in (\hat{L}_T, 1]$$

$$\hat{L}_T \in (0,1),$$

where $\hat{L}_T$ is a tourism development threshold beyond which tourism expansion leads to a fall in tourism revenues. This will be the case if the elasticity of the price is lower than one when L_T is below that threshold and higher than one when L_T is above it.[2]

In both scenarios we consider that:

$$\frac{d^2 TR}{dL_T^2} < 0$$

$$TR(L_T) > 0 \; \forall L_T \in (0,1].$$

The second condition implies that the intangible assets linked to land used in traditional activities are not essential for the resort to have tourism attractiveness since the tourism price is positive even in the case where all the land is occupied by tourism facilities.

2.4 Residents' Preferences

We consider that the economy is populated by a single representative agent that gives positive value to consumption and those cultural and natural assets that are contained in land devoted to traditional activities. His/her instantaneous utility function is:

$$U = U(C, L_{NT}) \quad U_C > 0, \; U_{CC} < 0, \; U_{LNT} > 0, \; U_{LNTLNT} < 0$$

3. THE OPTIMAL SOLUTION

The optimal solution results from solving the following problem:

$$MAX \int_0^\infty e^{-\rho t} U(C, L_{NT}) dt$$

subject to:

$$\dot{L}_T = \frac{\varphi}{\eta}[TR(L_T) + NTR(L_T) - C] \qquad (3.7)$$

$$C \geq 0$$

$$0 \leq L_T \leq 1$$

$$L_{NT} = 1 - L_T,$$

where (3.3) and (3.6) have been considered and ρ is the rate of time preference.

The first-order conditions of the maximum principle are:

$$U_C = \lambda \frac{\varphi}{\eta} \qquad (3.8)$$

$$- U_{L_{NT}} + \lambda \frac{\varphi}{\eta} [TR'(L_T) + NTR'(L_T)] = \rho\lambda - \dot{\lambda} \qquad (3.9)$$

and the transversality condition is:

$$\lim_{t \to \infty} e^{-\rho t} \lambda(t) L_T(t) = 0.$$

From (3.8) and (3.9) results:

$$TR'(L_T) = \frac{\eta}{\varphi} \left[\rho + \theta \frac{\dot{C}}{C} + \frac{U_{CL_{NT}}}{U_C} \dot{L}_T \right] - NTR'(L_T) + \frac{U_{L_{NT}}}{U_C}, \qquad (3.10)$$

where $\theta = - U_{CC} C/U_C$ is the elasticity of the marginal utility of consumption which is assumed constant.

Expression (3.10) is the Keynes–Ramsey rule that equates marginal returns to L_T (left-hand side) and the loss in utility and revenues from the traditional sector that arises from a marginal development of land aimed to accommodate tourism facilities (right-hand side). In equilibrium, marginal returns to L_T have to be larger the larger is the rate of time preference, since the occupation of land by tourism facilities requires an investment effort and therefore a delay in consumption. The second and third terms on the right-hand side measure the proportional change of the marginal utility of consumption, $- \dot{U}_C/U_C$. If, for instance, marginal utility of consumption falls through time,[3] the faster its fall, the lower the value of an increase in consumption capacity due to the expansion of tourism and, therefore, the higher the marginal return of L_T should be. The fourth term is the loss of revenues from the traditional sector due to a marginal transfer of land from that sector to the tourism sector. Finally, tourism expansion results in environmental, landscape and cultural losses whose value in terms of consumption is $U_{L_{NT}}/U_C$, that is, the last term of the right-hand side.

In the steady state all the variables remain constant. Therefore, and given (3.7) and (3.10) in the steady state the following conditions must be satisfied:

$$C_I = \frac{1}{v\theta} \left\{ (1 - L_T) \left[TR'(L_T) + NTR'(L_T) - \frac{\eta}{\varphi}\rho \right] \right.$$

$$\left. - v(1 - \theta)[TR(L_T) + NTR(L_T)] \right\} \qquad (3.11)$$

$$C_{II} = TR(L_T) + NTR(L_T) \qquad (3.12)$$
$$C_I = C_{II},$$

where we have considered the following utility function for the resident:

$$U = \frac{(CL_{NT}^v)^{1-\theta}}{1-\theta} \qquad (3.13)$$

Proposition 1. *In the optimal solution there is a unique steady state where the tourism sector is present if and only if the following condition is satisfied:*

$$TR'(0) > vNTR(0) - NTR'(0) + \frac{\eta}{\varphi}\rho. \qquad (3.14)$$

If (3.14) is satisfied, in the steady state C>0 and $L_T \in (0,1)$.
Proof: see Appendix I.

Let us assume that the economy is initially specialized in the traditional sector and condition (3.14) is satisfied. As is shown in Figure 3.1, there is an initial consumption level, C_0, that puts the economy on a path that

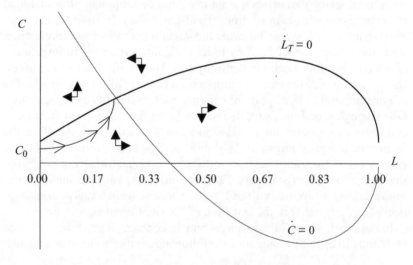

Note: [a] The following functional forms and parameter values have been used:
$Y_{NT} = B(L_{NT})^\beta$, $P_T = P_U[(L_{NT})^\alpha + j]$, $IT = AL_T P_T$, $B = 300\,000$, $A = 3\,000\,000$, $\alpha = 0.5$,
$\beta = 0.9$, $\eta = 100\,000$, $\varphi = 0.035$, $\theta = 0.8$, $\rho = 0.05$, $v = 0.5$, $j = 0.1$, $P_U = 1$.

Figure 3.1   Steady state and path of tourism development in the optimal solution[a]

converges to the steady state.[4] This path is characterized by a process of tourism development where capital accumulates, land is progressively occupied by tourism facilities and consumption and tourism revenues grow. This process of tourism expansion stops before reaching the physical carrying capacity due to three factors: the negative effect of congestion, loss of intangible assets on residents' and tourists' utility and the increase in marginal returns to land in the traditional sector.

Expression (3.14) can be interpreted as a necessary condition for a process of tourism development to be socially optimal. That is, for residents to be interested in the expansion of the tourism sector, revenues from the initial development of this sector, net of the revenue losses in the traditional sector, that is, $TR'(0) + NTR'(0)$, should be high enough; total revenues from the traditional sector when the economy is fully specialized in this sector, that is, $NTR(0)$, should be low enough; moreover, the weight on residents' utility of the intangible assets that are linked to land used in the traditional sector, v, as well as the rate of time preference, ρ, and investment per unit of land required for the building of tourism facilities, η/φ, should be low enough. Figure 3.2 shows a case when condition (3.14) is not satisfied. Regarding initial consumption, $C(t=0) > C^*$ is not possible, since it implies $\dot{L}_T(t=0) < 0$ and therefore a negative value of L_T. Any value of

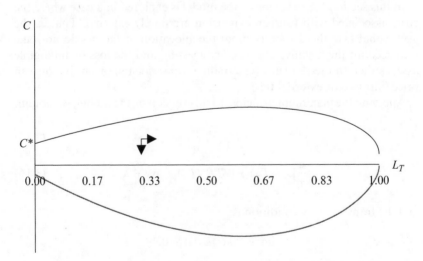

Note: [a] Same functional forms and parameter values as in Figure 3.1 except for P_U. Here $P_U = 0.5$.

Figure 3.2   A case where the expansion of the tourism sector is not socially optimal[a]

$C(t=0) < C^*$ would set the economy in a path where $C(t) < C^*$ $\forall t$, which is inferior to an alternative feasible path where $C(t) = C^*$ $\forall t$. Therefore, the optimal solution is $C(t) = C^*$, $L_T(t) = 0 \forall t$, that is, society is not interested in the tourism development.

4. SOLUTION WITH EXTERNALITIES

In a decentralized economy some of the costs associated with tourism expansion are not considered in the decisions about allocation of factors. For instance, lack of well-defined property rights on natural, environmental and landscape assets implies that, without public intervention, the tourism sector does not compensate the residents for the degradation of those assets linked to tourism expansion. Some of the costs of the tourism development fall on the tourism sector in the form of lower tourism attractiveness of the resort and a lower tourism price. However, the tourism price depends on the characteristics of the whole tourism resort regarding congestion and quality and abundance of intangible assets and, therefore, except for the case of perfect coordination in the tourism sector (for instance, in the case of a monopoly), the decisions of any of the tourism firms will cause negative externalities to the rest of the sector.

In this section the behavior of the model is explored in a case where the costs associated with tourism expansion are purely external. That is, the agents that take the decisions about the allocation of factors do not take into account the negative effects of congestion and the loss of intangible assets either on the residents (externalities on residents) or on the tourism price (intrasector externalities).

Applying the maximum principle to this version of the model, we obtain:

$$U_C = \lambda \frac{\varphi}{\eta} \tag{3.15}$$

$$\lambda \frac{\varphi}{\eta} [AP(L_T) + NTR'(L_T)] = \rho \lambda - \dot{\lambda} \tag{3.16}$$

and the transversality condition is:

$$\lim_{t \to \infty} e^{-\rho t} \lambda(t) L_T(t) = 0.$$

Condition (3.16) is different from (3.9) since in the former we assume that the effects of a change in the use of land on residents' utility and on the price of a night stay are not considered in the decisions of allocation of factors.

The behavior of the economy is determined by the transversality condition and the following dynamic system:

$$\frac{\dot{C}}{C} = \frac{1}{\theta}\frac{\varphi}{\eta}\left[AP(L_T) + NTR'(L_T) - v(1-\theta)\frac{1}{1-L_T}[TR(L_T) \right.$$

$$\left. + NTR(L_T) - C] - \frac{\eta}{\varphi}\rho \right] \qquad (3.17)$$

$$\dot{L}_T = \frac{\varphi}{\eta}[TR(L_T) + NTR(L_T) - C], \qquad (3.7)$$

where (3.13), (3.15) and (3.16) have been considered. The steady state satisfies the following conditions:

$$C_I = -\frac{(1-L_T)}{v(1-\theta)}\left[AP(L_T) + NTR'(L_T) - \frac{\eta}{\varphi}\rho \right] + TR(L_T) + NTR(L_T)$$

$$(3.18)$$

$$C_{II} = TR(L_T) + NTR(L_T) \qquad (3.19)$$
$$C_I = C_{II}.$$

Proposition 2. *In the solution with externalities there is a unique interior steady state if and only if the following condition is satisfied:*

$$AP(0) + NTR'(0) - \frac{\eta}{\varphi}\rho > 0. \qquad (3.20)$$

If (3.20) is satisfied, in the interior steady state $C > 0$, $L_T \in (0,1)$.
Proof: see Appendix II.

As is shown in Appendix II, the interior steady state is saddle-path stable and satisfies the transversality condition. Depending on the functional form of the tourism revenues function, there could exist a second steady state where $L_T = 1$. However, this steady state does not satisfy the transversality condition.

In the optimal solution, if the economy is initially specialized in traditional activities and condition (3.20) is satisfied, the economy will follow a path of tourism expansion characterized by the progressive occupation of land by tourism facilities, accumulation of capital and growth in consumption and tourism revenues. The condition that ensures that this process of tourism development stops before the whole land is occupied by tourism facilities is the assumption that marginal returns to land in the

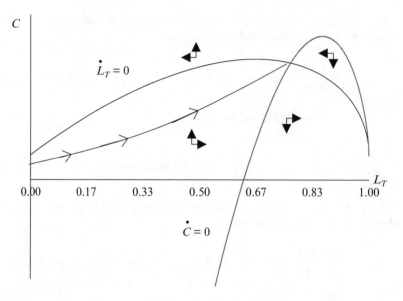

Note: ª Same functional forms and parameter values as in Figure 3.1.

*Figure 3.3   Steady state and path of tourism development in the solution
with externalities*ª

traditional sector go to infinity when L_{NT} tends to zero. Figure 3.3 shows
the steady state and the transitional path for the solution with externalities.

It is easy to show that in the solution with externalities tourism expansion is excessive from the social point of view. On the one hand, in the solution with externalities land occupied by tourism facilities when the steady
state is reached can be worked out from the following expression:

$$AP(L_T) + NTR'(L_T) = \frac{\eta}{\varphi}\rho, \tag{3.21}$$

where (3.18) and (3.19) have been considered.

On the other hand, from (3.11) and (3.12) it follows that in the optimal
solution:

$$AP(L_T) + NTR'(L_T) = \frac{v}{1 - L_T}[TR(L_T) + NTR(L_T)] - AL_TP'(L_T) + \frac{\eta}{\varphi}\rho$$

Given that $(v/(1 - L_T))[TR(L_T) + NTR(L_T)] - AL_TP'(L_T) > 0 \ \forall L_T \in (0,1)$
and that the left-hand side of both expressions is decreasing with L_T, it
follows that when the economic system does not consider the negative

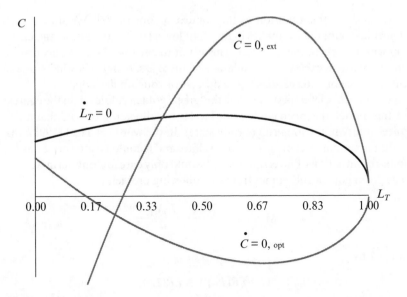

Note: [a]Same functional forms and parameter values as in Figure 3.1 except for the productivity parameter of the traditional sector.

Figure 3.4   A case where tourism expansion takes place despite being suboptimal[a]

external effects of the tourism sector the proportion of land occupied by tourism facilities as well as the accommodation capacity of the tourism resort are excessive from the social welfare point of view.

What is more, when the costs of the tourism expansion are not internalized, it could happen that a process of tourism development would take place despite this being socially suboptimal. This is what happens in the model when (3.20) is satisfied but (3.14) is not. Figure 3.4 shows a case of this sort.

5.   ENVIRONMENTAL DEGRADATION, DISCOUNTING AND EXTERNALITIES

Environmental degradation has often been explained by intergenerational conflict. That is, present generations, seeking to improve their own welfare and disregarding the welfare of future generations, overexploit natural resources leaving a bequest of degraded environment and low welfare. According to this explanation, a high discount factor is to blame for unsustainable development paths.

We address this question in the context of our model. We show that a higher discount factor implies higher (not lower) cultural, natural and environmental assets in the long run. This is not to say that the economy cannot end up with an excessive degradation of these assets but this will be due to the presence of externalities in the process of tourism development.

To show this, let us first calculate the 'green' golden rule level. In the context of this model, the green golden rule level is the allocation of land that maximizes utility in the long run (steady state). In the words of Heal (1998), this is the maximum level of sustainable welfare and it could be interpreted as the long-run situation of an economy that would only care for long-term welfare. The green golden rule comes from the following problem:

$$\underset{C,L_T}{\text{MAX}}\ U = \frac{[C(1-L_T)^\nu]^{1-\theta}}{1-\theta}$$

subject to

$$C = TR(L_T) + NTR(L_T),$$

which gives the following condition:

$$\Phi(L_T) = \frac{(1-L_T)}{\nu}[TR'(L_T) + NTR'(L_T)] - [TR(L_T) + NTR(L_T)] = 0.$$

$$(3.22)$$

The optimal solution and the green golden rule only differ in that in the former the welfare during the transition to the steady state is also considered in the economic decisions and, moreover, the future is discounted. In the optimal solution the economy ends up with a lower level of L_T than the green golden rule level. This can be shown if we combine (3.11) and (3.12) to get:

$$\Phi(L_T) = \frac{(1-L_T)}{\nu}[TR'(L_T) + NTR'(L_T)] - [TR(L_T) + NTR(L_T)]$$

$$= \frac{(1-L_T)}{\nu}\frac{\eta}{\varphi}\rho. \qquad (3.23)$$

Given that the right-hand side of (3.23) is positive when it is evaluated at the steady state of the optimal solution and that $\Phi'(L_T) < 0$ for the relevant range of values for L_T, we can conclude that in the optimal solution the economy ends up with a level of L_T that is lower than the green golden rule. That is, in this model it is not true that environmental degradation is a consequence of disregarding future generations' welfare since if society

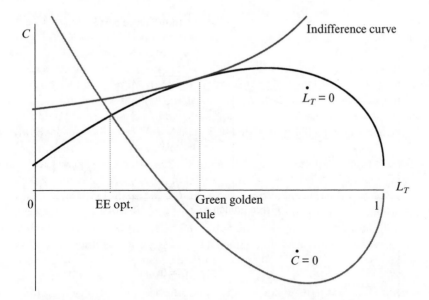

Figure 3.5   Optimal solution's steady state and green golden rule

were only worried about long-term welfare it would opt for a larger tourism expansion and lower long-term cultural, natural and environmental assets. This is due to the fact that tourism expansion and environmental degradation are linked to investment in the provision of tourism facilities. Precisely because in the optimal solution the future is discounted, current generations are not disposed to make the necessary sacrifices in terms of current consumption that are needed to reach the green golden rule. Figure 3.5 compares the steady state of the optimal solution with the green golden rule.

Contrary to the case of the optimal solution, when the environmental and cultural costs of tourism expansion are external to the decision makers, the economy can end up in the long run with a more degraded environment than what would follow from the maximization of long-run welfare. This is what happens if:

$$\frac{\eta}{\varphi}\rho < \frac{\nu}{1 - L_T}[TR(L_T) + NTR(L_T)] - AL_TP'(L_T),$$

the condition that results from the combination of (3.21) and (3.22) and where the right-hand side is evaluated at the green golden rule level.[5] This condition is satisfied for low values of the rate of time preference and investment requirements per unit of land. In this situation the solution with

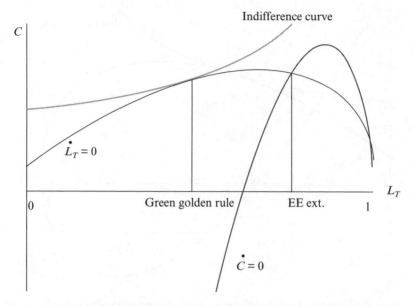

Figure 3.6   Steady state in the solution with externalities and green golden
          rule: a case of dynamic inefficiency

externalities is dynamically inefficient; that is, there are paths that imply higher welfare levels not only in the steady state but also during the transitional path and therefore long-term environmental degradation is not a symptom of intergenerational conflict but of inefficiencies due to the presence of external costs. Figure 3.6 represents a case where the solution with externalities implies excessive environmental degradation from the long-term welfare point of view.

6.   CONTINUOUS GROWTH AND ENVIRONMENTAL DEGRADATION

As set up, the model does not allow for long-run growth based on endogenous factors. On the one hand, consistent with a large body of the literature that stresses the existence of a carrying capacity in the tourism resorts (see for instance Butler, 1980), quantitative growth based on the increase in accommodation capacity and the number of visitors is not possible given a limited amount of space[6] and cultural and environmental assets. On the other hand, the model is constructed in a way that qualitative growth, for instance through the increase in capital per unit of accommodation, is not possible.[7] Therefore, if we want to analyze the effects of continuous growth on the allocation of land we have to rely on exogenous forces. A good candidate is the price of tourism relative to manufactures. Thus, in this section we explore the behavior of the model in a situation in which factors exogenous to the economy raise this relative price.

This assumption seems reasonable given several facts observed during the last decades. Specifically, since the 1950s international tourism expenditures have experienced faster growth than world GDP. At the micro level tourism expenditure has increased its share in households' expenditure in most developed countries. This behavior can be related to a broader phenomenon consistent with a shift of expenditure shares from manufactures to services. As is commented by Rowthorn and Ramaswamy (1997), this can mainly be explained by a rise in the price of services relative to manufactures since in real terms the change of expenditure shares in manufactures and services is quite small. The increase in this relative price can be explained by the combination of two factors. On the one hand, Clark (1957) considers the hypothesis that income effects could increase relative demand for services after a threshold of economic development has been passed. On the other hand, the higher productivity growth that the manufacturing sector has experienced tends to lower the price of manufactures relative to services. Figure 3.7 shows the effects of both explanations for the case of the price of tourism relative to manufactures. On the vertical axis there is the international relative price per night stay for a given perceived quality. *RD* is international relative demand tourism/manufactures that shifts to the right due to income effects[8] or possible changes in preferences. *RS* is relative supply tourism/manufactures that shifts to the left due to higher productivity growth in the manufacturing sector. The combined

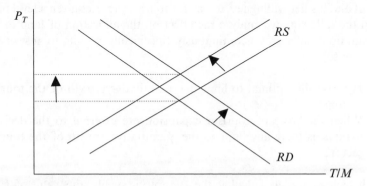

*Figure 3.7   Effects of shifts in relative demand and supply
tourism/manufactures on relative price of tourism*

effect is an increase in the relative price of tourism for a given perceived quality of the tourism product and an increase of the share of tourism expenditure in total expenditures.[9]

Lanza and Pigliaru (1994) set up a model where the international price of tourism relative to manufactures rises continuously due to a lower productivity growth in the former sector. In their model this relative price is endogenous since the economy specialized in tourism is large in international markets (in fact, it is the sole supplier of tourism). In contrast, in our model the economy is small in the sense that variations in its supply of accommodation capacity have a negligible effect on world tourism supply. Therefore, what we assume is that the rise in the international tourism price relative to manufactures is exogenous from the point of view of the economy. Regarding the price of the output of the traditional sector relative to manufactures we continue to assume that it remains constant through time.

Therefore, let us consider the following:

$$P_T = \tau P(L_T)$$

$$\frac{\dot{\tau}}{\tau} = g, \ \tau(t = 0) > 0, \ g > 0,$$

where τ is a parameter whose growth reflects upward pressure on the relative price of tourism for any perceived quality of tourism services, that is, for any level of L_T.

Therefore we identify two determinants of the relative price of tourism supplied by the economy: on the one hand, several factors that push up the price of tourism relative to manufactures and affect all the tourism destinations and all the market segments; on the other hand, those factors specific to the tourism destination, that is, congestion, landscape and natural and environmental assets that determine the satisfaction of a tourist visiting the resort and his/her willingness to pay for tourism services given a level of τ.

In the following we analyze the effect on the allocation of land of the assumption that τ grows continuously. Specifically, we aim to answer two questions:

1. Is it socially optimal to limit the quantitative growth of the tourism sector?
2. When the costs of tourism expansion are external to the decision makers, is there any limit to the quantitative growth of the tourism sector?

With such an aim, we calculate the asymptotic steady state value of L_T in the optimal solution and in the solution with externalities when τ grows continuously.

6.1 Optimal Solution

Considering (3.11) and (3.12) and inserting the parameter τ, the following condition is satisfied in the steady state of the optimal solution:

$$v[\tau TR(L_T) + NTR(L_T)] = (1 - L_T)\left[\tau TR'(L_T) + NTR'(L_T) - \frac{\eta}{\varphi}\rho\right]$$

(3.24)

or:

$$\tau = \frac{(1 - L_T)\left[NTR'(L_T) - \frac{\eta}{\varphi}\rho\right] - vNTR(L_T)}{vTR(L_T) - (1 - L_T)TR'(L_T)}.$$

(3.25)

The asymptotic value of L_T consistent with a τ that tends to infinity is the value that makes the denominator of the previous expression equal to zero,[10] that is:

$$TR'(L_T)(1 - L_T) = vTR(L_T).$$

(3.26)

From this reasoning we can derive the following proposition:

Proposition 3. *When the international relative tourism price grows continuously the steady state value of L_T tends asymptotically to a value $\bar{L}_T \in (0, 1)$.*
Proof: see Appendix III.

Proposition 3 implies that even when the relative price of tourism and therefore the attractiveness of tourism relative to other productive sectors grow continuously, it is socially optimal to limit the quantitative expansion of the tourism sector before it reaches its maximum capacity.

To show the dynamics of tourism development with the new assumption, let us consider expression (3.14) again, where we have now inserted parameter τ:

$$\tau TR'(0) > vNTR(0) - NTR'(0) + \frac{\eta}{\varphi}\rho.$$

(3.14′)

Remember that this expression is a necessary condition for a process of tourism development to be optimal. Therefore there is a threshold of τ under which it is not socially optimal to develop the tourism sector. If τ grows continuously, that condition will be satisfied sooner or later and from then on the economy will experience a non-balanced growth path characterized by an expansion of the tourism sector at the expense of the traditional sector.

Consumption and accommodation capacity grow but while the former grows continuously, the latter tends asymptotically to a level below the maximum capacity. Therefore we identify two sources of growth in the economy: sectoral change fueled by the reallocation of resources from other sectors to the tourism sector and exogenous improvements in the terms of trade of the economy. However, in the long term the former vanishes and only the latter remains. Figure 3.8 shows the behavior of the economy when τ grows continuously.

Notice that in the determination of $\bar{L}_T$ (expression 3.26), the traditional sector is absent. This is so because although this sector does not disappear (the asymptotic value of L_{NT} is positive), its share in the production value of the economy tends to zero as τ grows. Condition (3.26) has an interesting economic interpretation if we transform that expression into the following:

$$\tau TR'(L_T)[C^{-\theta}(1 - L_T)^{\nu(1-\theta)}] = \nu C^{(1-\theta)}(1 - L_T)^{\nu(1-\theta)-1}, \quad (3.26')$$

where $(1 - L_T)$ has gone to the right, we have multiplied both sides by $\tau C^{-\theta}(1 - L_T)^{\nu(1-\theta)}$ and we have considered that, when τ grows, the asymptotic value of consumption is equal to the asymptotic level of tourism revenues since investment tends asymptotically to zero and the revenues from the traditional sector tend to a constant value.

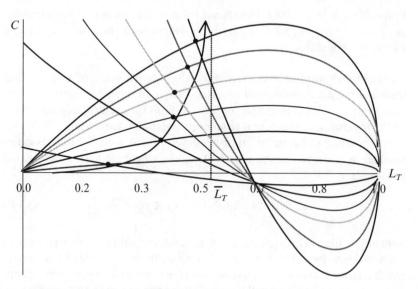

Note: [a] Same functional forms and parameter values as in Figure 3.1.

Figure 3.8 Steady state in the optimal solution when τ grows continuously[a]

The left-hand side of (3.26′) represents the contribution to residents' utility of an additional unit of consumption that comes from a marginal transfer of land to the tourism sector, disregarding the loss in the output of the traditional sector. The right-hand side is the negative impact on residents' utility due to the loss of intangible assets associated with that marginal transfer of land. Expression (3.26′) therefore equates marginal costs and marginal benefits of an increase in the accommodation capacity of the resort, disregarding the effects on the traditional sector. In summary, even in a context where the economic attractiveness of tourism relative to the traditional sector increases continuously, full specialization in tourism is not socially optimal, but the preservation of the traditional sector is not based on its direct productive contribution but on its role in the preservation of cultural, environmental and natural assets that are valued by the residents and are a source of tourism revenues.

6.2 Solution with Externalities

From (3.18) and (3.19), and inserting the parameter τ, the following condition is satisfied in the steady state of the solution with externalities:

$$\frac{(1 - L_T)}{v(1 - \theta)}\left[\tau AP(L_T) + NTR'(L_T) - \frac{\eta}{\varphi}\rho\right] = 0,$$

which, for the interior steady state, implies:

$$\left[\tau AP(L_T) + NTR'(L_T) - \frac{\eta}{\varphi}\rho\right] = 0$$

or

$$\tau = \frac{-NTR'(L_T) + \frac{\eta}{\varphi}\rho}{AP(L_T)}. \qquad (3.27)$$

Proposition 4. *The value of L_T in the interior steady state of the solution with externalities tends asymptotically to its maximum value, unity, when the relative tourism price grows continuously.*

Proof: we know that $\lim_{L_T \to 1^-} NTR'(L_T) = -\infty$ and $\lim_{L_T \to 1^-} P(L_T) > 0$, a finite value. Therefore, in (3.27) $\lim_{L_T \to 1^-} \tau = \infty$. Moreover, in (3.27) τ is a monotonous function of L_T for $L_T \in [0,1]$ since $NTR''(L_T) < 0$ and $P'(L_T) < 0$. We then conclude that $\lim_{\tau \to \infty} L_T = 1$.

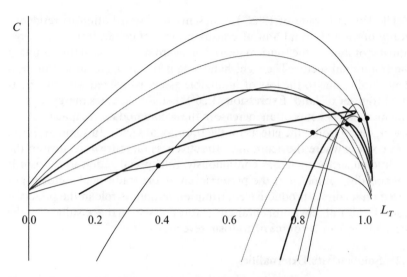

Note: [a] Same functional forms and parameter values as in Figure 3.1.

Figure 3.9   Steady state in the solution with externalities when τ grows continuously[a]

Proposition 4 implies that if the costs of tourism development are not considered by the decision makers, a continuous increase in the economic attractiveness of tourism relative to other sectors will generate incentives to expand tourism capacity with the only limit the total availability of land. The tourism sector fully crowds out other productive sectors even if full specialization in tourism is not socially optimal and society prefers to preserve part of the land from its occupation by tourism facilities not only as a source of amenities for the residents but also as a source of tourism revenues. Figure 3.9 shows the behavior of the economy with externalities when τ grows continuously.

7.   CONCLUSIONS

In this chapter we have constructed a dynamic general equilibrium model of tourism development based on the reallocation of land from a low productivity traditional sector to its use in the building of tourism facilities, where that reallocation is associated with investment efforts to provide those facilities. Tourism expansion allows for increases in consumption capabilities but also implies a loss of cultural, natural and environmental assets linked to land used in the traditional sector that are positively valued not only by the residents but also by the tourists.

In this framework, the social optimal solution is obtained. We identify a condition for the tourism development to be socially desirable. If this condition is met, the optimal solution implies convergence to a steady state where land is only partially occupied by tourism facilities. During the transition to the steady state the economy experiences economic growth based on sectoral change. Tourism development stops before reaching its maximum capacity due to the positive valuation of cultural, natural and environmental assets by the residents, the negative effect on tourism revenues of the loss of those assets and decreasing returns to land in the traditional sector.

It has also been shown that when the costs of tourism expansion are external to the decision makers, tourism development is excessive from the point of view of the residents' welfare. It could even happen that a process of tourism development would take place without it being socially desirable. It is also possible to end up in the long term with an environmental degradation that is not compensated with high enough consumption. However, in case this is so, the reason is not a problem of intergenerational conflict, since lower tourism development would increase welfare not only in the steady state but also during the transitional path, but rather the fact that the costs of tourism development are not fully internalized.

Finally, we consider an exogenous growth factor, that is, the increase in the price of tourism relative to manufactures in the international markets. In this context, the economic attractiveness of tourism relative to the traditional sector grows continuously but society is interested in preserving the latter not because it makes a significant contribution to income but because land used in this sector contains the cultural, natural and environmental assets that are valued by the residents and have a positive influence on tourism revenues. However, if the costs of tourism expansion are not considered in the decisions of factors allocation, the traditional sector and those intangible assets that are linked to this sector tend to disappear asymptotically.

NOTES

* We acknowledge the financial support of the Govern Balear (grant PRIB-2004-10142).
1. Given that the number of visits to the tourism resort is proportional to L_T, the allocation of land could also be a good approximation of the degree of congestion. This would reinforce the negative effect of L_T on tourists' satisfaction.
2. Tisdell (1987) considers a similar relationship between willingness to pay of tourists and the number of visits on the grounds of a combination of bandwagon and congestion effects, where the former would dominate in situations of low number of visitors and the latter when the number of tourists is high enough.
3. This is what happens when consumption grows and, if marginal utility of consumption is increasing with L_T, when the tourism sector expands. As is shown below, this is what happens in the transitional dynamics of the model.
4. In Appendix I it is shown that the steady state is saddle-path stable.
5. From (3.22) it follows that in the green golden rule $AP(L_T) + ITN'(L_T) = (v/(1 - L_T))[IT(L_T) + INT(L_T)] - AL_T P'(L_T)$. Moreover, $AP'(L_T) + ITN''(L_T) < 0$.

6. As shown in the previous sections, growth stops before reaching the maximum capacity of the resort.
7. See Gómez et al. (2003) for a model where qualitative growth is allowed.
8. Crouch (1995, 1996) reports high income elasticity of tourism demand.
9. Smeral (2003) documents a continuous increase in the price ratio of tourism exports to exports of manufactured goods in industrialized countries since 1980.
10. There is no value of $L_T \in [0,1]$ for which the numerator is infinity.

REFERENCES

Brunstad, R.J., Gaasland, I. and Vardal, E. (1999), 'Agricultural Production and the Optimal Level of Landscape Preservation', *Land Economics*, **75**(4), 538–46.

Butler, R.W. (1980), 'The Concept of a Tourist Area Cycle of Evolution: Implications for Management of Resources', *Canadian Geographer*, **XXIV**(1), 5–12.

Clark, C. (1957), *The Conditions of Economic Progress*, London: Macmillan.

Crouch, G.I. (1995), 'A Meta-Analysis of Tourism Demand', *Annals of Tourism Research*, **22**(1), 103–18.

Crouch, G.I. (1996), 'Demand Elasticities in International Marketing. A Meta-Analytical Application to Tourism', *Journal of Business Research*, **36**, 117–36.

Drake, L. (1992), 'The Non-Market Value of the Swedish Agricultural Landscape', *European Review of Agricultural Economics*, **19**(3), 351–64.

Drake, L. (1999), 'The Swedish Agricultural Landscape. Economic Characteristics, Valuations and Policy Options', *International Journal of Social Economics*, **26**(7/8/9), 1042–60.

Fleischer, A. and Tsur, Y. (2000), 'Measuring the Recreational Value of Agricultural Landscape', *European Review of Agricultural Economics*, **27**(3), 385–98.

Gómez, C.M., Lozano, J. and Rey-Maquieira, J. (2003), 'Environmental Policy in a Dynamic Model of an Economy Specialized in Tourism', mimeo, University of the Balearic Islands.

Heal, G. (1998), *Valuing the Future*, New York: Columbia University Press.

Huybers, T. and Bennett, J. (2000), 'Impact of the Environment on Holiday Destination Choices of Prospective UK Tourists: Implications for Tropical North Queensland', *Tourism Economics*, **6**(1), 21–46.

Lanza, A. and Pigliaru, F. (1994), 'The Tourist Sector in the Open Economy', *Rivista Internazionale di Economiche e Commerciali*, **41**(1), 15–28.

López, R.A., Shah, F.A. and Altobello, M.A. (1994), 'Amenity Benefits and the Optimal Allocation of Land', *Land Economics*, **70**, 53–62.

Piga, C. (2003), 'Pigouvian Taxation in Tourism', *Environmental and Resource Economics*, **26**(3), 343–59.

Pruckner, G.J. (1995), 'Agricultural Landscape Cultivation in Australia: An Application of the CVM', *European Review of Agricultural Economics*, **22**(2), 173–90.

Rowthorn, R.E. and Ramaswamy, R. (1997), 'Deindustrialization: Causes and Implications', IMF Working Paper WP97/42.

Rubio, S.J. and Goetz, R.U. (1998), 'Optimal Growth and Land Preservation', *Resource and Energy Economics*, **20**(4), 345–72.

Smeral, E. (2003), 'A Structural View of Tourism Growth', *Tourism Economics*, **9**(1), 77–93.

Tisdell, C.A. (1987), 'Tourism, the Environment and Profit', *Economic Analysis and Policy*, **17**(1), 13–30.

APPENDIX I   STEADY STATE AND STABILITY IN THE OPTIMAL SOLUTION

The steady state of the optimal solution satisfies the following conditions:

$$C_I = \frac{1}{v}(1 - L_T)\left[TR'(L_T) + NTR'(L_T) - \frac{\eta}{\varphi}\rho \right] \qquad (3AI.1)$$

$$C_{II} = TR(L_T) + NTR(L_T) \qquad (3AI.2)$$
$$C_I = C_{II},$$

where (3AI.1) comes from the combination of (3.11) and (3.12) and (3AI.2) is the same as (3.12). First of all we show that if (3.14) is satisfied, there exists at least one steady state where $C > 0$, $0 < L_T < 1$. To prove existence, given continuity in $L_T \in [0,1]$ of all functions, the following is enough:

(a) $C_{II} > 0 \ \forall L_T \in [0,1]$.
(b)   If (3.14) is satisfied, then $C_I > C_{II}$ for $L_T = 0$.
(c)   There is an $L_T = L_T^* \in (0,1)$ for which $C_I = 0$. Given (3AI.1), L_T^* satisfies:

$$\Omega(L_T) = TR'(L_T) + NTR'(L_T) - \frac{\eta}{\varphi}\rho = 0$$

There is only one level of L_T that satisfies this condition since: (i) $\Omega(0) > 0$ if (3.14) is satisfied; (ii) $\Omega(1) < 0$ given the properties of the traditional sector production function; (iii) $\Omega'(L_T) < 0$ in the unit interval given the assumption about the second derivatives of the tourism revenues function and the traditional sector production function. Therefore, C_I and C_{II} intersect at least once in the interval $L_T \in (0,1)$.

Second, it can be proved that the steady state is unique in the interval $L_T \in [0,1]$. On the one hand, if (3.14) is satisfied, then $L_T \neq 0$ in the steady state. Moreover, given that in the steady state:

$$\frac{1}{v}\left[TR'(L_T) + NTR'(L_T) - \frac{\eta}{\varphi} \right] = \frac{TR(L_T) + NTR(L_T)}{1 - L_T},$$

then $L_T \neq 1$ in the steady state since when $L_T = 1$ the left-hand side is minus infinity and the right-hand side is plus infinity.

On the other hand, given that $C_{II} > 0 \ \forall L_T \in (0,1)$, $C_I > 0 \ \forall L_T \in (0, L_T^*)$ and $C_I < 0 \ \forall L_T \in (L_T^*, 1)$, then $L_T \in (0, L_T^*)$ in the steady state. For this interval, C_I is always decreasing in L_T and, therefore, the steady state is unique if C_{II} is increasing in L_T for $L_T \in (0, L_T^*)$. Notice that C_{II} has a single maximum in the interval $L_T \in [0, 1]$ since $dC_{II}/dL_T > 0$ when $L_T = 0$ if (3.14) is satisfied, $dC_{II}/dL_T < 0$ when $L_T = 1$ given the properties of the traditional sector production function and finally $d^2C_{II}/dL_T^2 < 0$. C_{II} is maximum when $TR'(L_T) + NTR'(L_T) = 0$ while L_T^* satisfies the condition $TR'(L_T) + NTR'(L_T) = \eta \rho / \varphi$. Since $d^2C_{II}/dL_T^2 < 0$, the value of L_T that maximizes C_{II} is larger than L_T^* and therefore C_{II} is increasing in L_T in the interval $L_T \in (0, L_T^*)$.

Regarding stability, let us consider the system (3.7), (3.10), where in (3.10) it is assumed that the utility function of the resident is (3.13). Linearization around the steady state results in a linear system whose Jacobian is:

$$A = \begin{pmatrix} a_{11} & a_{12} \\ a_{21} & a_{22} \end{pmatrix}$$

and

$$a_{11} = v \frac{\bar{C}}{1 - \bar{L}_T} + \frac{\eta}{\varphi} \rho$$

$$a_{12} = -\frac{\varphi}{\eta}$$

$$a_{21} = \frac{\bar{C}}{\theta} \frac{\varphi}{\eta} \left\{ IT''(\bar{L}_T) + INT''(\bar{L}_T) - [v^2(1 - \theta) + v] \frac{\bar{C}}{(1 - \bar{L}_T)^2} - v(1 - \theta) \frac{\eta}{\varphi} \rho \right\}$$

$$a_{22} = -v \frac{\varphi}{\eta} \frac{\bar{C}}{1 - \bar{L}_T},$$

where $\bar{C}$ and $\bar{L}_T$ are steady state values.

It is clear that $a_{11} > 0$, $a_{12} < 0$, $a_{22} < 0$. If $\theta \leq 1$ then $a_{21} < 0$. In this case, $Det(A) < 0$ and therefore the eigenvalues are real and of opposite signs so the steady state is saddle-path.

Notice that $\theta \leq 1$ is a sufficient but not necessary condition for the steady state to be saddle-path. This assumption implies that marginal utility of consumption is increasing in L_{NT}.

APPENDIX II   STEADY STATE AND STABILITY IN THE SOLUTION WITH EXTERNALITIES

Conditions (3.18) and (3.19) imply:

$$\frac{(1-L_T)}{v(1-\theta)}\left[AP(L_T) + NTR'(L_T) - \frac{\eta}{\varphi}\rho\right] = 0 \qquad \text{(3AII.1)}$$

Leaving aside the case when $L_T = 1$ for the moment, (3AII.1) is satisfied if there is a value of $L_T \in [0,1)$ for which:

$$\psi(L_T) = AP(L_T) + NTR'(L_T) - \frac{\eta}{\varphi}\rho = 0$$

Given that:

(i) $\psi'(L_T) < 0\ \forall L_T \in (0,1)$, since $P'(L_T) < 0$, $NTR''(L_T) < 0$
(ii) $\psi(1) < 0$, since $AP(1) > 0$, $NTR'(1) = -\infty$,

there is a single value of $L_T \in [0,1)$ for which $\psi(L_T) = 0$ if:

$$\psi(0) = AP(0) + NTR'(0) - \frac{\eta}{\varphi}\rho \geq 0$$

In this steady state consumption is positive since $C_{II} > 0\ \forall \in [0,1)$. Moreover, this value of L_T is different from zero if the previous condition is satisfied as an strict inequality (condition 3.20).

Regarding the transversality condition, this can be expressed in the following way:

$$\lim_{t\to\infty} L_T(t)\lambda(t = 0)e^{\left[\frac{\dot\lambda(t)}{\lambda(t)} - \rho\right]t} = 0$$

L_T tends to a constant value since it belongs to the unit range. Moreover, $\lambda(t = 0) < \infty$, since $\lambda = \eta U_C/\varphi$, $0 < U_C < \infty\ \forall L_T \in [0,1)$. Regarding the growth rate of the shadow price, from (3.16) this can be expressed:

$$\frac{\dot\lambda}{\lambda} = \frac{\varphi}{\eta}[-AP'(L_T) - NTR'(L_T)] + \rho.$$

In the path that converges to the interior steady state the previous expression converges to zero since in the interior steady state the following condition is satisfied:

$$AP(L_T) + NTR'(L_T) = \frac{\eta}{\varphi}\rho > 0.$$

Therefore, the transversality condition is satisfied.

In case a second steady state existed where $L_T = 1$, the path that converges to this steady state does not satisfy the transversality condition. In this path $NTR'(L_T)$ goes to minus infinity and therefore the growth rate of the shadow price tends to infinity.

Regarding stability, the elements of the Jacobian in the solution with externalities are:

$$a_{11} = \frac{\varphi}{\eta}[TR'(L_T) + NTR'(L_T)]$$

$$a_{12} = -\frac{\varphi}{\eta}$$

$$a_{21} = \frac{C}{\theta}\frac{\varphi}{\eta}\left\{AP'(L_T) + NTR''(L_T) - v(1-\theta)\frac{1}{1-L_T}[TR'(L_T) + NTR'(L_T)]\right\}$$

$$a_{22} = v\frac{1-\theta}{\theta}\frac{\varphi}{\eta}\frac{C}{1-L_T}.$$

Therefore, the determinant is:

$$Det = -\frac{C}{\theta}\left(\frac{\varphi}{\eta}\right)^2[AP'(L_T) + NTR''(L_T)] < 0,$$

from which it can be concluded that the interior steady state is a saddle-path.

APPENDIX III   PROOF OF PROPOSITION 3

To prove proposition 3 we have first to show that there is a single value of $L_T \in (0,1)$ that satisfies (3.26). This proof requires a different treatment depending on the hypothesis regarding the behavior of the tourism revenues function that was considered in section 2.3.

In the case where $TR'(L_T) > 0 \; \forall L_T \in [0,1]$, the following is sufficient to prove that a single value of $L_T \in (0,1)$ satisfies (3.26):

(a)   when $L_T = 0$ left-hand side is larger than right-hand side;
(b)   when $L_T = 1$ left-hand side is smaller than right-hand side;
(c)   left-hand side is decreasing in L_T since $TR''(L_T) < 0$ and right-hand side is increasing in L_T for any $L_T \in [0,1]$.

In the alternative case when tourism revenues reach a maximum before reaching maximum tourism capacity, we can prove that a single value of $L_T \in (0,1)$ satisfies (3.26) in the following way. Condition (3.26) can be expressed as:

$$1 - L_T = v \frac{TR(L_T)}{TR'(L_T)} \qquad (3\text{AIII}.1)$$

The right-hand side of (3AIII.1) is zero when $L_T = 0$, infinity if L_T takes the value that maximizes tourism revenues, negative if L_T is larger than that value and increasing in L_T if this variable is below that value. Therefore, the level of L_T that satisfies (3AIII.1) and (3.26) is unique and it is strictly between zero and one.

We know that if L_T tends to the value that satisfies (3.26), the value of τ in expression (3.25) goes to infinity. The opposite is true; that is, if τ tends to infinity then the steady state level of L_T tends to the value that satisfies (3.26) if (3.25) is monotonically increasing. To show this, we have to prove that $d\tau/dL_T > 0$. To do this, we differentiate the steady state condition (3.24), which is equivalent to (3.25), with respect to τ and L_T to obtain:

$$\frac{d\tau}{dL_T} = \frac{(v+1)[\tau TR'(L_T) + NTR'(L_T)] - (1 - L_T)[\tau TR''(L_T) + NTR''(L_T)] - \dfrac{\eta}{\varphi}\rho}{(1 - L_T)TR'(L_T) - vTR(L_T)}$$

where L_T takes its steady state value. This expression is always positive since:

(a)   the denominator is positive since when steady state condition (3.24) is satisfied, then:

$$(1 - L_T)TR'(L_T) - \nu TR(L_T)$$
$$= \frac{NTR(L_T) - (1 - L_T)[NTR'(L_T) - \eta\rho/\varphi]}{\tau} > 0$$

(b) $\tau TR'(L_T) + NTR'(L_T) > 0$, since L_T in the steady state of the optimal solution is always below the golden rule.
(c) $\tau TR''(L_T) + NTR''(L_T) < 0$.
(d) $\tau TR'(L_T) + NTR'(L_T) > \eta\rho/\varphi$, since in Appendix I it is shown that L_T in the steady state of the optimal solution is below L_T^*, where $\tau TR'(L_T^*) + NTR'(L_T^*) = \eta\rho/\varphi$ and moreover $TR''(L_T) < 0$ and $NTR''(L_T) < 0$.

4. Tourism, increasing returns and welfare*

Jean-Jacques Nowak, Mondher Sahli and Pasquale Sgro

1. INTRODUCTION

Tourism has often been regarded as a major source of economic growth, and governments often invest in infrastructure to promote tourism and growth.[1] Tourism supplements the foreign exchange earnings already derived from trade in commodities and sometimes finances the imports of the capital goods necessary for the growth of the manufacturing sector.[2] Tourism has also been regarded as a mechanism for generating increased income and employment, both in the formal and informal sectors.[3] Hazari and Ng (1993) have also highlighted important differences between trade in commodities and tourism.[4] However, international tourism has also at times been considered an activity that imposes costs on the host country. Much attention in this context has been paid to inflationary and low multiplier effects of tourism expansion,[5] increased pollution, congestion and despoilation of fragile environments,[6] intra-generational inequity aggravation[7] and even to adverse sociocultural impacts.[8] Less obvious but more important costs of tourism have often been neglected, such as the adverse impacts of a tourism boom on other sectors resulting from general equilibrium effects. However, theoretical and empirical studies tell us that these effects can be quite substantial and have to be taken into account when assessing the net benefit of a tourism boom on an economy.[9]

The model used in this chapter captures the interdependence and interaction between tourism and the rest of the economy, in particular, agriculture and manufacturing. This is important in view of the public debate on the effects of tourism as it highlights the problem of competition for resources between two export-earning activities, agriculture and tourism. Furthermore, there is a concern as to whether tourism promotes or hinders the development of the manufacturing sector. Moreover, it is important to examine the welfare effects of tourism.

Specifically a tourist boom and its consequences are examined in a three-sector model of trade consisting of two internationally traded goods and one non-traded good. An important feature of the model is that the manufacturing good is produced with increasing returns to scale while the other goods are produced under constant returns to scale. A large proportion of a tourist's consumption is generally of non-traded goods and services and this consumption interacts with other sectors in a general equilibrium setting. Using this model, we analyse the effect of a tourism boom on structural adjustment, commodity and factor and product prices and most importantly resident welfare. An important result obtained is that the tourist boom may 'immiserize' the residents. This occurs because of two effects. The first is a favourable effect due to an increase in the relative price of the non-traded good which is termed the secondary terms of trade effect. The second is a negative effect due to an efficiency loss that occurs in the presence of increasing returns to scale in manufacturing. If this second effect outweighs the first effect, resident immiserization occurs.[10]

2. THE MODEL

Our analysis uses a hybrid of the Ricardo–Viner–Jones (RVJ) and Heckscher–Ohlin (H–O) models under the assumption of full employment. The economy consists of three sectors: one a non-traded goods sector producing X_N, an agricultural sector producing an exportable X_A, and a manufacturing sector producing an importable X_M. Assuming a small open economy, the terms of trade are given exogenously. It is assumed that commodities $X_j (j=N, A)$ are produced under constant returns to scale and X_M with increasing returns to scale. The production functions for the agriculture and non-traded goods sectors can be written as follows:

$$X_j = F_j(L_j, T_j) \quad j = A, N, \tag{4.1}$$

where L_j and T_j represent allocations of labour and land respectively utilized in the jth sector.[11]

These production functions exhibit positive and diminishing marginal products. In the manufacturing sector, the production functions for a typical firm and the industry as a whole are as follows:[12]

$$x_M^i = g_M^i (X_M) F_M^i (l_M^i, k_M^i) \quad i = 1, 2, \ldots N \tag{4.2a}$$

and

$$X_M = G_M(L_M, K_M) = g_M(X_M) F_M(L_M, K_M), \tag{4.2b}$$

where x^i_M is a typical firm's output of the manufactured good, X_M is the total output in the manufacturing sector; l^i_M and k^i_M are labour and capital respectively employed by a typical firm in this sector; and L_M and K_M are the total labour and specific capital employed in this sector. The increasing returns to scale in our model are output-generated and are external to the firm and internal to the industry. These assumptions ensure that perfect competition prevails at the firm level and that the economy will produce along its social transformation curve. Also note that the production function for the manufacturing sector, X_M, is multiplicatively separable.

The production function F_M in equation (4.2b) is linearly homogeneous in inputs. The increasing returns to scale are captured by the term $g_M(X_M)$, which is a positive function defined on the open interval $]0, +\infty[$ and is twice differentiable. This type of increasing returns to scale is 'neutral' in the sense that the capital intensity used in production is independent of the scale of production. It is assumed that X_M is homothetic in L_M and K_M.

Using the production function X_M defined in equation (4.2b), the rate of returns to scale, e_M, is specified below:

$$e_M = (dg_M/dX_M) \cdot (X_M/g_M) = F_M(L_M, K_M)g'_M(X_M), \qquad (4.3)$$

where e_M is defined over the open interval $]0, 1[$ in the case of increasing returns.

The full employment conditions can be specified as follows:

$$a_{LA}X_A + a_{LN}X_N = L_{AN} = \bar{L} - L_M \qquad (4.4)$$

$$a_{TA} X_A + a_{TN} X_N = \bar{T} \qquad (4.5)$$

$$a_{LM} X_M = L_M \qquad (4.6)$$

$$a_{KM} X_M = K_M = \bar{K} \qquad (4.7)$$

where the a_{ij}s denote the variable input coefficients, L_{AN} the amounts of labour used in the agriculture and non-traded goods sectors, L_M is the amount of labour used in the manufacturing sector, and $\bar{L}$, $\bar{T}$ and $\bar{K}$ are the inelastically supplied factors labour, land and capital respectively. Note that the subset of sectors A and N forms a Heckscher–Ohlin structure with an endogenous labour supply (equations (4.4) and (4.5)). The endogenous labour supply $(\bar{L} - L_M)$ is determined by the amount of labour used in the manufacturing sector.[13] There is an RVJ structure between this subset and the manufacturing sector.

Under the assumption of profit maximization, interior solution and competitive markets, the price side of our model is as follows:

$$a_{LA} w + a_{TA} t = 1 \qquad (4.8)$$

$$a_{LN} w + a_{TN} t = P_N \tag{4.9}$$

$$a_{LM} w + a_{KM} r = P, \tag{4.10}$$

where P_N and P are the relative price of the non-traded and manufactured good respectively; w, t and r are the wage rate, rental on land and the rental on capital. The agriculture good has been chosen as the numeraire. Assuming a small open economy, the terms of trade, P, are given. The relative price of the non-traded good, P_N, is determined domestically by the forces of demand and supply.

The quasi-concave aggregate utility function for the residents is as follows:

$$U = U(D_A, D_M, D_N), \tag{4.11}$$

where D_j, $(j = A, M, N)$ denotes the demand for the agriculture, manufactured and non-traded goods respectively by the residents.

Given utility maximization, it follows (from the equilibrium conditions) that:

$$\frac{\partial U}{\partial D_A} = \frac{1}{P_M} \frac{\partial U}{\partial D_M} = \frac{1}{P_N} \frac{\partial U}{\partial D_N}, \tag{4.12}$$

where $\partial U / \partial D_j$ $(j = A, M, N)$ denotes marginal utility.

The demand for the non-traded good consists of resident demand (D_N) and tourist demand (D_{NT}), which can be written as follows:

$$D_N = D_N(P, P_N, Y) \tag{4.13}$$

$$D_{NT} = D_{NT}(P, P_N, \Delta), \tag{4.14}$$

where Y is resident income and Δ is a variable that captures foreign income and other exogenous domestic amenities such as indigenous culture, fashion, special events and so on that distinguish tourist attractions in one country from another. All goods in consumption are substitutes and normal. We assume that $(\partial D_{NT}/\partial \Delta) > 0$ so that a tourist boom in our model is captured by an exogenous increase in Δ.

The market-clearing conditions for the non-traded good and the resident budget constraint are as follows:

$$D_N + D_{NT} = X_N \tag{4.15}$$

$$Y = P X_M + P_N X_N + X_A = P_N D_N + P D_M + D_A. \tag{4.16}$$

It is useful to represent the above model by using two diagrams, which highlight the interaction among the sectors and the factors of production. We represent the initial equilibrium of the model in Figure 4.1 where, in

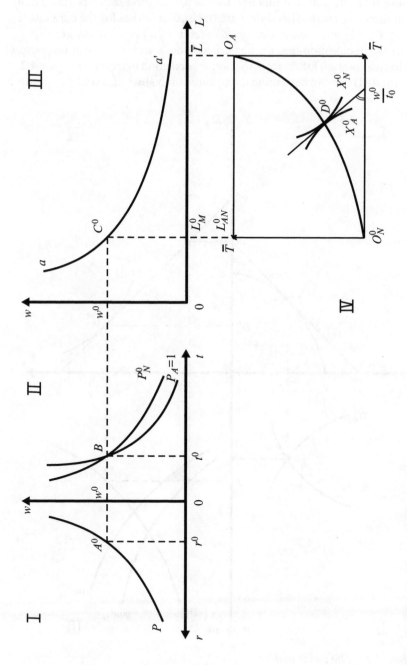

Figure 4.1   The factor markets

quadrant II, the unit cost function for the agricultural sector is drawn as a P_A in the space (w,t). Also shown are the isocost curves for the agriculture (given $P_A = 1$) and non-traded goods sector P_N^0. These curves are drawn under the assumption that the non-traded goods sector is labour intensive.

Given a solution for P_N from the non-traded good market (see Figure 4.2, quadrant II), we can determine the equilibrium values of w and t as shown

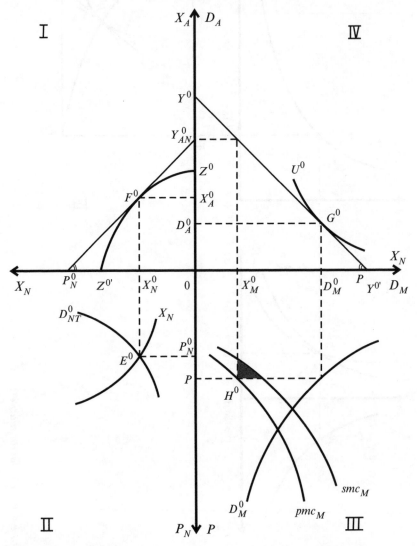

Figure 4.2   The goods market

by w^0 and t^0. In quadrant I, we have the isocost curve for the manufacturing sector P whose price is internationally given for the small country case.
The equilibrium solution for w^0 also determines the equilibrium value of r
as shown by r^0.

In quadrant III, the curve aa' is the marginal product of labour curve in
the manufacturing sector. The mathematical conditions necessary for this
case are derived in section 3. Generally the marginal product curve for an
increasing returns to scale technology can have any shape (Panagariya,
1986). From quadrant III, the equilibrium value w^0 enables us to determine
the employment level L_M^0 in the manufacturing sector. Since OL_M^0 of total
labour supply is used in the manufacturing sector, the residual $\bar{L} - OL_M^0$
determines the supply of labour for the other two sectors, L_{AN}^0.

Given this residual supply L_{AN}^0 and the quantity of land, $\bar{T}$, we can draw
the Edgeworth–Bowley box in quadrant IV of Figure 4.1. Also illustrated
is the contract curve $O_A O_N^0$, drawn under the assumption that the non-
traded good sector is labour intensive. Given the equilibrium wage/rental
ratio on land determined in quadrant II, we can identify the point
$D^0(X_A^0, X_N^0)$ on the contract curve which determines the allocation of
labour and land between the two sectors, agriculture and non-traded goods.
From the factor allocation in quadrant IV of Figure 4.1, we can derive the
production possibility curve $Z^0 Z^{0\prime}$ for goods X_A and X_N in quadrant I of
Figure 4.2, given the quantity of labour L_{AN}^0. In quadrant II of Figure 4.2,
we have drawn the tourist demand curve D_{NT} and the non-traded good
supply curve X_N. Note that for illustrative purposes only, we have made the
simplifying assumption that residents do not consume the non-traded
good. The actual results in the model presented in the following section are
derived for the general case of both resident and tourist demand for the
non-traded good. The equilibrium price and quantity are shown as
P_N^0 and X_N^0. In quadrant I, given P_N^0, we can determine the production
point $F^0(X_A^0, X_N^0)$, while in quadrant III, we have the demand (D_M^0) and
private (pmc_M) and social (smc_M) marginal cost curves for the manufacturing sector. Note that the axes are labelled X_M, D_M and P. Given the international price P, to satisfy the demand D_M^0, we import $D_M^0 X_M^0$ of the
manufacturing good. Due to the increasing returns to scale technology in
this sector, the social marginal cost curve is below the private marginal cost
curve, giving rise to a welfare loss represented by the shaded area. In quadrant IV, we determine resident welfare. The national income budget line is
represented by the line $Y^0 Y^{0\prime}$, while its slope is determined by the relative
price ratio P. The vertical intercept of this budget line $0Y^0$ is made up of
the sum of $X_A^0 + P_N^0 X_N^0 + PX_M^0$, the values of which can be read from
quadrants I and III. Also illustrated in quadrant I of Figure 4.2 is OY_{AN}^0,
which represents the income generated in the Heckscher–Ohlin subset of

the economy. Given the resident utility function U defined in equation (4.11), with the restriction that resident consumption of the non-traded good is zero, we can determine the social indifference curve U^0 with equilibrium at G^0. Note that the G^0 includes the imports $D_M^0 X_M^0$ of the manufactured good derived in quadrant III.

3.   RESULTS

In this section, we present the implications of a tourist boom on relative prices, outputs, factor incomes and resident welfare. The tourism boom is captured by change in Δ in equation (4.14).

By totally differentiating the cost equations (4.8) and (4.9) which make up the Heckscher–Ohlin bloc, we obtain the standard Stolper–Samuelson result:

$$\hat{w} = \frac{\theta_{TA}}{|\theta|} \hat{P}_N \tag{4.17}$$

$$\hat{t} = -\frac{\theta_{LA}}{|\theta|} \hat{P}_N \tag{4.18}$$

where the $\theta_{ij}s$ are the cost shares, the ($^\wedge$) notation denotes relative changes and $|\theta| = \theta_{LN} - \theta_{LA} = \theta_{TA} - \theta_{TN}$ describes the labour/land factor intensity which is positive for the case where the non-traded good is labour intensive *vis-à-vis* the agriculture good. Thus if the price of $\hat{P}_N$, the non-traded good, rises, w, the price of the factor used intensely in its production, rises and t falls.

Totally differentiating (4.2b), (4.10), using (4.3) and after some manipulation, we obtain:

$$e_M \hat{X}_M = \theta_{LM}\hat{w} + \theta_{KM}\hat{r}. \tag{4.19}$$

From equation (4.7), and (4.17)–(4.19) above, we obtain the following expression for $\hat{X}_M$:

$$\hat{X}_M = -\phi_M \hat{P}_N, \tag{4.20}$$

where

$$\phi_M = \frac{\theta_{LM}\theta_{TA}}{(1 - e_M)\xi_M|\theta|}, \quad \xi_M = \left(\frac{e_M}{1 - e_M}\right)\theta_{LM} - \frac{\theta_{KM}}{\sigma^M} \text{ and } \sigma^j$$

is the elasticity of substitution between the primary factors in sector j. The term ξ_M is the elasticity of the marginal physical product of labour with respect to a change in labour in X_M and is assumed to be negative for stability.[14]

From equations (4.6) and (4.20), we obtain the following expression for change in the labour demand in the manufacturing sector:

$$\hat{L}_M = -\frac{\theta_{TA}}{|\theta|(\xi_M)}\hat{P}_N \qquad (4.21)$$

By using equation (4.21), we have the change in the labour supply for the agriculture and non-traded goods sectors:

$$\hat{L}_{AN} = -\frac{\mu_M}{\mu_{AN}}\frac{\theta_{TA}}{|\theta|\xi_M}\hat{P}_N, \qquad (4.22)$$

where $\mu_j, (j = M, AN)$ is the labour share in j, e.g. $\mu_{AN} = L_{AN}/\bar{L}$.

From the full employment conditions in the Heckscher–Ohlin subset (equations (4.4), (4.5) and (4.22)), we obtain the following output changes for sectors X_A and X_N:

$$\hat{X}_A = -\phi_A \hat{P}_N \qquad (4.23)$$

$$\hat{X}_A = \phi_N \hat{P}_N, \qquad (4.24)$$

where

$$\phi_j = \left[(\lambda_{Li}\wp_T + \lambda_{Ti}\wp_L) - \lambda_{Ti}\frac{\mu_M}{\mu_{AN}}\frac{\theta_{TA}}{\xi_M} \right] \frac{1}{|\theta|\,|\lambda|}, \quad i, j = A, N, \quad i \neq j.$$

The term ϕ_j is the price elasticity of supply in sector j; λ_{Li} and λ_{Ti} are factor shares defined in sectors X_A and X_N. For example:

$$\lambda_{LA} = \frac{L_A}{L_{AN}}, \lambda_{TN} = \frac{T_N}{\bar{T}}.$$

Note that $|\lambda| = \lambda_{LN} - \lambda_{TN} = \lambda_{TA} - \lambda_{LA}$ has the same sign as $|\theta|$ since there are no distortions in the labour market. $\wp_i, i = T, L$ is the elasticity of factor i in sectors A and N with respect to (t/w) at constant outputs and factor endowments.

From the full employment conditions (4.4), (4.6), (4.7), the production function (4.2b), and using the definition of e_M, we obtain the following relationship between the slope of the production possibility surface and relative prices:

$$dX_A + P_N dX_N + P_M dX_M = e_M dX_M. \qquad (4.25)$$

Note that due to the presence of a distortion (here as increasing returns to scale), there is a non-tangency between the production possibility surface and relative prices.

Using equations (4.11), (4.12), (4.16) and (4.25), we obtain the following expression for the change in resident welfare:

$$\hat{y} = \gamma_N \hat{D}_N + \gamma_M \hat{D}_M + \gamma_A \hat{D}_A = \Psi \hat{P}_N, \tag{4.26}$$

where

$$\Psi = \left[\delta_{NT} + \left(\frac{e_M}{1 - e_M} \right) \frac{\theta_{TA}}{|\theta|} \frac{\delta_M}{\xi_M} \theta_{LM} \right] \begin{array}{c} \leq \\ > \end{array} 0,$$

δ_{NT} is the share of international tourist demand in national income, and δ_M is the share of manufacturing output in national income.

By differentiating (4.13)–(4.15), we obtain:

$$\hat{X}_N = \hat{D}_{NT} \alpha_{NT} + \hat{D}_N \alpha_N, \tag{4.27}$$

where

$$\alpha_N = \frac{D_N}{X_N}, \; \alpha_{NT} = \frac{D_{NT}}{X_N}$$

$$\hat{D}_{NT} = -\varepsilon_{NT} \hat{P}_N + \beta_{NT} \hat{\Delta} \tag{4.28}$$

$$\hat{D}_N = -\varepsilon_N \hat{P}_N + \eta_N \hat{y} \tag{4.29}$$

where $\varepsilon_i > 0$, $(i = N, NT)$ is the compensated price elasticity of demand, η_N is the resident income elasticity of the non-traded goods and β_{NT} measures the sensitivity of the tourist demand to the tourist shock.
Using (4.24), (4.26)–(4.29) we obtain:

$$\hat{P}_N = (\alpha_{NT} \beta_{NT}/\Omega) \hat{\Delta}, \tag{4.30}$$

where $\Omega = \phi_N + \alpha_{NT} \varepsilon_{NT} + \alpha_N \varepsilon_N - \alpha_N \varepsilon_N \Psi$ is the excess supply elasticity of the non-traded good in general equilibrium and is positive for stability in this market.

From the above equations, we are now able to describe the consequences of an increase in tourism on the key variables.

Irrespective of the labour intensity of the non-traded goods sector, its price and output always increase and the output of the agricultural sector falls. In our model, P_N can be interpreted as the relative price of an export and hence its increase is, in fact, an improvement in the terms of trade.

The response of the other key variables depends on the labour intensity of the non-traded goods sector. If this sector is labour intensive ($|\theta| > 0$), the wage rate increases and the rental on both land and capital falls. Due to the wage increase (and resultant increase in costs), the output of the manufacturing sector falls. Note that the tourist expansion comes at a cost to the manufacturing sector. Moreover, as the manufacturing output was already suboptimal at the initial market equilibrium (due to increasing returns to scale), this decrease in output worsens the welfare loss (second term in square brackets of Ψ in (4.26)). This welfare loss can outweigh the welfare gain (captured by δ_{NT} in Ψ in (4.26)) due to the terms of trade effect [$\hat{P}_N > 0$]. Hence resident welfare (income) may fall as a result of the increase in tourism. This may be a plausible hypothesis for small open economies of developed countries. On the other hand, 'green tourism', which consumes more land than labour, would be welfare enhancing for residents.

If the non-traded goods are land intensive ($|\theta| > 0$), the wage rate falls, the rental on capital and land rises and the outputs of both X_M and X_N rise. Hence the expansion in tourism helps the development of the manufacturing sector. Resident welfare (income) rises as both the effects referred to above are positive. That is, the terms of trade effect is still favourable while the expansion of the manufacturing sector reduces the welfare loss at the market equilibrium.[15]

It will be useful to use Figures 4.1 and 4.2 to illustrate some of the results. We will illustrate the case of immiserizing growth. In quadrant II of Figure 4.4, the increase in tourism induces an increase in P_N. Recall that, for illustrative purposes only, we assume that residents do not consume X_N. By the Stolper–Samuelson effect the wage rate, w, increases at the expense of the rental rates on land as described in quadrant II of Figure 4.3. The manufacturing sector reduces its demand for labour as shown in quadrant III of Figure 4.3, which results in an increased labour supply for the Heckscher–Ohlin–Samuelson (HOS) subset of the economy (X_A and X_N). In quadrant IV of Figure 4.3, we have represented both the factor prices and the labour supply effects on outputs X_A and X_N. The expansion of X_N and contraction of X_A production are illustrated in quadrant I of Figure 4.4 by the shift in the production point from F^o to F'. We can identify the terms of trade and increased labour supply effects on resident income in quadrant I of Figure 4.4 by the distance $Y^o_{AN} Y'_{AN}$.

As a result of the increases in P_N, both the (pmc_M) and (smc_M) curves shift to the left with the (pmc_M) curve shifting more than the (smc_M) curve

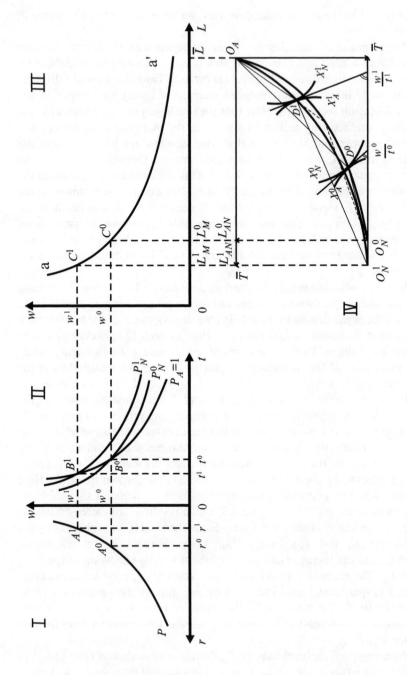

Figure 4.3 Tourism and factor markets

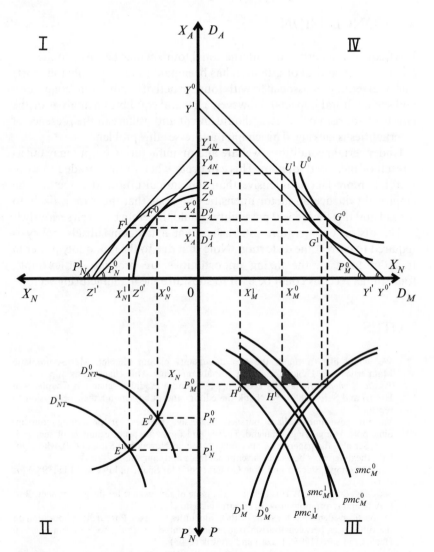

Figure 4.4   Tourism and welfare

because the private firms in X_M do not internalize the effects of the increasing returns to scale. As a result the welfare loss (represented by the shaded area) becomes largest. This increase in the welfare loss outweighs the increase in income from the terms of trade effect, as illustrated by the movement from the social indifference curve U^0 to U^1 in quadrant IV of Figure 4.4.

4. CONCLUSION

It is frequently asserted that international tourism may be costly to the host country. A great deal of attention has been paid to the most obvious costs due to externalities associated with tourism activity (pollution, congestion and sociocultural impacts). However, a general equilibrium analysis of the effects of tourism on structural adjustment and welfare in the presence of externalities is lacking. This chapter addresses this problem.

Under certain conditions, welfare and manufacturing output may fall as a result of increased tourism. This can occur when the non-traded tourism sector is more labour intensive than the agricultural traded sector. The empirical evidence on factor intensities suggests that this case is likely to prevail and this theoretical possibility should therefore be taken seriously.[16]

The distortion literature establishes that a tax-cum-subsidy policy is required to correct the distortion. Note that due to the monopoly power in trade in tourism, the taxing opportunities are broader; for example, tourism tax receipts could be used to subsidize the manufacturing sector.

NOTES

*   We would like to thank the two discussants of our chapter, Marie-Antoniette Maupertuis and Fabio Cerina, for useful comments. This chapter has appeared in *Pacific Economic Review*, **8**(3), October 2003 and a modified version as Chapter 9 in Hazari and Sgro (2004). We thank the editors and publishers for their permission to reprint.
1.   Various governments have pursued aggressive policies for promoting tourism. Singapore, Hong Kong, Thailand, Tunisia and Egypt are prime examples of such policies. See also the papers by Copeland (1991), and Nowak and Sahli (1999), who highlight the differences between conventional trade and tourism.
2.   See for example Sinclair and Bote Gomez (1996) for Spain and Pye and Lin (1983) for Asian NIC.
3.   See de Kadt, (1979), WTO (1998); on the issue of tax revenue for the government, Bird (1992), and to promote growth, Hazari and Sgro (1995).
4.   Domestic residents pay for some of these amenities via taxes. For further elaboration on the differences between tourism trade and commodities trade, see Copeland (1991), Hazari and Sgro (1995), Hazari and Nowak (2003).
5.   See for example Cazes (1992) and Sheldon (1990).
6.   See for example Cater and Goodall (1992), Eber (1992).
7.   See for example Long (1991).
8.   See for example Krippendorf (1991).
9.   Empirical evidence shows that in some cases tourism development is detrimental to agriculture, as on the Spanish Mediterranean coast (Tyrakowski, 1986), in Caribbean countries (Bryden, 1973; Weaver, 1988), in Bali or in many parts of Mexico (Latimer, 1986). Computable general equilibrium modelling experiments in Australia (Adams and Parmenter, 1995) and Hawaii (Zhou et al., 1997) also suggest that an increase in the demand for tourism may seriously crowd out agriculture and manufacturing activities, with no change in overall output.

10. In the 'Dutch disease' literature, Corden and Neary (1982), and Neary and Van Wijnbergen (1986) have emphasized the detrimental consequences of a booming traded goods sector and other traded goods sectors, especially on manufacturing industry. In our model, since the foreign tourists consume the local non-traded good, the booming sector is the non-traded sector, which makes our analysis different to the 'Dutch disease' model, although structural effects may still exist.

11. Several studies stress competition for use of land and labour between agriculture and tourism; see Bryden (1973), Latimer (1986), Telfer and Wall (1996).

12. This particular formulation is used, for example, by Panagariya (1980, 1986), Herberg and Kemp (1969) and Choi and Yu (1984).

13. In general with endogenous labour supply the price–output response may be perverse and the production possibility curve may not be concave (Kemp and Jones, 1962; Martin and Neary, 1980). To avoid this problem in the H–O subset we impose restrictions on the price elasticities.

14. Panagariya (1986) proved that a necessary and sufficient condition for stability in the RVJ model is that the weighted sum of the sectoral marginal physical product of labour be negative. In this case the price–output response is normal and the production possibility curve is concave. Given that there are no production or factor market distortions from the H–O subset (sectors X_A and X_N), and given note 13 above, it is easy to show that the corresponding elasticity is always negative for this subset. Therefore it is sufficient to assume $\xi_M < 0$ for stability in our model.

15. Note also that both the Heckscher–Ohlin–Komiya (HOK) and the RVJ models can be derived from our more general model by making specific simplifying assumptions. In the HOK model, by allowing capital mobility between all the sectors, we obtain the price and output results of Komiya (1967) and the welfare result does not have a terms of trade effect. Welfare will rise or fall depending on the labour intensity of X_N *vis-à-vis* the other two sectors. To obtain the RVJ model, we add land immobility between X_A and X_N. In this case the rise in P_N always increases the wage rate and the results are qualitatively identical to the case above where $(|\theta| > 0)$, i.e. the non-traded good sector is labour intensive. Note also that the return to the specific factor in the non-traded good sector in the RVJ model rises but in our model decreases. Our model is also based on the assumption of competitive markets, full employment and interior solutions.

16. See for example Krueger et al. (1983). One might conclude that if the non-traded good is labour intensive, more tourism is a good strategy for a small open economy which is predominately made up of increasing returns to scale (IRS) manufacturers (Hong Kong, Thailand). It may also be a good strategy for countries such as Corsica or the West Indies where manufacturing is essentially handcrafts without IRS.

REFERENCES

Adams, P.D. and B.R. Parmenter (1995), 'An Applied General Equilibrium Analysis of the Economic Effects of Tourism in a Quite Small, Quite Open Economy', *Applied Economics*, **27**(10), 985–94.

Bird, R.M. (1992), 'Taxing Tourism in Developing Countries', *World Development*, **20**(8), 1145–58.

Bryden, J.M. (1973), *Tourism and Development: A Case Study of the Commonwealth Caribbean*, London: Cambridge University Press.

Cater, E. and B. Goodall (1992), 'Must Tourism Destroy its Resource Base?', in A.M. Mannion and S.R. Bowlby (eds), *Environmental Issues in the 1990s*, Chichester: John Wiley.

Cazes, G. (1992), *Tourisme et Tiers-Monde: un bilan controversé*, Paris: L'Harmattan.

Choi, J.-Y. and E.S.H. Yu (1984), 'Gains from Trade under Variable Returns to Scale', *Southern Economic Journal*, **49**, 979–92.

Copeland, B.R. (1991), 'Tourism, Welfare and Industrialization in a Small Open Economy', *Economica*, **58**, 515–29.

Corden, W.M. and J.P. Neary (1982), 'Booming Sector and De-industrialisation in a Small Open Economy', *Economic Journal*, **92**, 825–48.

de Kadt, E. (1979), *Tourism: Passport to Development*, Oxford: Oxford University Press.

Eber, S. (ed.) (1992), *Beyond the Green Horizon. Principles for Sustainable Tourism*, Godalming: World Wide Fund for Nature.

Hazari, B.R. and A. Ng (1993), 'An Analysis of Tourists' Consumption of Non-traded Goods and Services on the Welfare of the Domestic Consumers', *International Review of Economics and Finance*, **2**, 3–58.

Hazari, B.R. and J.J. Nowak (2003), 'Tourism, Taxes and Immiserization: A Trade Theoretic Analysis', *Pacific Economic Review*, **8**(3), 279–87.

Hazari, B.R. and P.M. Sgro (1995), 'Tourism and Growth in a Dynamic Model of Trade', *Journal of International Trade and Economic Development*, **4**(2), 243–52.

Hazari, B.R. and P.M. Sgro (2004), *Tourism, Trade and National Welfare*, Contributions to Economic Analysis Series No. 265, edited by B. Baltagi, E. Sadka and D. Wildasin, Amsterdam: Elsevier.

Herberg, H. and M.C. Kemp (1969), 'Some Implications of Variable Returns to Scale', *Canadian Journal of Economics*, **2**, 403–15.

Kemp, M.C. and R.W. Jones (1962), 'Variable Labour Supply and the Theory of International Trade', *Journal of Political Economy*, **70**, 30–6.

Komiya, R. (1967), 'Non-traded Goods and the Pure Theory of International Trade', *International Economic Review*, **8**(2), 132–52.

Krippendorf, J. (1991), 'Towards New Tourism Policies', in S. Medlik (ed.), *Managing Tourism*, London: Butterworth Heinemann, pp. 301–6.

Krueger, A.O. et al. (1983), *Trade and Employment in Developing Countries: Synthesis and Conclusions*, NBER, Chicago: The University of Chicago Press.

Latimer, H. (1986), 'Developing Island Economies: Tourism v Agriculture', *Tourism Management*, **6**, 32–42.

Long, V.H. (1991), 'Government–Industry–Community Interaction in Tourism Development in Mexico', in M.T. Sinclair and M.J. Stabler (eds), *The Tourism Industry: An International Analysis*, Wallingford: C.A.B. International.

Martin, Q.P. and J.P. Neary (1980), 'Variable Labour Supply and the Purse Theory of International Trade', *Journal of International Economics*, **10**, 549–59.

Neary, J.P. and S. Van Wijnbergen (eds) (1986), *Natural Resources and the Macroeconomy*, Oxford: Basil Blackwell.

Nowak, J.-J. and M. Sahli (1999), 'L'analyse d'un boom touristique dans une petite économie ouverte', *Revue d' Economique Politique*, **105**(5), 729–49.

Panagariya, A. (1980), 'Variable Returns to Scale in General Equilibrium Theory Once Again', *Journal of International Economics*, **10**, 499–526.

Panagariya, A. (1986), 'Increasing Returns and the Specific Factor Model', *Southern Economic Journal*, **86**, 1–17.

Pye, E.A. and T.B. Lin (eds) (1983), *Tourism in Asia: The Economic Impact*, Singapore: Singapore University Press.

Sheldon P.J. (1990), 'A Review of Tourism Expenditure Research', in C.P. Cooper (ed.), *Progress in Tourism, Recreation and Hospitality Management*, vol. 2, London: Belhaven.

Sinclair, M.T. and V. Bote Gomez (1996), 'Tourism, the Spanish Economy and the Balance of Payments', in M. Barke, M. Newton and J. Towner (eds), *Tourism in Spain: Critical Perspectives*, Wallingford: C.A.B. International.

Telfer, D.J. and G. Wall (1996), 'Linkages between Tourism and Food Productions', *Annals of Tourism Research*, **23**(3), 635–53.

Tyrakowski, K. (1986), 'The Role of Tourism in Land Utilization Conflicts on the Spanish Mediterranean Coast', *Geojournal*, **13**, 19–26.

Weaver, D. (1988), 'The Evolution of a Plantation Tourism Landscape on the Caribbean Island of Antigua', *Tidschrift voor Economische en Sociale Geographie*, **79**, 319–31.

World Tourism Organization (1998), *Tourism Economic Report*, Madrid.

Zhou, D., J.F. Yanagida, U. Chakravorty and P. Leung (1997), 'Estimating Economic Impacts from Tourism', *Annals of Tourism Research*, **24**(1), 76–89.

5. How to develop an accounting framework for ecologically sustainable tourism

Cesare Costantino and Angelica Tudini

INTRODUCTION

Tourism is an area of specific interest in economic analysis, especially in a macroeconomic perspective. It has become even more so with the increasing importance attached to issues related to sustainable development, given the many important implications of the sector in the economic and social sphere, as well as the pressure it may exert on the natural environment locally and world-wide.

In the debate on ecologically sustainable development, tourism is included among target sectors of environmental policy. Since integrated environmental and economic accounting is acknowledged as an important instrument for implementing a sustainability strategy, it would be interesting to develop a specific accounting module focused on tourism and its interrelationships with the natural environment. Such a work can build on methodological achievements now available within official statistics.

A preliminary step towards the development of an integrated environmental and economic accounting module specific for tourism is the definition of a system of economic accounts concerning the sector. Since a thorough economic analysis cannot be pursued within the central framework of the conventional economic accounts, what is needed is an economic satellite account for tourism. The internationally agreed 'Tourism Satellite Account – Recommended Methodological Framework' (TSARMF) is the answer to this need. It is essential to take this framework into account, if an accounting framework for tourism is to be developed which addresses environmental issues while ensuring proper links with official economic information on the same sector.

The following step addresses the economic and environmental dimensions of sustainable development at once; this is crucial in general for a sustainability strategy to be successful, and the same applies in particular to tourism. The main methodological reference for the analysis of the inter-relationships between the environment and the economy in a satellite account form is the handbook *Integrated Environmental and Economic Accounts 2003* (SEEA2003).

Finally, as far as environmental pressures are concerned, the results of projects carried out in the 1990s in the framework of the European System of Environmental Pressure Indices (ESEPI) are to be taken into account in order to derive suitable inputs to the definition of an accounting framework for ecologically sustainable tourism.

In the following paragraphs, tourism is first considered in a macroeconomic perspective and a presentation of the TSARMF is given (section 1). The structure of this accounting framework is analysed, highlighting that it offers a set of relevant indicators of the size of tourism in an economy. Then the sector is considered in a sustainability perspective, with focus on environmental aspects and with the aim of arriving at a methodological proposal for an accounting framework (section 2). After a brief introduction on analytical and accounting frameworks for ecologically sustainable development (subsection 2.1), the SEEA2003 is introduced in 2.2.1; although none of the SEEA2003 accounts addresses tourism as a sector and its interaction with the natural environment, one of the SEEA schemes, i.e. 'hybrid flow accounts' – which combines national accounts in monetary terms (economic module) and flow accounts in physical units (environmental module) in a common matrix presentation – is proposed as a possible reference framework for analysing the interrelationship between tourism and the natural environment. A presentation of ESEPI follows in 2.2.2, highlighting how the sector environmental pressures proposed in that framework suit the proposed scheme, which combines physical indicators with national accounting monetary aggregates. Finally, subsection 2.3 presents a proposal for an application of the 'hybrid accounts' methodology to the tourism sector; on the basis of the SEEA2003 reference framework, the main input for the economic module derives from the economic satellite account for tourism as envisaged by the TSARMF, while the proposed content of the environmental module is based on the results of Eurostat projects carried out in the framework of ESEPI. A first evaluation of the feasibility of the proposed hybrid flow account for the tourism sector is then made in subsection 2.4, with reference to a simplified framework for the case of Italy.

1.   TOURISM IN A MACROECONOMIC PERSPECTIVE

1.1   The Tourism Sector: a Case for Satellite Analysis and Accounting

Tourism is one of the special cases for which a thorough economic analysis cannot be pursued within the central framework of the SNA, so that one cannot fully identify its related activities and products. The main feature distinguishing tourism from other activities – which are, instead, fully described and analysed through the same central framework – is that there are many examples in which a given activity or product is related to tourism if tourists make use of it, while, if this is not the case, the same activity or product does not belong to tourism. This is, for example, the case of transport activities. The identification of economic activities covered within the central framework of the SNA does not, instead, depend on the use that is made of them. Furthermore, tourists are a special type of consumers in that they can only be defined as such with reference to a temporary situation, whereas in the central framework of the SNA more permanent features, such as place of residence, are used to identify transactors. For this and other special cases that do not fit into the central framework, the SNA envisions the development of satellite accounts or systems,[1] which 'expand the analytical capacity of national accounting for selected areas of social concern in a flexible manner, without overburdening or disrupting the central system' (United Nations, 1993, §21.4).

There are two main types of satellite accounts:

1.   The so-called 'functional satellite accounts', also known as 'internal satellite accounts', which maintain a fundamental consistency with the central framework core concepts, while introducing some additional elements, expanding and rearranging specific items so as to make the analysis of fields such as tourism possible.[2]
2.   The 'external satellite accounts', which introduce substantial alternative concepts such as an enlarged production boundary or set of assets, thus allowing, for example, the analysis of natural resources.

While the SNA itself provides the reference concepts for the development of satellite accounts in general, the detailed framework and the operational guidelines for each individual account need to be defined in specific manuals by the experts in the field.

1.2   Tourism Satellite Account – Recommended Methodological Framework (TSARMF)

In the case of tourism, efforts for the development of a tourism satellite account (TSA) led to the publication, in 2001, of the Recommended Methodological Framework (TSARMF) for the development of a TSA, jointly defined by the Commission of the European Communities – Eurostat, the Organisation for Economic Co-operation and Development (OECD), the World Tourism Organization (WTO) and the United Nations Statistics Division (UNSD).[3] The manual aims to provide the basic guidelines for the regular national production of statistical data on the effects of tourism on the economy on an annual basis in a way that is internationally comparable, internally consistent and presented within widely recognized macroeconomic frameworks.[4]

The main purposes of the TSA are (see TSARMF §1.14):

- to analyse in detail all the aspects of demand for goods and services which might be associated with tourism within the economy;
- to observe the operational interface with the supply of such goods and services within the same economy of reference; and
- to describe how this supply interacts with other economic activities.

To this aim the TSARMF presents reference definitions and classifications for the identification of the scope of the TSA as well as the tables and aggregates that constitute the satellite account itself.

As for any specific field in a satellite account framework, the starting point for the statistical representation of the tourism sector is – according to the SNA recommendations – the analysis of the uses in order to find an answer to the question 'how many resources are devoted to the specific field under examination?' These uses, that is, the expenditures for the specific function at issue, are already included in the core framework of the SNA, but they need to be separately identified by specifying the scope of the TSA, that is:

- by defining the field of analysis: this is done through the definition of tourism, which 'comprises the activities of persons travelling to and staying in places outside their usual environment for not more than one consecutive year for leisure, business and other purposes not related to the exercise of an activity remunerated from within the place visited' (TSARMF §2.1); persons conforming to this definition are called 'visitors';
- by identifying and classifying goods and services that are specific to the field, that is, products whose supply would cease to exist in

meaningful quantity in the absence of visitors, whose absence might significantly affect tourism consumption and that represent a significant share of tourism consumption (TSARMF §3.19); due to measurement difficulties, the proposed list of tourism-specific products includes up to now services only (TSARMF – Annex 1). Among specific products, tourism-characteristic products and tourism-connected products are distinguished; the first group covers specific products that can be considered characteristic for purposes of the international comparability of results in TSA compilation; connected products are 'a residual category, including those that have been identified as Tourism-specific in a given country but for which this attribute has not been acknowledged on a worldwide basis' (TSARMF §3.17);

- by identifying and classifying the characteristic activities, that is, activities that are typical of the field under study; in our case, they are productive activities that produce a principal output which has been identified as characteristic of tourism.

For the development of the TSA, a basic set of tables, a list of tourism-characteristic products and a list of tourism-characteristic activities are recommended (TSARMF §4.25); these are reported in Table 5.1.

Table 5.1   Tourism-characteristic products and activities and their correspondence

Tourism-characteristic products	Tourism-characteristic activities
1 Accommodation	
1.1 Hotels and other lodging services	1 Hotels and similar
1.2 Second home services on own account of for free	2 Second home ownership (imputed)
2 Food and beverage serving	3 Restaurants and similar
3 Passenger transport services	
3.1 Interurban railway transport services	4 Railway passenger transport services
3.2 Road transport services	5 Road passenger transport services
3.3 Water transport services	6 Water passenger transport services
3.4 Air transport services	7 Air passenger transport services
3.5 Supporting passenger transport services	8 Transport supporting services

Table 5.1   (continued)

Tourism-characteristic products	Tourism-characteristic activities
3.6 Passenger transport equipment rental	9 Transport equipment rental
3.7 Maintenance and repair services of passenger transport equipment[a]	
4 Travel agency, tour operator and tourist guide services	10 Travel agencies and similar
4.1 Travel agency services	
4.2 Tour operator services	
4.3 Tourist information and tourist guide services	
5 Cultural services	11 Cultural services
5.1 Performing arts	
5.2 Museum and other cultural services	
6 Recreation and other entertainment services	12 Sporting and other recreational services
6.1 Sports and recreational sport services	
6.2 Other amusement and recreational services	
7 Miscellaneous tourism services	
7.1 Financial and insurance services	
7.2 Other good rental services	
7.3 Other tourism services	

Note: [a]Does not correspond to a characteristic activity.

Source: Adapted from TSARMF, p. 58.

In relation to the concept of 'visitor consumption' and the place where this occurs, as well as the need to distinguish resident and non-resident visitors, the following concepts are also defined (TSARMF §2.61):

- domestic tourism: the tourism of resident visitors within the economic territory of the country of reference;
- domestic tourism consumption: the consumption of resident visitors within the economic territory of the country of reference;

- inbound tourism: the tourism of non-resident visitors within the economic territory of the country of reference;
- inbound tourism consumption: the consumption of non-resident visitors within the economic territory of the country of reference and/or that provided by residents;
- outbound tourism: the tourism of resident visitors outside the economic territory of the country of reference;
- outbound tourism consumption: the consumption of resident visitors outside the economic territory of the country of reference and provided by non-residents;
- internal tourism: the tourism of visitors both resident and non-resident, within the economic territory of the country of reference;
- internal tourism consumption: the consumption of both resident and non-resident visitors within the economic territory of the country of reference and/or that provided by residents;
- national tourism: the tourism of resident visitors, within and outside the economic territory of the country of reference;
- national tourism consumption: the consumption of resident visitors, within and outside the economic territory of the country of reference.

On the basis of the concepts, definitions and classifications presented above, which define the boundaries of the sector under investigation, the TSARMF foresees the development of ten main accounting tables that enable the analysis of the economic features of tourism, encompassing demand, supply, impact on employment as well as other aspects. All tables are reported in Appendix I. The ten tables can be grouped into two different sets according to their degree of priority.

Specifically, Tables 1 to 7 and Table 10 are regarded as high priority as they include the minimum set of accounts needed to pursue a comprehensive analysis of tourism within a satellite framework; by contrast, Tables 8 and 9 have lower priority because of their complex nature and because of the burden posed on compilers in terms of data requirements. For the first group, a brief description of the tables is given below:

- Tables 1 to 4 focus on the demand perspective and analyse consumption. In all tables, rows record consumption by product classified consistently with the first column of Table 5.1. Tables 1, 2 and 3, devoted – respectively – to inbound, domestic and outbound tourism, record visitor final consumption expenditure in cash. Table 4, devoted to internal tourism consumption, records tourism consumption in cash as well as in kind.

- Table 5 focuses on the supply perspective and analyses production of tourism-characteristic industries as well as other industries.
- Table 6, which includes the confrontation between supply and internal tourism consumption, is regarded as the core of the TSA.
- Table 7 provides a detailed description of employment in the tourism sector.
- Table 10 presents a number of non-monetary indicators related to tourism such as the number of trips and overnight stays, the number of establishments in tourism-characteristic and -connected activities, etc.

The compilation of TSA tables includes the calculation of the following aggregates:

- internal tourism consumption in cash;
- internal tourism consumption (in cash and in kind);
- value added of the tourism industries;
- tourism value added;
- tourism GDP.

These aggregates, to be used for international comparison in the first stage of TSA implementation, are considered as a set of relevant indicators of the size of tourism in an economy (TSARMF §§4.77 and 4.78).

2. TOURISM IN A SUSTAINABILITY PERSPECTIVE

2.1 Analytical and Accounting Frameworks for Ecologically Sustainable Development

While the development of a TSA for a given country offers great possibilities for economic analysis, the investigation of environmental issues related to tourism is outside the scope of the TSARMF described in subsection 1.2.

In order to study the interaction between tourism, the economy and the natural environment, a specific statistical tool needs to be developed starting from the consideration of frameworks for ecologically sustainable development. Indeed, 'frameworks are important for linking information pertaining to different areas, and for relating indicators to analytical questions and policy issues' (De Haan and Kee, 2003, p. 2).

Two types of frameworks can be distinguished: analytical and statistical, the latter including accounting frameworks. Each type has its own specific

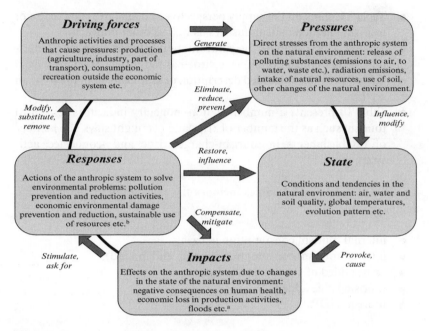

Notes:
[a]The social system at large, and not just the economy, is affected by changes in the state of the natural environment. This may be an important source of demand for ecological sustainability policy and may retroact on the economy. To the extent that this occurs, impacts on the social system are accounted for in the environmental/economic interaction circuit even though they do not have, *per se*, an economic or an environmental dimension.
[b]There are examples of responses aimed at solving environmental problems which are addressed to the social system, e.g. information campaigns directed to changing social behaviour as a response to the need for energy saving. They are accounted for in the environmental/economic interaction circuit in so far as they imply economic costs and/or retroact on economic behaviour.

Figure 5.1   The DPSIR circuit

features; both are important for developing statistical tools to be used in a sustainability perspective.

The best-known example of an analytical framework in the environmental field is the Driving Force–Pressure–State–Impact–Response (DPSIR) model developed by the European Environment Agency (EEA) on the basis of the original OECD Pressure–State–Response (PSR) model.[5]

Figure 5.1 depicts the environmental/economic interaction circuit provided by the DPSIR model: man, with all his activities (driving forces), causes stress (pressures) to the natural environment, whose conditions (state) tend to be modified as a consequence of this stress;[6] wherever these modifications of environmental conditions turn out to be undesirable for man (impact), the anthropic system tends, in turn, to react (response) to the environmental change, to eliminate the causes or the consequences; when these responses are intended to eliminate the causes, they retroact more or less effectively on the pressures carried out by man on nature.

A map of the relevant relationships in the technosphere/ecosphere dialectic can thus be identified starting from the DPSIR model, in view of developing an organic and, to the extent possible, complete statistical description of the interrelationships between the economic and environmental dimensions of development. This does not mean, however – partly due to the heterogeneity of the elements that are included in the model and partly due to insufficient knowledge of complex interactions – that one can rely on a series of identities that tie all the elements of this environmental/economic interaction circuit in a unique accounting framework, in the same way as with the 'income circuit' and the national accounts. In other words, there is no way to derive directly from the DPSIR model a framework for describing the interrelationships between economy and environment in an accounting fashion.

Accounting frameworks are useful for analytical purposes, decision taking and policy making in the economic realm, as is recognized through the world-wide adoption of the System of National Accounts (SNA)[7] and, at the European level, of its fully consistent counterpart, the 1995 European System of National and Regional Accounts (ESA) (Eurostat, 1996).[8] In this context, 'an account is a means of recording, for a given aspect of economic life, the uses and resources or the changes in assets and the changes in liabilities during the accounting period, or the stock of assets and liabilities existing at the beginning or at the end of this period' (Eurostat, 1996, §1.48).

In the broader domain of sustainable development, which requires the consideration of economic, environmental and social issues at the same time, there is no accounting framework comparable to the SNA or the ESA as regards the degree of standardization across countries and the widespread adoption. Nevertheless, accounting frameworks are increasingly adopted at the national level to measure the interrelationships between the economic, social and environmental dimensions.[9]

Specifically, for the analysis of the interrelationships between the environment and the economy, the main reference is the handbook *Integrated Environmental and Economic Accounts 2003* (SEEA2003), released on the web by the UN, the European Commission, the International Monetary Fund, the OECD and the World Bank.[10] The SEEA2003 provides, within an overall accounting framework, an articulated system of environmental accounts, concerning various aspects and moments of the environmental/economic interaction circuit (as represented by the DPSIR model) and integrated through a common basis of concepts, definitions and classifications.

Each specific accounting scheme is supposed to contribute to the measurement of economic/ecological aspects of sustainable development.[11]

A general advantage of accounting frameworks is that, through a well-structured and systematic organization of basic statistics, they allow 'making more out of primary data' (Steurer, 2003, p. 9). Their value added is manifold; in particular, according to the Task Force 'European Strategy for Environmental Accounting', the value added of environmental accounts stems from the fact that they:

- allow to integrate and make good use of otherwise scattered and incomplete primary data, help structure existing data, improve consistency and provide the basis for estimates (e.g. when primary data are not available annually)
- are integrated with other data sets (especially with economic accounts and hence also aspects of the social dimension of sustainable development) thereby linking environmental information to the economic actors
- allow to derive coherent sets of indicators that are linked to one another
- are therefore a key basis for integrated economic and environmental analysis and modelling, including cost-effectiveness analyses, scenario modelling and economic and environmental forecasts
- through an integrative framework, allow to put sectoral policies and indicators in a comprehensive economic and environmental context
- ensure international comparability of results through common frameworks, concepts and methods
- play a role within the statistical system where environmental accounts frameworks can help guide and develop environmental statistics so as to ensure greater coherence with economic and social statistics, provide input, extra uses and positive feedback for other areas of statistics. (Eurostat, 2002, p. 4)

Subsection 2.2 will investigate – starting with a presentation of the above-mentioned SEEA2003 – the extent to which existing statistical frameworks centred on environmental aspects enable development of an accounting statistical tool for the description and analysis of tourism and sustainable economic development, with focus on the interrelationships between the environment and the economy.

2.2 Relevant Statistical Frameworks for Studying the Interaction between Tourism and the Natural Environment

In addition to the TSARMF discussed in subsection 1.2 – which deals with the impact of tourism on the economy – two international statistical frameworks are worth considering in order to develop an accounting framework for ecologically sustainable tourism. They deal with:

- the interrelationships between the economy and the environment (overall integrated environmental and economic accounting – SEEA2003)

- the environmental pressures exerted on the natural environment by the anthropic system, specifically by environmental policy target sectors, among which is tourism (European System of Environmental Pressure Indices – ESEPI).

2.2.1 Integrated Environmental and Economic Accounts 2003 (SEEA2003)

The most comprehensive international approach to the analysis of the relationship between the environment and the economy in a satellite account form is the handbook *Integrated Environmental and Economic Accounts 2003* (SEEA2003), the final version of which has been released on the web by the UN, the European Commission, the International Monetary Fund, the OECD and the World Bank.

The SEEA2003 covers physical flow accounts, hybrid flow accounts (integration of physical and monetary accounts), accounting for economic activities and products related to the environment, accounting for other environmentally related transactions and asset accounts, including the valuation of natural resource stocks; it also deals with valuation techniques for measuring degradation as well as with environmental adjustments to the flow accounts.

None of the SEEA2003 accounts addresses tourism as a sector and its interaction with the natural environment. For the purpose of developing a specific environmental accounting framework for tourism, among the different types of accounting modules dealt with in the SEEA2003, hybrid flow accounts are a possible starting point.[12]

In hybrid flow accounts, national accounts in monetary terms (economic module) and flow accounts in physical units (environmental module) based on common national accounts principles are presented in a common matrix presentation (hence the use of the term 'hybrid'). Both the economic module and the environmental module can assume different forms, depending on the purposes of the analysis and data availability. The economic module generally consists of a supply and use table, an input–output table or a National Account Matrix (NAM).[13] The reference framework for the environmental module is the physical flow accounts describing how natural resources and ecosystem inputs are used in the economic system and how residuals are created by the economy itself.[14]

Table 5.2 presents an example of a hybrid flow account where the monetary supply and use table represented by the bold type is extended by adding physical flow accounts.

Most applications (mainly in the EU countries) of hybrid flow accounts have taken the form of hybrid supply and use tables and developed the residuals accounts within the environmental module focusing specifically

Table 5.2   Hybrid supply and use table

	Products	Industries	Consumption	Capital	Exports	Residuals
Products		**Products used by industry (intermediate consumption)**	**Products consumed by households**	**Products converted to capital**	**Products exported**	
Industries	**Products made by industry**					Residuals generated by industry
Consumption						Residuals generated by households
Capital						Residuals generated by capital
Imports	**Products imported**					Residuals imported
Margins	**Trade and transport margins**					
Value added		**Value added by industry**				
Monetary totals	**Total products supplied**	**Total industry inputs**	**Total household consumption**	**Total capital supplied**	**Total exports**	
Natural resources[a]		Natural resources used by industry	Natural resources consumed by households		Natural resources exported	
Ecosystem inputs[b]		Ecosystem inputs used by industry	Ecosystem inputs consumed by households		Ecosystem inputs exported	
Residuals[c]		Residuals reabsorbed by industry		Residuals going to landfill	Residuals exported	
Other information		Employment Energy use	Energy use			

Notes:
Bold type indicates the economic module.
[a]Minerals, energy resources, water and biological resources are included (SEEA §2.31).
[b]Includes 'water and other natural inputs (e.g. nutrients, carbon dioxide) required by plants and animals for growth and the oxygen necessary for combustion' (SEEA §2.31).
[c]Includes solid, liquid and gaseous wastes (SEEA §2.31).

Source: SEEA, pp. 4–9.

on air emission accounts. These applications are known under the name of NAMEAs (National Account Matrix including Environmental Accounts) despite the fact that they are not always based on an NAM.[15]

Interest in hybrid accounts is also due to their many potential analytical and policy uses;[16] among the most common ones are:

- the comparison of economic and environmental indicators at the national level or at a sectoral level. In both cases the time trends of national accounts figures such as GDP, employment, etc. can be supplemented by, for example, air emissions or waste time trends. Moreover, for a given grouping of industries, the 'economic contribution' – represented for example by their percentage share of total value added, total output and total employment – is compared to the 'environmental burden' – represented for example by their percentage share of total air emissions; this comparison is called the environmental–economic profile (see SEEA §§4.99–4.107);
- the calculation of direct coefficients of environmental pressure intensity by industry, where environmental pressure can be represented for example by residuals generation, material or energy use; these indicators are obtained by dividing indicators of environmental pressure due to one industry by the output of the industry itself (see SEEA §11.15);
- the measurement of direct and indirect environmental pressures – that is, material and energy requirements and residuals generation – due to final demand (see SEEA §§4.119–4.135);
- the assessment of different sources of change in environmental pressure over time through decomposition analysis (see SEEA §§4.136–4.143 and 11.21–11.26); and
- dynamic modelling for strategic planning (see SEEA, ch. 11, section B 2).

A proposal for an application of the 'hybrid accounts' methodology for the tourism sector is presented in subsection 2.3, following a brief discussion of the possible input provided by ESEPI to the definition of the proposed accounting framework.

2.2.2   European System of Environmental Pressure Indices (ESEPI)

In a communication addressed to the Council and the European Parliament in 1994, the Commission of the European Communities defined the 'Directions for the EU on Environmental Indicators and Green National Accounting' (Commission of the European Communities, 1994); such directions included, among other things, the development of a European System of Environmental Pressure Indices – 'ESEPI action'. As a follow-up, Eurostat then launched a number of projects, including six Sectoral Infrastructure Projects (SIPs), focused on sector environmental pressure indicators. The different SIPs concerned the five target sectors identified as areas of special attention in the 5th Environmental Action Programme for the European Communities[17] – that is, agriculture, energy, industry, transport, tourism – plus waste management.[18]

In this context, a project for the tourism sector was carried out jointly by Istat and Statistics Sweden,[19] followed by another project carried out by Istat with the aim of harmonizing the results obtained by the SIPs for the different sectors.[20] The focus here is on the results of these two projects.[21]

In the two studies human action at large has been taken into account, with no limitation, in principle, to economic activities as dealt with by national accounts.[22] A national accounting rationale has nevertheless inspired the approach followed, leading to methodological solutions that incorporate national accounting concepts.

A crucial step has been the delimitation of the target sectors under examination in terms of activities causing environmental pressures. With reference to this, a first distinction has been made between production and consumption activities recorded in the national accounts and other human activities that are to be taken into consideration according to the chosen perspective.[23] This distinction is basically tantamount to identifying, in addition to the production activities recorded in the national accounts, other possible activities that may or may not have a direct counterpart in transactions recorded in this system, but which create environmental pressures to be considered in addition to those already associated with production activities.

The approach followed is described in Figure 5.2, which shows the application of the adopted basic scheme to the tourism sector. As can be seen, different sets of activities are distinguished. On one side are the production activities at the service of tourism and on the other side tourists' activities;[24] within the latter, furthermore, the use of services and the use of goods by tourists plus other important tourist activities are distinguished. As far as the use of services by tourists is concerned, there is concomitance between the purchase and the use by tourists of the products at issue, while the use of material goods bought as such can be postponed in time with respect to the act of purchasing them. The consumption of services provided by activities included in the NACE Rev. 1 does not create separate environmental pressures, as those generated at the time of use of a service – for example, a trip in a taxi – coincide with those due to its production, already accounted for among those considered in the relevant sector. Acts of postponed consumption plus other tourists' activities which do not immediately involve economic transactions[25] may generate, on the contrary, specific environmental pressures[26] that do not depend on the use of any particular

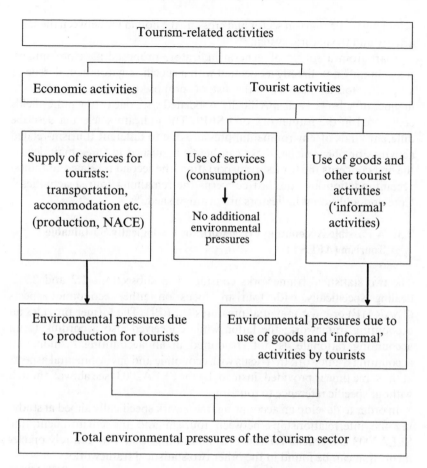

Figure 5.2   Delimitation and schematic representation of the
environmental pressures due to the tourism sector

product; for this reason they are labelled 'informal' activities and constitute a distinct set of activities with respect to supply and use of services. Activities carried out within the economic system (supply of services for tourists) and 'informal' activities exhaust, then, the set of human activities, and the union of their respective environmental pressures gives the set of all anthropogenic environmental pressures.[27]

Based on the concepts developed for the delimitation of the sector as described above, an extensive set of possible environmental pressures for tourism has been identified; the proposed list is reported in the tables in Appendix II. They are intended as flows directly generated by given activities belonging to the tourism sector and crossing the boundary between the same activity and the natural system.[28]

Apart from a subset of general indicators proposed as a preliminary step – mainly not directly associated with a specific environmental issue or a specific tourist activity – the list of proposed indicators includes a number of subsets, each specifically associated with one of the policy fields considered in the framework of ESEPI. The indicators selected describe different kinds of environmental pressure due to different tourism-related activities or phenomena; these can be distinguished in three main levels: the first concerns the tourist transportation, the second is related to tourist accommodation and the last concerns the remaining tourist activities.[29] Core and additional indicators are distinguished.[30]

2.3   A Possible Accounting Framework for Ecologically Sustainable Tourism (AFEST)

The two statistical frameworks considered in subsections 1.2 and 2.2.2, dealing specifically with tourism, focus on either economic aspects (TSARMF) or environmental pressures (ESEPI). The former provides an accounting framework; the latter, while conceived also according to an accounting rationale, is not structured in an accounting fashion. An accounting framework that deals with economic and environmental aspects at the same time is provided, instead, by the SEEA2003 (see above), though without specific reference to tourism.

In order to develop an accounting framework specifically aimed at studying the interrelationships between tourism and the environment, the SEEA2003 is a crucial reference. In addition to that, one can rely on elements that can be found in the other two statistical frameworks.

One possible framework could be designed according to the SEEA2003 'hybrid accounts' concept and, specifically, on the basis of Table 5.2, a hybrid supply and use table.

Table 5.3 shows the AFEST scheme that results from applying to the SEEA hybrid supply and use model the key inputs provided by the TSARMF and ESEPI statistical frameworks, concerning tourism-specific economic and environmental aspects respectively.

Given the focus of the SEEA2003 on the interrelationship between the economy and the natural environment, and for the sake of maximizing consistency with the SNA, the ESEPI approach is followed as far as environmental pressures are concerned, but not to the extent of considering human action at large. In practice, the key input from ESEPI is given by the proposed list of tourism environmental pressure indicators, without going into tourist 'informal activities'.

Table 5.3 Schematic diagram of a possible AFEST

	Products (TSA breakdown)	Industries (TSA breakdown)	Consumption	Residuals
Products (by CPC with TSA breakdown)		**Products used by industry (intermediate consumption) N.B. only CPC breakdown required**	**Products consumed by tourists**	
Industries (TSA breakdown)	**Products made by industry**			Residuals generated by industry
Consumption				Residuals generated by tourists
Imports	**Products imported**			Residuals imported
Taxes less subsidies on products	**Taxes less subsidies on products**			
Value added		**Value added by industry**		
Monetary totals	**Total products supplied**	**Total industry inputs**	**Total tourists' consumption**	
Natural resources[a]		Natural resources used by industry	Natural resources consumed by tourists	
Ecosystem inputs[b]		Ecosystem inputs used by industry	Ecosystem inputs consumed by tourists	
Residuals[c]		Residuals reabsorbed by industry		
Other information		Employment Energy use	Energy use	

Notes:
Bold type indicates the economic module.
[a]Minerals, energy resources, water and biological resources are included (SEEA §2.31).
[b]Includes 'water and other natural inputs (e.g. nutrients, carbon dioxide) required by plants and animals for growth and the oxygen necessary for combustion' (SEEA §2.31).
[c]Includes solid, liquid and gaseous wastes (SEEA §2.31).

The economic module in Table 5.3 (identified by bold type) includes all the items of the corresponding economic module of Table 5.2 that are relevant in the case of tourism; they can be derived from the TSA tables, particularly from Table 6, 'Domestic supply and internal tourism consumption by products'.[31] In order to maintain the focus on tourism, TSA-consistent classifications are introduced; specifically:

- For products, the classification is the Central Product Classification (CPC)[32] with the additional breakdown of some CPC items into tourism-characteristic and -connected products (see Table 5.1); the tourism-specific product breakdown is required for all the items that sum up to obtain total supply at purchasers' prices – i.e. output, imports, taxes less subsidies on products – as well as for internal tourism consumption. In the case of intermediate consumption, instead, consistently with the structure of TSA Table 6, only the CPC first digit breakdown is needed.[33]
- For industries, the TSA classification (see Table 5.4) is used. As in TSA Table 6, for each item of the industry classification, both total output and the specific tourism share are provided.

The environmental module, taking as a reference the tourism environmental pressure indicators developed in the context of the 'ESEPI action' (see above), could include, for example:

- for the category 'natural resources' – the use of mineral oil or natural gas as a fuel, the use of energy and water abstraction due to tourism;
- for the category 'residuals' – air emissions, water emissions, waste.

However, the category 'ecosystem inputs' cannot be directly related to tourism.

At present, since 'products' in the TSA only refer to services, 'Residuals generated by tourists' cannot be filled in. In a more general framework, residual generation by tourists would include, for example, the emissions due to tourists' private transport; the corresponding item in the economic module, under 'Products consumed by tourists', would be related to expenditure for fuels used for tourists' private transport.

2.4   Preliminary Feasibility Assessment of an AFEST: the Italian Example

As far as the economic dimension is concerned, the spur coming from the TSARMF as well as the economic importance of tourism for Italy have

Table 5.4   Link between the TSA and the NAMEA industry classification

Industry classification in Table 6 of the TSA	NACE Rev. 1 codes of the TSA industry breakdown	NACE Rev. 1 codes of the industry breakdown available for emissions in the Italian NAMEA
Tourism-characteristic industries		
1 Hotels and similar	55.11, 12, 21, 22, 23	55
2 Second home ownership (imputed)	70.2	70–74
3 Restaurants and similar	55.30, 40, 51, 52	55
4 Railway passenger transport services	60.1	60.1
5 Road passenger transport services	60.21, 22, 23	60.2 + 60.3
6 Water passenger transport services	61	61
7 Air passenger transport services	62.1; 62.2	62 (includes 62.3)
8 Transport supporting services	63.2	63
9 Transport equipment rental	71.1; 71.21, 22, 23	70–74
10 Travel agencies and similar	63.3	63
11 Cultural services	92.31, 32; 92.52, 53	92
12 Sporting and other recreational services	92.61*; 92.62; 92.33; 92.71, 92.72*	92
Tourism-connected industries	50.2; 50.4, 60.24, 92.34, 92.51	50–52, 60.2 + 60.3, 92
Non-specific industries	All other	All other

Note: * part of.

called for the development of a TSA within official statistics. A group of Istat experts produced a first feasibility study on the possibility of building a TSA for Italy consistent with the international guidelines, thus forming the basis for carrying out a first pilot implementation of a TSA for Italy.[34] The same group has carried out, in the framework of Eurostat projects, the first attempt to compile some of the tables that constitute the TSA. Table 6 is not included in the implementation exercise. Future work will allow us, *inter alia*, to realise to what extent Table 6, that is, the main source for the economic module of the AFEST, can be compiled.

As regards the environmental dimension, the focus could be on residuals generated by industry and specifically on the case of air emissions. The steps needed to build the accounts for this kind of environmental pressure should reflect the Istat experience gained from the construction of air emission accounts within the NAMEA framework.[35] The objective would be the calculation of emissions with the industry breakdown appearing in the columns of Table 6 of the TSA (see first column of Table 5.4). For each activity both total emissions and tourism share need to be distinguished consistently with the structure of the economic module.

As regards total emissions by industry, since the Italian NAMEA actually includes air emissions data by economic activity, the first step is to look at the extent to which NAMEA data can be used to achieve the objective of calculating emissions with the Table 6 industry breakdown.[36] To this purpose columns 2 and 3 of Table 5.4 show the link between the various industries of Table 6 (listed in column 1) and the industry breakdown available for emissions in the Italian NAMEA, in terms of NACE Rev. 1 codes.

As shown in Table 5.4, only in the case of the characteristic activity '4 Railway passenger transport services' can the required total emissions be directly derived from the NAMEA as they are available at the same breakdown level. In all other cases NAMEA data are available at a more aggregated level than necessary. Hence, for these activities, the specific AFEST industry emissions can be calculated by applying the coefficient

$$\frac{\text{output of the AFEST activity}}{\text{output of the NAMEA activity}}$$

to the corresponding NAMEA total emissions number.

The tourism share of the total emissions for each AFEST activity can be assumed to be equal to the tourism output share for the same activity.

NOTES

1. See United Nations (1993), ch. XXI.
2. Another example of a functional satellite account is the Environmental Protection Expenditure Account (EPEA). The Italian EPEA is available on the Istat web site http://www.istat.it/Economia/Conti-nazi/index.htm under the section 'Dati'. References to the EPEA are also included.
3. See Commission of the European Communities et al. (2001).
4. There is no obligation on countries to produce TSAs. Up to now obligations exist only with reference to agriculture and social protection satellite accounts.
5. Another variant is the Driving Force–State–Response (DSR) framework used initially by the United Nations Commission on Sustainable Development (UNCSD) in its work on sustainable development indicators.

6.   The fact that the conditions of the natural environment are the result of the combined effect of stress produced by the anthropic system and the spontaneous evolution of the natural system is not considered here.
7.   See United Nations (1993).
8.   See Eurostat (1996).
9.   See, *inter alia*, the papers presented at the OECD Workshop 'Accounting Frameworks in Sustainable Development', held on 14–16 May 2003 in Paris.
10. See United Nations et al. (2003).
11. As regards the analysis of the relationship between the economic and social aspects of sustainable development – not considered here – an important reference framework is the Social Accounting Matrix (SAM), which can be derived from an expansion of national accounts matrices, as explained in *Handbook on Social Accounting Matrices and Labour Accounts* (see Battellini et al., 2003, and De Haan, 2003).
12. See United Nations et al. (2003), ch. 4.
13. For more details on matrix style accounts see United Nations (1993), chs. XV and XX.
14. See United Nations et al. (2003), ch. 3.
15. See Eurostat (1999 and 2001).
16. Some of the analytical applications described below require the availability of hybrid input–output tables; in addition, in some cases time series of hybrid accounts tables are necessary.
17. See Commission of the European Communities (1993).
18. It should be noted that, even if the sectors at issue are looked at separately, they are not necessarily unlinked, given possible overlapping such as that between, for example, the transport and the energy sectors.
19. See Cammarrota et al. (1999).
20. See Costantino and Femia (2002).
21. Both projects obtained financial contribution from the European Commission.
22. Paragraph 2.3 of Cammarrota et al. (1999) reads: 'Tourism is not treated as a sector in the statistical classification of economic activities, NACE. This means that a "translation" of the sector Tourism, as defined in the 5th Environmental Action Programme for the European Communities, into activities within the NACE system is an important, even if not a straightforward, step to take. In addition to that, it has to be mentioned that the impacts of the sector tourism depend also on activities outside the formal classification system of NACE. The influence on the environment of e.g. holiday travels by private cars, changes of area occupied by privately owned secondary houses or trips with an increasing number of privately owned pleasure boats could be considerable, even if there are few data that can confirm this. In some groups or classes of NACE activities related to the sector Tourism can be identified. A specification of activities related to Tourism from the supply side has already been published by Istat (1991).'
23. As said, the focus is on human action at large.
24. The practical implication of the distinctions at issue relates to the fact that the identification of those activities that are not 'economic activities' may not be immediate and may require *ad hoc* investigations (no standard classification, such as NACE for production activities, is available).
25. E.g. recreational activities such as hunting.
26. E.g. more animals killed through hunting by tourists.
27. From an institutional sector accounting standpoint one can see that, in addition to the relevant production activities, some activities carried out by households that come under the realm of target sector policies, but that are not economic activities, have been explicitly taken into consideration. Such activities generate environmental pressures that are additional to those put down to production. These additional environmental pressures are generated either during a consumption phase which is separate from the production of the goods being consumed, or in activities that, as such, do not have any counterpart in terms of production, although their execution contributes – as, for example, in the case of many recreational activities – to satisfying households' needs.

28. Environmental pressures indirectly generated via other activities that are either 'upstream' or 'downstream' from the activity at issue – in an organizational or technical sense – are excluded. As for value added and employment in national accounting, however, indirect environmental pressures are important from an analytical and normative point of view. They can be calculated starting from direct environmental pressures, provided that these are known for all the relevant intermediate steps; for example, this can be done via the vertical integration of sectors with the input–output technique, at the branch-of-activity level.

29. In addition to transportation and accommodation aspects, tourists staying in a certain area may themselves generate some environmental burdens. The presence of tourists within a limited area, first of all, will increase energy consumption, water use as well as waste generation. Moreover, all open space activities related to tourism such as trips on mountains, in wooded areas and the countryside, riding, tracking and sport activities (skiing, golf, climbing, sailing, hunting, fishing, etc.) can cause damage to the environment.

30. Core indicators had been originally identified by scientific advisory groups of experts, within *ad hoc* ESEPI projects; additional indicators have been proposed for the first time in Cammarrota et al. (1999), already mentioned.

31. The correspondence between the cells of the economic module in Table 5.3 and parts of Table 6 (TSA) is shown in Appendix I: Table 6 and link to Table 5.3.

32. See United Nations (1993), Annex V, Part I, G.

33. Intermediate consumption is not required for tourism-connected industries and for non-specific industries.

34. See Cerroni et al. (2001).

35. Data and explanatory notes on the Italian NAMEAs are available on the Istat web site http://www.istat.it/Economia/Conti-nazi/index.htm.

36. In the absence of any source of air emissions data by industry, the calculation would start from the official data source for air emissions, i.e. the Italian CORINAIR, in which data are classified according to the process-based SNAP97 classification. In order to shift from the CORINAIR process-based classification to the AFEST economic activity-based classification, three main steps would be needed:
  ● analysis of the qualitative link between each SNAP97 process and AFEST activities, i.e. identification of the AFEST activities in which a process takes place;
  ● allocation of the emissions of each SNAP97 process to the related AFEST activities either directly (for processes linked to one activity only) or through specific indicators (for processes linked to more than one activity);
  ● calculation of total emissions by AFEST activity.

REFERENCES

Battellini, F., Coli, A. and Tartamella, F. (2003), 'A Pilot SAM for Italy: Methodology and Results', paper presented to the OECD Workshop for Accounting Frameworks in Sustainable Development, May, OECD, Paris.

Cammarrota, M., Costantino, C. and Fängström, I. (1999), 'Joint final report of the sectoral infrastructure project – Tourism', in Eurostat, *Towards Environmental Pressure Indicators for the EU: An Examination of the Sectors*, Luxembourg.

Cerroni, F., Di Leo, F., Maresca, S., Mirto, A.P., Perez, M. and Siesto, G. (2001), 'Tourism Satellite Account: Italy's Approach', paper presented at the International Conference on Tourism Satellite Account: Credible Numbers for Good Business Decision, 8–10 May, Vancouver.

Commission of the European Communities (1993), 'Community programme of policy and action in relation to the environment and sustainable development', *Official Journal* C 138, 17/05/1993.

Commission of the European Communities (1994), 'Communication from the Commission to the Council and the European Parliament on Directions for the EU on Environmental Indicators and Green National Accounting (COM (94) 670 final)', Brussels.

Commission of the European Communities, Eurostat, Organisation for Economic Co-operation and Development, World Tourism Organization and United Nations Statistics Division (2001), 'Tourism Satellite Account: Recommended Methodological Framework', Luxembourg, Madrid, New York and Paris.

Costantino, C. and Femia, A. (2002), 'Environmental Pressure Indicators – Sectoral Indicators Project: Harmonisation of the SIP Results', Eurostat, Luxembourg.

Costantino, C., Falcitelli, F., Femia, A. and Tudini, A. (2003), 'Integrated Environmental and Economic Accounting in Italy', paper presented to the OECD Workshop for Accounting Frameworks in Sustainable Development, May, OECD, Paris.

De Haan, M. (2003), 'Findings of the Leadership Group on Social Accounting Matrices: An Overview of the Handbook on Social Accounting Matrices and Labour Accounts', paper presented to the OECD Workshop for Accounting Frameworks in Sustainable Development, May, OECD, Paris.

De Haan, M. and Kee, P. (2003), 'Accounting for Sustainable Development', background paper for the OECD Workshop for Accounting Frameworks in Sustainable Development, May, OECD, Paris.

Eurostat (1996), 'European System of Accounts – ESA 1995', Luxembourg.

Eurostat (1999), 'Pilot Studies on NAMEAs for Air Emissions with a Comparison at European Level', Office for Official Publications of the European Communities, Theme 2: Economy and Finance, Collection: Studies and Research (catalogue number: CA-23-99-338-EN-C), Luxembourg.

Eurostat (2001), *NAMEAs for air emissions – Results of Pilot Studies*, Office for Official Publications of the European Communities, Theme 2: Economy and Finance, Collection: Studies and Research (catalogue number: CA-23-99-338-EN-C), Luxembourg.

Eurostat (2002), 'The European Strategy for Environmental Accounting Task Force – Report to the Statistical Programme Committee', document for discussion by the Working Party Economic Accounts for the Environment at its 1–3 October meeting, Luxembourg.

Steurer, A. (2003), 'The Use of National Accounts in Developing SD Indicators', paper presented to the Second Meeting of the ESS Task Force on Methodological Issues for Sustainable Development Indicators, Luxembourg.

United Nations (1993), 'System of National Accounts', New York.

United Nations, European Commission, International Monetary Fund, Organisation for Economic Co-operation and Development and World Bank (2003), 'Integrated Environmental and Economic Accounting 2003', available on the web site.

APPENDIX I: TABLES OF THE TSA

Table 1   Inbound tourism consumption by products and categories of visitors (visitor final consumption expenditure in cash) (net valuation)

Products	Same-day visitors (1,1)	Tourists (1,2)	Total visitors (1,3) = (1,1) + (1,2)
A. Specific products			
A.1 Characteristic products			
1 – Accommodation services			
1.1 Hotels and other lodging services (3)	X		
1.2 Second homes services on own account of for free	X		
2 – Food and beverage serving services (3)	X	X	X
3 – Passenger transport services (3)			
3.1 Interurban railway (3)			
3.2 Road (3)			
3.3 Water (3)			
3.4 Air (3)			
3.5 Supporting services			
3.6 Transport equipment rental			
3.7 Maintenance and repair services			
4 – Travel agency, tour operator and tourist guide services			
4.1 Travel agency (1)			
4.2 Tour operator (2)			
4.3 Tourist information and tourist guide			
5 – Cultural services (3)			
5.1 Performing arts			
5.2 Museum and preservation services			
6 – Recreation and other entertainment services (3)			
6.1 Sports and recreational sport services			
6.2 Other amusement and recreational services			

Table 1   (continued)

Products	Same-day visitors (1,1)	Tourists (1,2)	Total visitors (1,3) = (1,1) + (1,2)
7 – Miscellaneous tourism services			
7.1 Financial and insurance services			
7.2 Other good rental services			
7.3 Other tourism services			
A.2 Connected products			
distribution margins			
goods (4)			
services			
B. Non-specific products			
distribution margins			
goods (4)			
services			
TOTAL			
number of trips			
number of overnights			

Notes:
X = does not apply.
(1) Corresponds to the margins of the travel agencies.
(2) Corresponds to the margins of the tour operators.
(3) The value is net of the amounts paid to travel agencies and tour operators.
(4) The value is net of distribution margins.

Source: Commission of the European Communities et al. (2001).

Table 2   Domestic tourism consumption by products and ad hoc sets of resident visitors (visitor final consumption expenditure in cash) (net valuation)

Products	Resident visitors travelling only within the country of reference			Resident visitors travelling to a different country (*)			All resident visitors (**)		
	Same-day visitors (2,1)	Tourists (2,2)	Total visitors (2,3) = (2,1)+(2,2)	Same-day visitors (2,4)	Tourists (2,5)	Total visitors (2,6) = (2,4)+(2,5)	Same-day visitors (2,7) = (2,1)+(2,4)	Tourists (2,8) = (2,2)+(2,5)	Total visitors (2,9) = (2,3)+(2,6)
A. Specific products									
A.1 Characteristic products									
1 – Accommodation services	X			X			X		
1.1 Hotels and other lodging services (3)	X			X			X		
1.2 Second homes services on own account of for free	X	X	X	X	X	X	X	X	X
2 – Food and beverage serving services (3)									
3 – Passenger transport services (3)									
3.1 Interurban railway (3)									

130

Table 2 (continued)

Products	Resident visitors travelling only within the country of reference			Resident visitors travelling to a different country (*)			All resident visitors (**)		
	Same-day visitors (2,1)	Tourists (2,2)	Total visitors (2,3) = (2,1)+(2,2)	Same-day visitors (2,4)	Tourists (2,5)	Total visitors (2,6) = (2,4)+(2,5)	Same-day visitors (2,7) = (2,1)+(2,4)	Tourists (2,8) = (2,2)+(2,5)	Total visitors (2,9) = (2,3)+(2,6)
6 – Recreation and other entertainment services (3)									
6.1 Sports and recreational sport services									
6.2 Other amusement and recreational services									
7 – Miscellaneous tourism services									
7.1 Financial and insurance services									
7.2 Other good rental services									
7.3 Other tourism services									

A.2 Connected products

distribution margins
goods (4)
services

B. Non-specific products

distribution margins
goods (4)
services

TOTAL

number of trips
number of overnights

Notes:

X = does not apply.

(*) This set of visitors refers to those resident visitors which trip will take them outside the economic territory of the country of reference and, consequently, this columns will include the corresponding consumption expenditure in the country of reference before leaving it.

(**) Due to the fact that some expenditures cannot be associated separately in both ad hoc sets of categories of visitors (for instance, single purpose consumer durable bought or purchased outside the context of any trip) the estimation of domestic tourism consumption (which corresponds to the last column of the table) will require some specific adjustments. Consequently, the process for obtaining the visitors final consumption in cash referred to all resident visitors does not correspond exactly with the adition of its components.

(1) Corresponds to the margins of the travel agencies.

(2) Corresponds to the margins of the tour operators.

(3) The value is net of the amounts paid to travel agencies and tour operators.

(4) The value is net of distribution margins.

Source: Commission of the European Communities et al. (2001).

133

*Table 3   Outbound tourism consumption by products and categories of
visitors (visitor final consumption expenditure in cash)
(net valuation)*

Products	Same-day visitors (3,1)	Tourists (3,2)	Total visitors (3,3) = (3,1) + (3,2)
A. Specific products			
A.1 Characteristic products			
1 – Accommodation services	X		
1.1 Hotels and other lodging services (3)	X		
1.2 Second homes services on own account of for free	X	X	X
2 – Food and beverage serving services (3)			
3 – Passenger transport services (3)			
3.1 Interurban railway (3)			
3.2 Road (3)			
3.3 Water (3)			
3.4 Air (3)			
3.5 Supporting services			
3.6 Transport equipment rental			
3.7 Maintenance and repair services			
4 – Travel agency, tour operator and tourist guide services			
4.1 Travel agency (1)			
4.2 Tour operator (2)			
4.3 Tourist information and tourist guide			
5 – Cultural services (3)			
5.1 Performing arts			
5.2 Museum and preservation services			
6 – Recreation and other entertainment services (3)			
6.1 Sports and recreational sport services			

Table 3   (continued)

Products	Same-day visitors (3,1)	Tourists (3,2)	Total visitors (3,3) = (3,1)+(3,2)
6.2 Other amusement and recreational services			
7 – Miscellaneous tourism services			
7.1 Financial and insurance services			
7.2 Other good rental services			
7.3 Other tourism services			
A.2 Connected products			
distribution margins			
goods (4)			
services			
B. Non-specific products			
distribution margins			
goods (4)			
services			

TOTAL

number of trips
number of overnights

Notes:
X = does not apply.
(1) Corresponds to the margins of the travel agencies.
(2) Corresponds to the margins of the tour operators.
(3) The value is net of the amounts paid to travel agencies and tour operators.
(4) The value is net of distribution margins.

Source: Commission of the European Communities et al. (2001).

Table 4 Internal tourism consumption by products and types of tourism (net valuation)

Products	Visitor final consumption expenditure in cash			Other components of visitor consumption $(4,4)^{***}$	Internal tourism consumption (in cash and in kind) $(4,5)=(4,3)+(4,4)$
	Inbound tourism consumption $(4,1)^*$	Domestic tourism consumption $(4,2)^{**}$	Internal tourism consumption in cash $(4,1)+(4,2)=(4,3)$		
A. Specific products					
A.1 Characteristic products					
1 – Accommodation services					
1.1 Hotels and other lodging services (3)	X	X	X		
1.2 Second homes services on own account of for free					
2 – Food and beverage serving services (3)					
3 – Passenger transport services (3)					
3.1 Interurban railway (3)					
3.2 Road (3)					
3.3 Water (3)					
3.4 Air (3)					
3.5 Supporting services					
3.6 Transport equipment rental					
3.7 Maintenance and repair services					
4 – Travel agency, tour operator and tourist guide services					
4.1 Travel agency (1)					
4.2 Tour operator (2)					
4.3 Tourist information and tourist guide					
5 – Cultural services (3)					
5.1 Performing arts					

5.2 Museum and preservation services

6 – Recreation and other entertainment services (3)

6.1 Sports and recreational sport services

6.2 Other amusement and recreational services

7 – Miscellaneous tourism services

7.1 Financial and insurance services

7.2 Other good rental services

7.3 Other tourism services

A.2 Connected products

distribution margins

services

B. Non-specific products

distribution margins

services

Value of domestic produced goods net of distribution margins

Value of imported goods net of distribution margins

TOTAL

Notes:
X = does not apply.
(*) Corresponds to 1.3 in Table 1.
(**) Corresponds to 2.9 in Table 2.
(***) These components (referred to as visitor final consumption expenditure in kind, tourism social transfer in kind and tourism business spenses) are recorded separately as they are not easily attributable by types of tourism.
(1) Corresponds to the margins of the travel agencies.
(2) Corresponds to the margins of the tour operators.
(3) The value is net of the amounts paid to travel agencies and tour operators.

Source: Commission of the European Communities et al. (2001).

Table 5   Production accounts of tourism industries and other industries (net valuation)

| | | | | | | TOURISM | |
	1 – Hotels and similar	2 – Second home ownership (imputed)	3 – Restaurants and similar	4 – Railway passenger transport	5 – Road passenger transport	6 – Water passenger transport	7 – Air passenger transport
Products							
A. Specific products							
A.1 Characteristic products							
1 – Accommodation services							
1.1 Hotels and other lodging services (3)		X					
1.2 Second homes services on own account of for free	X		X	X	X	X	X
2 – Food and beverage serving services (3)		X					
3 – Passenger transport services (3)		X					
3.1 Interurban railway (3)		X					
3.2 Road (3)		X					
3.3 Water (3)		X					
3.4 Air (3)		X					
3.5 Supporting services		X					
3.6 Transport equipment rental		X					
3.7 Maintenance and repair services		X					
4 – Travel agency, tour operator and tourist guide services		X					
4.1 Travel agency (1)		X					
4.2 Tour operator (2)		X					
4.3 Tourist information and tourist guide		X					

INDUSTRIES					TOTAL tourism industries	Tourism-connected industries	Non-specific industries	TOTAL output of domestic producers (at basic prices)
8 – Passenger transport supporting services	9 – Passenger transport equipment rental	10 – Travel agencies and similar	11 – Cultural services	12 – Sporting and other recreational services				
x	x	x	x	x		x		

Table 5   (continued)

	1 – Hotels and similar	2 – Second home ownership (imputed)	3 – Restaurants and similar	4 – Railway passenger transport	5 – Road passenger transport	6 – Water passenger transport	7 – Air passenger transport
							TOURISM
5 – Cultural services (3)		X					
5.1 Performing arts		X					
5.2 Museum and preservation services		X					
6 – Recreation and other entertainment services (3)		X					
6.1 Sports and recreational sport services		X					
6.2 Other amusement and recreational services		X					
7 – Miscellaneous tourism services							
7.1 Financial and insurance services							
7.2 Other good rental services							
7.3 Other tourism services							
A.2 Connected products distribution margins services							
B. Non-specific products distribution margins services		X					
Value of domestic produced goods net of distribution margins		X					
Value of imported goods net of distribution margins	X	X	X	X	X	X	X
TOTAL output (at basic prices)							

INDUSTRIES					TOTAL tourism industries	Tourism-connected industries	Non-specific industries	TOTAL output of domestic producers (at basic prices)
8 – Passenger transport supporting services	9 – Passenger transport equipment rental	10 – Travel agencies and similar	11 – Cultural services	12 – Sporting and other recreational services				
X	X	X	X	X	X	X	X	X

Table 5 (continued)

	1 – Hotels and similar	2 – Second home ownership (imputed)	3 – Restaurants and similar	4 – Railway passenger transport	5 – Road passenger transport	6 – Water passenger transport	7 – Air passenger transport
							TOURISM
1. Agriculture, forestry and fishery products							
2. Ores and minerals							
3. Electricity, gas and water							
4. Manufacturing							
5. Construction work and construction							
6. Trade services, restaurants and hotel services							
7. Transport, storage and communication services							
8. Business services							
9. Community, social and personal services							
Total intermediate consumption (at purchasers' price)							
Total gross value added of activities (at basic prices)							
Compensation of employees							
Other taxes less subsidies on production							
Gross Mixed income							
Gross Operating surplus							

Notes:
X = does not apply.
(1) Corresponds to the margins of the travel agencies.
(2) Corresponds to the margins of the tour operators.
(3) The value is net of the amounts paid to travel agencies and tour operators.

Source: Commission of the European Communities et al. (2001).

INDUSTRIES					TOTAL tourism industries	Tourism-connected industries	Non-specific industries	TOTAL output of domestic producers (at basic prices)
8 – Passenger transport supporting services	9 – Passenger transport equipment rental	10 – Travel agencies and similar	11 – Cultural services	12 – Sporting and other recreational services				
						X	X	X
						X	X	X
						X	X	X
						X	X	X
						X	X	X
						X	X	X
						X	X	X
						X	X	X
						X	X	X

Table 6   *Domestic supply and internal tourism consumption by products (net valuation)*

	TOURISM INDUSTRIES								
	1 – Hotels and similar		2 – Second home ownership (imputed)		* * *		12 – Sporting and other recreational services		TOTAL tourism indus-tries
	output	tourism share	output	tourism share	output	tourism share	output	tourism share	output
Products									
A. Specific products									
A.1 Characteristic products									
1 – Accommodation services									
1.1 Hotels and other lodging services (3)			X	X					
1.2 Second homes services on own account of for free	X	X			X	X	X	X	
2 – Food and beverage serving services (3)			X	X					
3 – Passenger transport services (3)			X	X					
3.1 Interurban railway (3)			X	X					
3.2 Road (3)			X	X					
3.3 Water (3)			X	X					
3.4 Air (3)			X	X					
3.5 Supporting services			X	X					
3.6 Transport equipment rental			X	X					
3.7 Maintenance and repair services			X	X					
4 – Travel agency, tour operator and tourist guide services			X	X					
4.1 Travel agency (1)			X	X					
4.2 Tour operator (2)			X	X					
4.3 Tourist information and tourist guide			X	X					
5 – Cultural services (3)			X	X					
5.1 Performing arts			X	X					

TOTAL tourism indus- tries		Tourism- connected industries		Non-specific industries		Total output of domestic producers (at basic prices)	Imports*	Taxes less subsidies on products of domestic output and imports	Domestic supply (at pur- chasers' price)	Internal tourism consump- tion	Tourism ratio on supply
tourism share	output	tourism share	output	tourism share							
X		X	X	X	X		X	X			

Table 6   (continued)

	TOURISM INDUSTRIES								
	1 – Hotels and similar		2 – Second home ownership (imputed)		* * *		12 – Sporting and other recreational services		TOTAL tourism indus- tries
	output	tourism share	output	tourism share	output	tourism share	output	tourism share	output
5.2 Museum and preservation services			X	X					
6 – Recreation and other entertainment services (3)			X	X					
6.1 Sports and recreational sport services			X	X					
6.2 Other amusement and recreational services			X	X					
7 – Miscellaneous tourism services									
7.1 Financial and insurance services									
7.2 Other good rental services									
7.3 Other tourism services									
A.2 Connected products distribution margins services									
B. Non-specific products distribution margins services			X	X					
Value of domestic produced goods net of distribution margins			X	X					
Value of imported goods net of distribution margins	X	X	X	X	X	X	X	X	X
TOTAL output (at basic prices)									

1. Agriculture, forestry
   and fishery products
2. Ores and minerals

TOTAL tourism industries	Tourism-connected industries		Non-specific industries		Total output of domestic producers (at basic prices)	Imports*	Taxes less subsidies on products of domestic output and imports	Domestic supply (at purchasers' price)	Internal tourism consumption	Tourism ratio on supply
tourism share	output	tourism share	output	tourism share						
									X	X
X	X	X	X	X	X		X	X	X	X
	X	X	X	X	X					
	X	X	X	X	X					

Table 6 (continued)

	TOURISM INDUSTRIES				
	1 – Hotels and similar	2 – Second home ownership (imputed)	* * *	12 – Sporting and other recreational services	TOTAL tourism indus- tries
	output / tourism share	output / tourism share	output / tourism share	output / tourism share	output
3. Electricity, gas and water					
4. Manufacturing					
5. Construction work and construction					
6. Trade services, restaurants and hotel services					
7. Transport, storage and communication services					
8. Business services					
9. Community, social and personal services					
Total intermediate consumption (at purchasers' price)					
Total gross value added of activities (at basic prices)					
Compensation of employees					
Other taxes less subsidies on production					
Gross Mixed income					
Gross Operating surplus					

Notes:
X = does not apply.
*** Means that all tourism industries of the proposed list have to be considered one by one in the enumeration.
* The imports referred to here are exclusively those which are purchased within the country of reference.
(1) Corresponds to the margins of the travel agencies.
(2) Corresponds to the margins of the tour operators.
(3) The value is net of the amounts paid to travel agencies and tour operators.

Source: Commission of the European Communities et al. (2001).

TOTAL tourism industries	Tourism-connected industries		Non-specific industries		Total output of domestic producers (at basic prices)	Imports*	Taxes less subsidies on products of domestic output and imports	Domestic supply (at purchasers' price)	Internal tourism consumption	Tourism ratio on supply
tourism share	output	tourism share	output	tourism share						
	X	X	X	X	X					
	X	X	X	X	X					
	X	X	X	X	X					
	X	X	X	X	X					
	X	X	X	X	X					
	X	X	X	X	X					
	X	X	X	X	X					

Table 6 (and link to Table 5.3)   *Domestic supply and internal tourism consumption by products (net valuation)*

	TOURISM INDUSTRIES								
	1 – Hotels and similar		2 – Second home ownership (imputed)		***		12 – Sporting and other recreational services		TOTAL tourism indus- tries
	output	tourism share	output	tourism share	output	tourism share	output	tourism share	output
Products									
A. Specific products									
A.1 Characteristic products									
1 – Accommodation services									
1.1 Hotels and other lodging services (3)			X	X					
1.2 Second homes services on own account of for free	X	X			X	X	X	X	
2 – Food and beverage serving services (3)			X	X					
3 – Passenger transport services (3)			X	X					
3.1 Interurban railway (3)			X	X					
3.2 Road (3)			X	X					
3.3 Water (3)			X	X					
3.4 Air (3)			X	X					
3.5 Supporting services			X	X					
3.6 Transport equipment rental			X	X					
3.7 Maintenance and repair services			X	X					
4 – Travel agency, tour operator and tourist guide services			X	X					
4.1 Travel agency (1)			X	X					
4.2 Tour operator (2)			X	X					
4.3 Tourist information and tourist guide			X	X					
5 – Cultural services (3)			X	X					
5.1 Performing arts			X	X					

TOTAL tourism industries	Tourism-connected industries		Non-specific industries		Total output of domestic producers (at basic prices)	Imports*	Taxes less subsidies on products of domestic output and imports	Domestic supply (at purchasers' price)	Internal tourism consumption	Tourism ratio on supply
tourism share	output	tourism share	output	tourism share						
x	x	x	x			x	x			

Table 6 (and link to Table 5.3)　　(continued)

	TOURISM INDUSTRIES								
	1 – Hotels and similar		2 – Second home ownership (imputed)		* * *		12 – Sporting and other recreational services		TOTAL tourism indus- tries
	output	tourism share	output	tourism share	output	tourism share	output	tourism share	output
5.2 Museum and preservation services			X	X					
6 – Recreation and other entertainment services (3)			X	X					
6.1 Sports and recreational sport services			X	X					
6.2 Other amusement and recreational services			X	X					
7 – Miscellaneous tourism services									
7.1 Financial and insurance services									
7.2 Other good rental services									
7.3 Other tourism services									
A.2 Connected products distribution margins services									
B. Non-specific products distribution margins services			X	X					
Value of domestic produced goods net of distribution margins			X	X					
Value of imported goods net of distribution margins	X	X	X	X	X	X	X	X	X

TOTAL output (at basic prices)

1. Agriculture, forestry and fishery products
2. Ores and minerals

TOTAL tourism industries		Tourism-connected industries		Non-specific industries		Total output of domestic producers (at basic prices)	Imports*	Taxes less subsidies on products of domestic output and imports	Domestic supply (at purchasers' price)	Internal tourism consumption	Tourism ratio on supply
tourism share	output	tourism share	output	tourism share	output						
										X	X
X	X	X	X	X	X	X		X	X	X	X
X	X	X	X	X							
X	X	X	X	X							

Table 6 (and link to Table 5.3)   (continued)

	TOURISM INDUSTRIES				
	1 – Hotels and similar	2 – Second home ownership (imputed)	***	12 – Sporting and other recreational services	TOTAL tourism indus- tries
	output tourism share	output tourism share	output tourism share	output tourism share	output
3. Electricity, gas and water					
4. Manufacturing					
5. Construction work and construction					
6. Trade services, restaurants and hotel services					
7. Transport, storage and communication services					
8. Business services					
9. Community, social and personal services					
Total intermediate consumption (at purchasers' price)					
Total gross value added of activities (at basic prices)					
Compensation of employees					
Other taxes less subsidies on production					
Gross Mixed income					
Gross Operating surplus					

Notes:
X = does not apply.
*** Means that all tourism industries of the proposed list have to be considered one by one in the enumeration.
* The imports referred to here are exclusively those which are purchased within the country of reference.
(1) Corresponds to the margins of the travel agencies.
(2) Corresponds to the margins of the tour operators.
(3) The value is net of the amounts paid to travel agencies and tour operators.

Source: Commission of the European Communities et al. (2001).

TOTAL tourism indus-tries	Tourism-connected industries		Non-specific industries		Total output of domestic producers (at basic prices)	Imports*	Taxes less subsidies on products of domestic output and imports	Domestic supply (at pur-chasers' price)	Internal tourism consump-tion	Tourism ratio on supply
tourism share	output	tourism share	output	tourism share						
X	X	X	X	X	X	Cells of Table 5.3				
X	X	X	X	X	X					
X	X	X	X	X	X					
X	X	X	X	X	X					
X	X	X	X	X	X					
X	X	X	X	X	X					
X	X	X	X	X	X					

products made by industry

products used by industry

products imported

taxes less subsidies on products

products consumed by tourists

value added by industry

Table 7 Employment in the tourism industries

Tourism industries	Number of establishments	Number of jobs			Status in employment						Number of employed persons		
		total			employees			other			total		
		Male	Female	Total	Male	Female	Total	Male	Female	Total	Male	Female	Total
1 – Hotels and similar													
2 – Second home ownership (imputed)													
3 – Restaurants and similar		X	X	X	X	X	X	X	X	X	X	X	X
4 – Railway passenger transport													
5 – Road passenger transport													
6 – Water passenger transport													
7 – Air passenger transport													
8 – Passenger transport supporting services													
9 – Passenger transport equipment rental													

10 – Travel agencies and
     similar
11 – Cultural services
12 – Sporting and other
     recreational services

TOTAL

Note: X = does not apply.

Source: Commission of the European Communities et al. (2001).

Table 8   *Tourism gross fixed capital formation of tourism industries and other industries*

Capital goods	TOURISM						
	1 – Hotels and similar	2 – Second home ownership (imputed)	3 – Restaurants and similar	4 – Railway passenger transport	5 – Road passenger transport	6 – Water passenger transport	7 – Air passenger transport
A. Produced non-financial assets							
A.1 Tangible fixed assets							
1 – Tourism accommodation							
1.1 Hotel and others collective accommodation	X						
1.2 Dwellings for tourism use							
2 – Other buildings and structures							
2.1 Restaurants and similar buildings	X						
2.2 Construction or infrastructure for passenger transport by road, rail, water, air	X						
2.3 Buildings for cultural services and similar	X						
2.4 Construction for sport, recreation and entertainment	X						
2.5 Other constructions and structures	X						
3 – Passenger transport equipment							
3.1 Road and rail	X						
3.2 Water	X						
3.3 Air							
4 – Machinery and equipment							
A.2 Intangibles fixed assets	X						

INDUSTRIES						Other industries			Total tourism gross fixed capital formation of tourism industries and others
8 – Passenger transport supporting services	9 – Passenger transport equipment rental	10 – Travel agencies and similar	11 – Cultural services	12 – Sporting and other recreational services	TOTAL tourism industries	Public Adminis- tration	Others	Total	
					(1)				
						(1)	(1)		
						(1)	(1)		
						(1)	(1)		

Table 8　(continued)

Capital goods	TOURISM						
	1 – Hotels and similar	2 – Second home ownership (imputed)	3 – Restaurants and similar	4 – Railway passenger transport	5 – Road passenger transport	6 – Water passenger transport	7 – Air passenger transport
B. Improvement of land used for tourism purposes							
TOTAL							
Memo:							
C. Non-produced non-financial assets **1 – Tangibles** **2 – Intangibles**							
TOTAL							

Notes:
X = does not apply.
(1) Only of tourism purpose.

Source:　Commission of the European Communities et al. (2001).

INDUSTRIES						Other industries			Total tourism gross fixed capital formation of tourism industries and others
8 – Passenger transport supporting services	9 – Passenger transport equipment rental	10 – Travel agencies and similar	11 – Cultural services	12 – Sporting and other recreational services	TOTAL tourism industries	Public Adminis- tration	Others	Total	

Table 9 Tourism collective consumption by functions and levels of government

Functions	National level (9,1)	Regional (state) level (9,2)	Local level (9,3)	Total tourism collective consumption (9,4) = (9,1) + (9,2) + (9,3)	Memo (*) Intermediate consumption by the tourism industries
Tourism promotion					
General planning and coordination related to tourism affairs					X
Generation of statistics and of basic information on tourism					X
Administration of information bureaus					
Control and regulation of establishments in contact with visitors					X
Specific control to residents and non-resident visitors					X
Special civil defence services related to the protection of visitors					
Other services					
TOTAL					

Notes:
X = does not apply.
(*) This column reflects the expenditure by the tourism industries in tourism promotion or other services related to the functions described, when relevant.

Source: Commission of the European Communities et al. (2001).

Table 10   Non-monetary indicators

10 a)   Number of trips and overnights by type of tourism and categories of visitors

	Inbound tourism			Domestic tourism			Outbound tourism		
	Same-day visitors	Tourists	Total visitors	Same-day visitors	Tourists	Total visitors	Same-day visitors	Tourists	Total visitors
Number of trips									
Number of overnights									

Source: Commission of the European Communities et al. (2001).

10 b)   Number of arrivals and overnights by means of transport (*)

	Number of arrivals	Number of overnights
1. Air		
1.1 Scheduled flights		
1.2 Non-scheduled flights		
1.3 Other services		
2. Waterway		
2.1 Passenger lines and ferries		
2.2 Cruise		
2.3 Other		
3. Land		
3.1 Railway		
3.2 Motor coach or bus and other public road transportation		
3.3 Private vehicles		
3.4 Vehicle rental		
3.5 Other means of land transport		
TOTAL		

Note: (*) Only for inbound tourism.

Source: Commission of the European Communities et al. (2001).

10 c)   Number of establishments and capacity by forms of accommodation

	Collective tourism establishments		Private tourism accommodation	
	Hotels and similar	Others	Second homes	Others
Number of establishments				
Capacity (rooms)				
Capacity (beds)				
Capacity utilization (rooms)				
Capacity utilization (beds)				

Source: Commission of the European Communities et al. (2001).

10 d)   Number of establishments according to tourism characteristic and connected activities and number of employed persons

	1–4	5–9	10–19	20–49	50–99	100–249	250–499	500–999	>1000	TOTAL
Characteristic activities (tourism industries)										
1 – Hotels and similar										
2 – Second home ownership (imputed)										
3 – Restaurants and similar										
4 – Railway passenger transport										
5 – Road passenger transport										
6 – Water passenger transport										

10 d) (continued)

	1–4	5–9	10–19	20–49	50–99	100–249	250–499	500–999	>1000	TOTAL
7 – Air passenger transport										
8 – Passenger transport supporting services										
9 – Passenger transport equipment rental										
10 – Travel agencies and similar										
11 – Cultural services										
12 – Sporting and other recreational services										
Connected activities										
TOTAL										

Source: Commission of the European Communities et al. (2001).

APPENDIX II: ENVIRONMENTAL PRESSURE INDICATORS PROPOSED IN THE FRAMEWORK OF ESEPI

Table A   General indicators

1 Ratio tourists/residents
2 Ratio tourist overnight stays/residents * $(365 - k)$, where k is the number of days spent by residents outside the area considered
3 Number of tourists/km^2 (in the reference period and in peak season)
4 Passenger-km travelled by tourists in relation to total passenger-km, divided by type of transport

Table B   Air pollution

Core indicators	Unit of measurement and reference period
Emissions of NO_x due to tourist transportation	tonnes, yr
Emissions of NO_x due to energy used for tourist accommodation	tonnes, yr
Emissions of NMVOC due to tourist transportation	tonnes, yr
Emissions of NMVOC due to energy used for tourist accommodation	tonnes, yr
Emissions of SO_2 due to tourist transportation	tonnes, yr
Emissions of SO_2 due to energy used for tourist accommodation	tonnes, yr
Emissions of particles due to tourist transportation	tonnes, yr
Emissions of particles due to energy used for tourist accommodation	tonnes, yr
Emissions of CO due to tourist transportation	tonnes, yr
Emissions of CO due to energy used for tourist accommodation	tonnes, yr

Additional indicators

Number of air-conditioned rooms in hotels (for emissions of chlorofluorocarbons (CFCs) and halons)
Number of refrigerators in hotels (for emissions of chlorofluorocarbons (CFCs) and halons)

Table C Climate change

Core indicators	Unit of measurement and reference period
Emissions of CH_4 due to tourist transportation	tonnes, yr
Emissions of CO_2 due to tourist transportation	tonnes, yr
Emissions of CO_2 due to energy used for tourist accommodation	tonnes, yr
Emissions of N_2O due to tourist transportation	tonnes, yr
Emissions of N_2O due to energy used for tourist accommodation	tonnes, yr
Emissions of NO_x due to tourist transportation	tonnes, yr
Emissions of NO_x due to energy used for tourist accommodation	tonnes, yr
Number of air-conditioned rooms in hotels (for emissions of chlorofluorocarbons (CFCs) and halons)	number, yr
Number of refrigerators in hotels (for emissions of chlorofluorocarbons (CFCs) and halons)	number, yr
Emissions of particles due to tourist transportation	tonnes, yr
Emissions of particles due to energy used for tourist accommodation	tonnes, yr

Additional indicators
Emissions of CO due to tourist transportation
Emissions of CO due to energy used for tourist accommodation
Emissions of NMVOC due to tourist transportation
Emissions of NMVOC due to energy used for tourist accommodation

Table D   Loss of biodiversity

Core indicators	Unit of measurement and reference period
Percentage of area occupied by tourist establishments in relation to total land area within certain types of land, e.g. mountain area, beaches	%, yr
Percentage of area changed for tourism purposes (time series of the previous one)	%, yr
No. of visitors per km² in protected areas	no./km², yr
Area occupied by roads, railways, ports, airports, with regard to the total area of a given country	% or km², yr

Additional indicators
Percentage of animals killed through hunting by tourists in relation to all animals killed through hunting
Percentage of fish catch of certain valuable species taken by tourists

Table E   Marine environment and coastal zones

Core indicators	Unit of measurement and reference period
Percentage of nutrients (N and P) discharged through sewage water attributable to tourism	%, yr
Percentage of coastal zones occupied by tourist establishments in relation to total land area in coastal zones	%, yr
Change in the percentage of coastal zones, etc. (time series of the previous one)	%, yr
Percentage of coastal zones covered by roads, railways, ports, airports in relation to total land area in coastal zones	%, yr
Total no. of tourists arriving into the country by sea in relation to total no. of sea passengers	%, yr
Total no. of yachts and other pleasure boats arriving to countries	no., yr
Amount of waste discharged from the increased no. of ships during the tourist season	tonnes, yr
Discharge of sewage water to coastal water by type of treatment	tonnes, yr

Table E   (continued)

Core indicators	Unit of measurement and reference period
Percentage of organic substances (BOD) discharged through sewage water attributable to tourism	%, yr
Number of boats, yachts rented by tourists	number, yr
Additional indicators	
Percentage of certain fish and other marine species caught by tourists (e.g. lobster, salmon)	
Number of tourist ports	

Table F   *Ozone layer depletion*

Core indicators	Unit of measurement and reference period
Number of air-conditioned rooms in hotels (for emissions of chlorofluorocarbons (CFCs) and halons)	number, yr
Number of refrigerators in hotels (for emissions of chlorofluorocarbons (CFCs) and halons)	number, yr
Emissions of NO_x due to tourist transportation	tonnes, yr
Emissions of NO_x due to energy used for tourist accommodation	tonnes, yr

Table G   *Resource depletion*

Core indicators	Unit of measurement and reference period
Annual use of mineral oil or natural gas as a fuel attributable to tourism	tonnes or km^3, yr
Water abstraction due to tourism in relation to total water abstraction for household purposes, divided by groundwater and surface water	%, yr
Additional indicators	
Percentage of area occupied by tourist establishments in relation to total land area within certain types of land, e.g. mountain area, beaches	
Percentage of area occupied by tourist establishments in relation to total residential area	

Table G (continued)

Core indicators	Unit of measurement and reference period
Percentage of area changed for tourism purposes (e.g. ski centres, golf courses, beach areas owned by hotels, pleasure ports, etc.)	
No. of visitors per year and per km^2 in protected areas	
Percentage of area occupied by roads, railways, ports, airports, with regard to the total area of a given country	
Percentage of fish catch of certain valuable species taken by tourists	
Percentage of animals killed through hunting by tourists in relation to all animals killed through hunting	
Annual use of energy attributable to tourism	

Table H   Dispersion of toxics

No core indicator was selected.

Additional indicators
Percentage of batteries in municipal wastes during tourist seasons in comparison to other periods of the year
Amount of petrol containing lead sold per month during tourist seasons in relation to the same amount outside tourist seasons
Emissions of lead from the transport sector due to tourism

Table I   Urban environmental problems

Core indicators	Unit of measurement and reference period
Discharge of sewage water within 'tourist urban areas' attributable to tourism, by type of treatment	tonnes, yr
Water supply to the tourism sector within 'tourist urban areas'	litres, yr
Percentage of waste attributable to tourism within 'tourist urban areas'	%, yr

Additional indicators
Emissions of air pollutants due to tourist transport in 'tourist urban areas'

Table I   (continued)

Core indicators	Unit of measurement and reference period
Road traffic density during the tourist season in relation to road traffic density during other periods of the year within 'tourist urban areas' (for noise)	
Air traffic density during the tourist season in relation to air traffic density during other periods of the year within 'tourist urban areas' (for noise)	
Railways traffic density during the tourist season in relation to railways traffic density during other periods of the year within 'tourist urban areas' (for noise)	
Boat traffic density during the tourist season (for example: Venice, Amsterdam) in relation to boat traffic density during other periods of the year within 'tourist urban areas' (for noise)	
Number of discotheques in open spaces within 'tourist urban areas'	
Number of water-based theme parks within 'tourist urban areas'	

Table J   *Waste*

Core indicators	Unit of measurement and reference period
Percentage of waste attributable to tourism	%, yr
Additional indicators	
Amount of sludge from sewage treatment plants attributable to tourism	
Emissions of CH_4 due to the percentage of waste attributable to tourism	
Emissions of NO_x due to the percentage of waste attributable to tourism	

Table K   *Water pollution and water resources*

Core indicators	Unit of measurement and reference period
Water abstraction due to tourism in relation to total water abstraction for household purposes, divided by groundwater and surface water	%, yr
Total no. of tourists arriving into the country by inland boat in relation to total no. of inland boat passengers	%, yr
Discharge of sewage water to lakes and rivers attributable to tourism, by type of treatment	tonnes, yr

Table K   (continued)

Core indicators	Unit of measurement and reference period
Additional indicators	

Total no. of yachts and other pleasure boats arriving at inland ports

Amount of waste discharged from the increased no. of ships during the tourist season

Percentage of organic substances (BOD) discharged through sewage water attributable to tourism

Percentage of nutrients (N and P) discharged through sewage water attributable to tourism

6. The effect of climate change and extreme weather events on tourism

Andrea Bigano, Alessandra Goria, Jacqueline Hamilton and Richard S.J. Tol

1. INTRODUCTION

Decisions about whether to take a holiday and where to spend that holiday are by no means secondary ones. Such decisions are relevant for our well-being, but, more importantly, are economically relevant because billions of people in the world make analogous decisions every year, many of them more than once per year.[1] This makes tourism an industry of primary importance for the world economy: it generates about 7.3 per cent of total worldwide exports.[2] For some countries, tourism is the first source of income and foreign currency, and many local economies heavily depend on it.

Among the factors taken into account by tourists when they decide upon their holidays, the destinations' climate characteristics rank very high (Hu and Ritchie, 1993; Lohmann and Kaim, 1999). Hence tourists are sensitive to climate and to climate change (Maddison, 2001; Lise and Tol, 2002; Hamilton, 2003). Climate change will affect the relative attractiveness of destinations and hence the motive for international tourists to leave their country of origin. Yet, until recently, the attention devoted by the tourism literature to climate change and by the climate change literature to tourism has been quite limited.

The degree of interest is now slowly increasing, and various aspects of the relationship between climate change and tourism are being covered. We review this literature in section 2. Five branches of literature have started to grow. First, there are a few studies (e.g. Maddison, 2001) that build statistical models of the behaviour of certain groups of tourists as a function of weather and climate. Second, there are a few studies (e.g. Abegg, 1996) that relate the fates of particular tourist destinations to climate change. Third, there are studies (e.g. Matzarakis, 2002) that try to define indicators of the attractiveness of certain weather conditions to tourists. Fourth, there are a few studies (e.g. Hamilton et al., 2003) that use simulation models of the tourism sector to study the impacts of climate change on tourist flows and on the tourist potential of destinations. Finally, a handful of studies (e.g. Berritella et al., 2004) analyse the economic implications of tourism in the face of climate change.

Section 3 illustrates an empirical study, which represents a first attempt to cover one of the gaps in the literature, namely the relationship between tourism demand and extreme weather events. More specifically, the study looks at the relationship between climate characteristics, weather extremes and domestic and international tourism demand for Italy. This study draws on the results on the Italian tourist sector of the WISE project, a multi-sector research project that investigates the impacts of extreme weather events (very warm summers, mild winters and storms) on the socioeconomic systems of some European countries. The results considered in section 3 cover the quantitative analysis of the impacts of climate extremes on the socioeconomic system in Italy and the qualitative analysis of individuals' perception of climate extremes based on results from individuals' surveys. In order to put these results in a broader perspective, they are briefly compared with the results for other European countries. Our conclusions and a brief discussion of future research directions are in section 4.

2.   REVIEW OF THE RELEVANT LITERATURE

2.1   Tourism Demand

Tourism demand forecasting continues to be a popular theme in the tourism literature. Reviews of this literature by Witt and Witt (1995) and Lim (1995) show that demand forecasting, in the majority of studies, is focused on economic factors. Morley (1992) criticizes typical demand studies because they do not consider utility in the decision-making process. Moreover, he suggests an alternative way to estimate demand based on the expected utility derived from the characteristics of the product. Lancaster (1966) originally developed the concept that the characteristics of a good are more important to the consumer than the actual good itself. How these characteristics are perceived will determine the expected utility from the consumption of the good. In the case of tourism, the product is the holiday at a certain destination and at a certain time, and this product will have certain characteristics. Most importantly, Morley (1992) argues that climate and landscape attributes of countries should be included in the characteristics set. Seddighi and Theocharous (2002) have applied this theory using a logit analysis. Political stability was the focus of their study rather than environmental characteristics such as climate or landscape. Rather than just examining the demand for a single country, demand systems provide the opportunity to examine the pattern of flows of tourists to different destination countries. Recent studies, however, do not include natural resource characteristics (see Lyssiotou, 2000; Divisekera, 2003; Lanza et al., 2003).

2.2 Tourism and Climate

There is a consensus that destination image plays an important role in destination choice, and this area has been the subject of much research. What role does climate play in destination image? Not all studies of destination image include climate as an image-defining attribute, as can be seen in the extensive review of destination image studies by Gallarza et al. (2002). Of the 25 destination image studies reviewed by them, climate was included as an attribute in 12 studies. Nevertheless, from their list of 20 attributes, climate is the seventh most frequently used attribute. Studies of destination image, which include climate/weather as an attribute, find that it is one of most important attributes. Measuring the importance of destination characteristics is also the focus of a study by Hu and Ritchie (1993), where they review several studies from the 1970s and find that 'natural beauty and climate' were of universal importance in defining destinations attractiveness. A good climate and the possibility to sunbathe were included in Shoemaker's (1994) list of destination attributes. There are, however, differences in the preferences shown by different types of tourists and for tourists from different places (Hu and Ritchie, 1993; Shoemaker, 1994; Kozak, 2002; Beerli and Martin, 2004).

Only one of the 142 destination image papers reviewed by Pike (2002) deals specifically with weather. This was a study by Lohmann and Kaim (1999), who assess, using a representative survey of German citizens, the importance of certain destination characteristics. Landscape was found to be the most important aspect even before price considerations. Weather and bio-climate were ranked third and eighth respectively for all destinations. Moreover, the authors found that although weather is an important factor, destinations are also chosen in spite of the likely bad weather. In a study by Gössling et al. (2004) of tourists surveyed in Zanzibar, tourists were asked to rate climate's importance for their decision to travel to Zanzibar. More than half rated climate important but a small share of the respondents (17 per cent) stated that climate was not important at all.

De Freitas (2001) classifies climate according to its aesthetic, physical and thermal aspects. The thermal aspect is assumed to be a composite of temperature, wind, humidity and radiation. There is growing evidence, however, that climate has significant neurological and psychological effects

(Parker, 2000), which may also have some influence on the choice of holiday destination. Many numerical indices have been developed to measure the thermal aspect of climate and to allow comparison of the suitability of different destinations for different tourism activities. De Freitas (1990) found that the relationship between HEBIDEX, a body–atmosphere energy budget index, and the subjective rating of the weather by beach users was highly correlated. Furthermore, he found that the optimal thermal conditions for beach users were not at the minimum heat stress level but at a point of mild heat stress. Matzarakis (2002) uses an index of thermal comfort to identify areas of Greece where there is high likelihood of heat stress.

2.3 Tourism and Climate Change

Qualitative impact studies of climate change have been carried out for the Mediterranean (Nicholls and Hoozemans, 1996; Perry, 2000), the Caribbean (Gable, 1997), wetland areas in Canada (Wall, 1998) and the German coast (Krupp, 1997; Lohmann, 2001). These studies vary in their focus and techniques. Krupp (1997) and Lohmann (2001) used surveys, scenarios and consulted both tourist and tourist industry discussion groups in their analysis. Viner and Agnew (1999) examine the current climate and market situation for the most popular tourist destinations of the British. The consequences for demand for these destinations under a changed climate are discussed.

While these studies provide information about vulnerabilities and the likely direction of change, they do not provide estimates of changes in demand. Four groups of quantitative climate change studies exist: predicting changes to the supply of tourism services; using tourism climate indices coupled with demand data; estimating the statistical relationship between demand and weather or climate; and finally studies that have their foundations in economic theory. First, predicting changes in the supply of tourism services has been applied to the winter sports industry. Abegg (1996) analysed the impact of changes in temperature on snow depth and coverage and the consequences of these changes on ski season length and the usability of ski facilities in the Swiss Alps. Similar studies were carried out for winter sports tourism in Scotland, Switzerland, alpine Austria and Canada (Harrison et al., 1999; Kromp-Kolb and Formayer, 2001; Elsasser and Bürki, 2002; Scott et al., 2001). These studies rely on the assessment of physical conditions that make tourism possible in these areas for a certain activity, that is the supply of tourism services for a specific market segment.

Second, the index approach has been used. Scott and McBoyle (2001) apply the tourism index approach to assess the impact of climate change on city tourism in several North American cities. Cities are ranked according to their climatic appropriateness for tourism and the relationship between tourist accommodation expenditures is examined. Then this ranking is recalculated using data from a scenario of climate change. The authors predict an increase in revenue from tourist accommodation for Canadian cities. In the above studies, changes in the relative market position of the destinations or the sites examined are neglected, as well as the change in climate relative to the origin climate of tourists. Amelung and Viner (2004) have produced detailed data on the climatic attractiveness of Europe. Using monthly climate data, they calculate the tourism climate index for Europe with a spatial resolution of $0.5° \times 0.5°$. They then recalculate the indices using climate data for a scenario of climate change. Their detailed maps show that higher latitudes will become more attractive for tourists.

Third, some studies use the statistical relationship between demand and weather. For example, Agnew and Palutikof (2001), within the same research framework of section 3,[3] model domestic tourism and international inbound and outbound tourism using a time series of tourism and weather data. In a similar study for the Netherlands, Tol (2000) finds that Dutch tourists show no significant response to the weather, but that more foreigners visit the country during hot summers.

Fourth, we have the studies that are grounded in economic theory. The impact of climate change in the USA on eight recreation activities is examined by Loomis and Crespi (1999). They estimate demand equations relating the number of activity days to temperature and precipitation. Under a scenario of a $+ 2.5°C$ change in temperature and a 7 per cent reduction in precipitation, they predict sharp reductions in the number of skiing days (-52 per cent) and increases in the number of days spent playing golf (14 per cent), at the beach (14 per cent) and at reservoirs (9 per cent). Mendelsohn and Markowski (1999) also estimate the impact of climate change on a range of recreation activities. The aggregate impact is estimated in terms of welfare and ranges from a reduction of 0.8 billion 1991$ to an increase of 26.5 billion 1991$. Using the contingent visitation approach, Richardson and Loomis (2004) find that temperature is a positive determinant of demand for visits. Moreover, depending on the climate change scenario, they estimate an increase in recreational visits from 9.9 per cent to 13.6 per cent in 2020. Snow-dependent activities are the focus of a study by Englin and Moeltner (2004). Using data on price, weekly conditions at ski resorts and the participants' income, they find that although demand increases as snow amount increases, trip demand is more responsive to changes in price.

A development of the travel cost model, the 'Pooled Travel Cost Model' (PTCM), has been applied to tourists from the UK, the Netherlands and Germany (Maddison, 2001; Lise and Tol, 2002; Hamilton, 2003).

Nevertheless, they have estimated the relationship between demand and certain climate variables. The possibility of taking a vacation in the origin country was included in the study by Hamilton. In addition to the travel cost approach, Lise and Tol (2002) study the holiday travel patterns of tourists from a range of OECD countries. They find that people from different climates have the same climate preferences for their holidays. Similar results were found by Bigano et al. (2004a), who find that people from countries with a warmer climate are more particular about their destination climate. This can be seen by a peaked temperature–demand relationship.

2.4 Global Models on Climate Change and Tourism

Hamilton et al. (2003) present a simulation model (the Hamburg Tourism Model) that traces the flows of international tourists from and to 207 countries. The model is calibrated for 1995, using data for total international departures and arrivals. Bilateral tourism flows are generated by the model. The simulations are driven by four variables: distance, population, income and temperature. Population growth leads to more tourists. Income growth causes changes in trip frequency, and since tourists avoid poor countries, developing countries become more attractive as tourist destinations.

Climate change has two effects. First, cool destinations become more attractive as they get warmer, and warm destinations become less attractive. Second, cool countries generate fewer international tourists as they get warmer, and warm countries generate more. Put together, these two effects generate an interesting pattern. Climate change leads tourists to seek out cooler regions in higher latitudes and at higher altitudes. However, climate change also reduces the total number of tourists, because international tourism is dominated by the Germans and the British, who prefer to take their holidays in their home countries. The reduction in international tourism because of climate change is, however, dwarfed by the growth due to population and economic growth. A modification of the model, presented in Hamilton et al. (2004), examines the effect of demand saturation, that is, a limit on the number of tourists who can be accommodated in a given location. This does not drastically change the results. In addition, the Hamburg Tourism Model is used as an input to a computable general equilibrium model, which is used to examine the economy-wide implications of climate change. The results show that the global impact of climate change on tourism is negligible (Berritella et al., 2004). There is substantial redistribution, however. Countries in Western Europe, the subtropics and the tropics are negatively affected. North America, Eastern Europe and the former Soviet Union, and Australasia are positively affected. The negative impacts may amount to −0.3 per cent of GDP by 2050, the positive impacts to +0.5 per cent of GDP. These numbers are large compared to other monetized impacts of climate change (e.g. Smith et al., 2001).

As can be seen from this review, there has been an extensive variety of research carried out on tourism and climate and on tourism and climate change. The majority of these studies look at the role that climate plays in destination choice or in determining demand. Climate data, however, are based on 30-year averages, and so do not account for extreme conditions, which may affect short-term decision making. Hence these studies neglect the influence that such extreme weather conditions have on demand, whether this is through the choice of destination, change to the length of the trip, or changing the departure time of the holiday. The following sections of this chapter describe one first attempt to investigate the effects of weather extremes on tourism demand.

3. THE IMPACTS OF CLIMATE EXTREMES ON THE TOURISM SECTOR ACROSS EUROPE: THE WISE PROJECT

A recent, European Commission sponsored study addresses the impacts of extreme weather events on tourism across Europe, using time series of tourism and weather data in selected European countries. The tourism impact study is part of a wider project (the WISE project: Weather Impacts on Natural, Social and Economic Systems), conducted in 1997–99 in four European countries, namely Italy, the UK, Germany and the Netherlands. The project addresses the evaluation of the overall impact of extreme weather events on the natural, social and economic systems in Europe, and provides, where possible, a monetary evaluation of these impacts. Beside tourism, the other key sectors studied in the project include agriculture, energy consumption, forest fires and health.

The project was carried out in Italy by the Fondazione Eni Enrico Mattei,[4] following a methodology jointly agreed upon by all partners.

3.1 The WISE Methodology

All country studies consist of a qualitative analysis and a quantitative analysis. The qualitative analysis investigates, by means of mail and telephone surveys, the individuals' perception of climate change impacts on their daily life, including tourism behaviour. The quantitative analysis estimates weather extremes' impacts on tourism and other key economic sectors, through econometric models and national statistics data which cover all regions for the last three decades. In the first part of this section, the methodology and the main results of the quantitative analysis will be presented in depth. The second part illustrates the results of the quantitative analysis carried out in Italy. Finally, we present a brief comparison of qualitative and quantitative results across partner countries.

More specifically, indicators of productivity and key variables in the social and economic sectors of interest are expressed as a linear function of weather parameters, and a linear estimation procedure is applied to estimate the weather impacts on the socioeconomic system over the years and across regions.

Therefore the methodology used is not 'sector-specific', and the analysis of the impacts of climate change and extreme weather events on tourism is based on the general modelling framework applied to the various sectors of interest.

The general model used for annual and national observations is:

$$X_t = \alpha_0 + \alpha_1 X_{t-1} + \alpha_2 T + \alpha_3 W_t + \alpha_4 W_{t-1} + u_t,$$

where t expresses the time series dimension of the model, X denotes the index of interest (i.e. number of bed-nights/tourist arrivals in the tourism impact Italian study). X depends on its lagged value to indicate that most influences other than weather (income, technology, institutions) are much the same now and in the past.

T denotes time: for annual observations T indicates the year of observation.[5] Time is taken up as an explanatory variable to capture all unexplained trends.

W denotes the weather variable that it is assumed to influence X. W is a vector including only those climate variables that are supposed to have an influence on X: the climate variables selected vary depending on the core sector under analysis.

The weather variable consists of the average value over the time dimension t of the climate variable under consideration; when yearly observations on X are available, the weather variable W generally consists of the yearly average of the climate variable. However, when specific seasons during the year are thought to have a stronger influence on the dependent variable, the average value of the climate variable over that season in each year is used in the regressions.

The lagged value of W is taken up to address a dynamic dimension in the model, and because past weather may influence current behaviour, particularly in the tourism sector. u denotes the error term. The intercept is included, assuming that at least one of the variables is not expressed in deviations from its mean. Under the assumption that u is i.i.d.[6] and has normal distribution, the model is estimated by ordinary least squares (OLS) estimators, based on the following procedure: after a first estimation insignificant explanatory variables are removed and the model is re-estimated, checking whether the residuals are stationary.

When monthly observations on X are available, lagged values of X and W for both the month before and the corresponding month in the year before are used. If in addition regional observations are available, the general model is applied to a panel data structure, covering the time series and cross-section regional data.

The availability of regional and monthly data on tourism demand makes it possible to carry out a panel estimation of the effects of climate change and extreme weather events in Italy.

The panel model estimated across regions (indexed by i) and over a monthly time series (indexed by t) is:

$$X_{it} = \alpha_0 + \alpha_1 X_{it-1} + \alpha_2 X_{it-12} + \alpha_3 T + \alpha_4 W_{it} + \alpha_5 W_{it-1} + \alpha_6 W_{it-12} + u_{it}$$

In the panel estimation of the general model, dummy variables are used for the years showing patterns of extreme weather to capture the effect of extreme seasons on the dependent variable, as well as for regions or macro-regions in order to identify specific regional effects on the dependent variables.

Following the estimation, a direct cost evaluation method is used to assess the impact of climate change on some of the core sectors identified. The direct cost method assumes that the welfare change induced by the weather extremes can be approximated by the quantity change in the relevant variable times its price. The direct cost thus imputed would be a fair approximation of the change in consumer surplus if the price did not change much. The use of dummy variables for extreme seasons in the time series and panel estimations allows an evaluation in monetary terms of the relative impacts of those extreme seasons on the various sectors, exploiting estimates of quantity changes in those seasons and the corresponding seasonal prices, if available.

3.2 The Italian WISE Case Study on Tourism

3.2.1 Data on climate

Climate data in Italy are available[7] for most variables on a monthly basis, at the regional level, from 1966 until 1995.[8] Italy seems to show weather patterns that differ from those identified by Northern and Central European countries. The UK, the Netherlands and Germany identify the summers of 1995 and 1992 as the most extreme. In the 1990s Italy indeed experienced extremely high summer temperatures and anomalies in 1994. During the

1980s, a strong temperature anomaly was recorded in the summer of 1982. The year 1994 was recorded as one of the driest summers, together with the summer of 1985. In addition, the summer of 1985 had a very high sunshine rate, comparable only to the late 1960s (in particular 1967).

With regard to extreme winter seasons, the 1989 winter is definitely the mildest winter recorded, showing strong anomalies in temperature, in exposure to sunshine and lack of precipitation. The winter of 1989 was followed by relatively mild winters, reaching very high peaks in temperature again in the year 1994.

In contrast with the evidence collected by the other European partner countries, where the 1990 winter was recorded as mild and wet, the 1990 winter season in Italy was mild and extremely dry all over the country. Anomalies in yearly precipitation versus yearly temperature, as well as anomalies of winter precipitation versus winter sunshine rates, show the highest negative correlation. Overall, the summers of 1994 and 1985, and the 1989 winter can be identified as the most extreme seasons in Italy. With regard to the regional variability of weather data, it can be generally observed that there is a low variance of weather variables across regions in the extreme seasons with respect to the other seasons: this shows a relative homogeneity of weather extremes within the country.

3.2.2 Data on tourism

The data on tourism demand include data on the number of bed-nights and on the number of arrivals for both domestic and foreign tourism. Monthly data are available at the national level for a period of two decades, starting from 1976 for domestic tourism and from 1967 for foreign tourism, and at the regional level starting from 1983.[9]

Since 1990, due to a new legislation, the data refer only to accommodation provided by registered firms (thus excluding accommodation provided by private individuals) and consequently both series show a structural break. Separate analyses are carried out for the two time periods. Both variables generally show an increasing trend over the three decades, and a seasonal peak during the summer season for both domestic and foreign tourism.

Focusing on the second period under analysis, a high positive correlation exists between the monthly number of bed-nights and the monthly temperature (0.7072), as well as the monthly temperature in the year before (0.6310), all measured at the national level. The national number of bed-nights during the summer is highly correlated with the summer national temperature (0.6838) and even more correlated with the summer national temperature in the year before (0.9486). The regional number of bed-nights over winter is highly and negatively correlated with the monthly regional temperature in the previous year.

Looking at the correlation coefficients between bed-nights and temperatures, in 1986–95, temperature is positively correlated with tourism during the month of May, and the summer months of June, July and August. A very high positive correlation exists between temperature and tourism in March: this evidence suggests a very sensitive demand for tourism in the spring intermediate season. A relatively strong negative correlation indeed exists between temperatures and monthly tourism in December, perhaps due the negative effect of high temperatures on the skiing season in the Alps and in the Apennines. Data for the first period under analysis, between 1976 and 1989, generally show much higher correlation coefficients, certainly due to the fact that the data include accommodation provided by private individuals, which meets a high share of tourism demand.

3.2.3 Main results
The national monthly data on bed-nights of domestic tourism is non-stationary. The analysis is based on the regional data on domestic tourism, which are available on a monthly basis starting from 1983; due to a structural break in the data, separate analyses are carried out for the period 1983–89 and for the period 1990–95.

During mild winters we may expect a decrease in domestic tourism to mountain regions due to the shortening of the skiing seasons and a general increase of domestic tourism across the country due to warmer weather. The expected sign of the net outcome across the whole country could be slightly positive or uncertain. During extremely hot summer months we would expect a decrease in domestic tourism since domestic tourists may prefer to take their summer holidays abroad, particularly in northern countries, where it is cooler than in Italy. We may also expect an increase in domestic tourism during summer months due to more weekend trips because of hotter weather. The relative strength of the latter effect is tested.

In both periods, following the methodology previously described, OLS fixed effects panel estimation regressions are performed, first over all months in the year and then over selected summer and winter months. Dummy variables are included for the years that show extreme weather patterns and for each region.

The final results of the OLS fixed effects panel estimation for all the months of the year for both periods are presented in Table 6.1. The most interesting results can be summarized as follows. In both periods higher monthly regional temperature is estimated to have a positive effect on domestic tourism flows. In the first period under analysis, even last year's temperature in the corresponding month appears to trigger monthly domestic tourism. In the second period under analysis, last year's rainfall in the corresponding month appears to work as a deterrent to monthly

Table 6.1   OLS fixed effects panel estimation of the monthly regional number of bed-nights of domestic tourism across Italy throughout the year

Independent variables	Coefficient estimates for the period 1983–89	t-statistics	Coefficient estimates for the period 1990–95	t-statistics
Constant	−203610.7***	−2.803	−118313**	−1.999
One-month-lagged no. of regional bed-nights	0.2545983***	12.248	0.3748518***	15.590
12-months-lagged no. of regional bed-nights	0.5831289***	27.063	0.4085923***	16.741
Time trend				
Monthly regional temperature	84619.3***	4.454	44203.16***	8.207
One-month-lagged regional temperature	−25735.59***	−3.285	−23126.96***	−4.224
12-months-lagged regional temperature	−32630.28*	−1.736		
Monthly regional precipitation			1150.442**	2.174
One-month-lagged regional precipitation			1086.217***	2.662
12-months-lagged regional precipitation			−2865.918***	−5.541
No. of observations	1364		1131	
F-test	402.06		223.68	
R-squared				
Within	0.6002		0.5860	
Between	0.4652		0.6085	
Overall	0.5866		0.5922	

Notes: * significant at 95%; **significant at 97.5%; ***significant at 99%.

domestic tourism flows, as expected. However, in the same period, monthly precipitation unexpectedly has a positive influence on domestic tourism. In both periods model estimates are robust.

The OLS panel estimation including the dummy variables for each region shows that in the period 1983–89 the regions where Italian tourists spend the highest number of bed-nights are Emilia-Romagna, Trentino, Liguria and Lazio.

The same procedure is applied to the estimation of climate predictors of domestic tourism during the summer months over the two periods under analysis (Table 6.2).

In both periods the summer regional temperature has a high positive effect on the number of bed-nights, and the 12-months-lagged value of temperature has an even stronger positive effect. In line with the hypotheses initially formulated, these results suggest the important role that temperatures and expectations play on tourism demand: not only do the number of bed-nights tend to increase during hot summers, but also a hot summer in the previous year influences the number of bed-nights that domestic tourists decide to take.

When we re-estimate the panel model including extreme season dummies,[10] the dummy for the 1994 extreme season has a significant and negative effect on the number of bed-nights of domestic tourists during the summer months.

Tables 6.3–6.7 report results from the estimation of the climate predictors of domestic tourism bed-nights across Italy in selected months, representative of the main seasons.

It is interesting to note that tourism in February is strongly and negatively influenced by high temperatures in January: as it was initially formulated, this may be due to the negative influence of high temperatures on the skiing season, at least in the Alps and Apennines, or to anticipated winter trips or vacations due to good weather in the month of January.

Higher temperatures in the intermediate seasons of spring and autumn turn out to trigger domestic tourism flows; the results suggest a relatively higher elasticity of domestic tourism to climate factors in the intermediate seasons.

However, precipitation in July works as a deterrent to domestic tourism flows in that month, and higher temperatures in July reduce domestic tourism considerably in the month of August. Following our initial considerations, this result may be partly due to a 'substitution effect' between domestic and foreign destinations in tourism demand due to climate variability.

Overall, domestic tourism demand seems to be quite sensitive to climate factors, and extreme seasons seriously affect tourism demand.

Table 6.2 OLS fixed effects panel estimation of the monthly regional number of bed-nights of domestic tourism across Italy during the summer months June, July and August

Independent variables	Coefficient estimates for the period 1983–89	t-statistics	Coefficient estimates for the period 1990–95	t-statistics
Constant	−2853644***	−6.511	−1638962***	−6.746
One-month-lagged no. of regional bed-nights	1.011495***	27.607	1.123286***	39.348
12-months-lagged no. of regional bed-nights	0.0881233***	2.791		
Time trend				
Monthly regional temperature	80178.66***	3.506	41022.48***	2.864
One-month-lagged regional temperature				
12-months-lagged regional temperature	93467.5***	4.091	49305.5***	3.665
Monthly regional precipitation			1595.653**	2.269
One-month-lagged regional precipitation			1698.946***	2.953
12-months-lagged regional precipitation				
No. of observations	342			240
F-test	507.90			510.92
R-squared				
Within	0.8647			0.9210
Between	0.9234			0.9663
Overall	0.8408			0.9201

Notes: * significant at 95%; **significant at 97.5%; ***significant at 99%.

Table 6.3   OLS fixed effects panel estimation of number of bed-nights of domestic tourism across Italy in February, 1983–89

Independent variables	Coefficient estimates	t-statistics
Constant	390832.9***	6.978
Regional bed-nights in January	0.9285***	7.810
Regional bed-nights in February of the year before	−0.6450***	−6.556
Regional temperature in January	−12887.39***	−2.959
Dummy for the winter 1988	57988.49***	2.989
No. of observations	108	
F-test (4, 86)	20.79	
R-squared		
Within	0.4916	
Between	0.9126	
Overall	0.8722	

Notes: * significant at 95%; **significant at 97.5%; ***significant at 99%.

Table 6.4   OLS fixed effects panel estimation of number of bed-nights of domestic tourism across Italy in May, 1986–95

Independent variables	Coefficient estimates	t-statistics
Constant	372574.3***	4.299
Regional bed-nights in April	0.3264***	2.672
Regional temperature in May	6135.286**	2.246
Regional temperature in May of the year before	−9748.003***	−3.526
No. of observations	98	
F-test (3, 78)	8.85	
R-squared		
Within	0.2539	
Between	0.9454	
Overall	0.9224	

Notes: * significant at 95%; **significant at 97.5%; ***significant at 99%.

To summarize some of the most interesting results, based on estimates over the last ten years, a 1 °C temperature increase in July in the coastal regions is estimated to increase the number of bed-nights by 24 783 in those regions. In the month of August a 1 °C temperature increase would imply

Table 6.5   OLS fixed effects panel estimation of number of bed-nights of domestic tourism across Italy in July, 1983–89

Independent variables	Coefficient estimates	t-statistics
Constant	7.34e+07***	2.680
Regional bed-nights in June	2.1685 ***	9.205
Regional bed-nights in July of the year before	0.5816***	7.429
Time trend	−37375.1***	−2.705
Regional precipitation in July	−2014.282***	−3.029
No. of observations	120	
F-test (4, 96)	45.44	
R-squared		
Within	0.6544	
Between	0.8876	
Overall	0.8805	

Notes: * significant at 95%; **significant at 97.5%; ***significant at 99%.

Table 6.6   OLS fixed effects panel estimation of number of bed-nights of domestic tourism across Italy in August, 1983–89

Independent variables	Coefficient estimates for the period 1983–89	t-statistics
Constant	1044081**	2.074
Regional bed-nights in July	1.1424***	3.477
Regional bed-nights in August of the year before	0.2119**	−2.037
Regional temperature in July	−39493.91**	−2.037
No. of observations	107	
F-test (3, 86)	148.18	
R-squared		
Within	0.8379	
Between	0.9919	
Overall	0.9885	

Notes: * significant at 95%; **significant at 97.5%; ***significant at 99%.

an increase of 62 294 bed-nights. These effects are likely to increase welfare in those regions.

Focusing on winter temperatures and Alpine regions, over the same period the model instead estimates that a 1 °C increase in winter temperature

Table 6.7   OLS fixed effects panel estimation of number of bed-nights of domestic tourism across Italy in October, 1986–95

Independent variables	Coefficient estimates	*t*-statistics
Constant	−271016.3**	−2.150
Regional bed-nights in September	0.1731***	2.468
Regional bed-nights in October of the year before	0.2787***	2.741
Regional temperature in October	11540.6***	2.787
Regional temperature in October of the year before	14488.39***	4.108
No. of observations	78	
F-test (3, 78)	10.13	
R-squared		
Within	0.4112	
Between	0.7562	
Overall	0.7496	

Notes: * significant at 95%; **significant at 97.5%; *** significant at 99%.

would result in a decrease in local domestic tourism equal to 30 368 bed-nights, with a reduction in welfare.

On average across all regions, the model estimates that anomalous hot weather in July would diminish domestic tourists' flows in the following month by 39 494 bed-nights. However, in the intermediate seasons an increase in temperature is estimated to have a positive effect on domestic tourism: a 1 °C increase in temperature in May and October may explain an increase in domestic tourism, for every region, by 6135 and 11 540 bed-nights respectively. Therefore the net welfare effect of climate extremes on tourism across regions and during the year is unclear.

The computed elasticity of domestic tourism bed-nights to climate, including accommodation provided by private individuals, suggests a 0.071 percentage increase in tourism per marginal percentage increase in monthly temperature, and a 0.49 percentage increase per marginal percentage increase in summer monthly temperature, which reaches a 0.79 per marginal percentage increase in summer monthly temperature when private accommodation is not included.

3.3   Comparison of WISE Results across Europe

The quantitative results from the Italian study correspond to the results from the other European partner countries.[11]

In general, temperature is the strongest indicator of domestic tourism. The relationship is generally positive in the same month all across Europe, except in a winter sports region. A summer warming of 1 °C is estimated to increase domestic holidays by 0.8–4.7 per cent with respect to the period's average.

The climate impact also depends on destination type: for example, coastal resorts respond more favourably to summer temperature increases than inland resorts.

In the UK, where data on international tourism are available, the evidence suggests that outbound tourism is more sensitive to climate than inbound tourism. Temperature is generally regarded as having the greatest influence on international tourism. For example, a 1 °C increase in temperature in the Netherlands increases outbound tourism in the following year by 3.1 per cent. Globally the optimal summer temperature at the destination country is estimated to be 21 °C.[12] There is little deviation from country to country. Moreover, there is little evidence that in extremely hot seasons Dutch tourists prefer domestic to foreign beach holidays.

As to the qualitative results, a very brief overview of the surveys of individuals' perception across the European partner countries shows that, during an unusually hot summer, day trips are more climate-responsive than short breaks, and short breaks are more climate-responsive than main holidays. In an unusually hot summer, most people tend not to change plans for their main vacation: those that do change either stay at home or in their own country. However, several regional differences in the adaptive response to climate extremes can be noted.

Results of the management perception surveys, conducted among operators in the tourist supply system, indeed show the relevance of weather/climate for short holiday trips, domestic trips and spontaneous trips. Weather conditions (actual and anticipated) are found to be very important for determining the attractiveness of a holiday destination: tourists have great freedom of destination choice, and climate is a significant consideration in tourist destination choice decision making. Nevertheless, it is not always easy to tease out the impact of climate from the many other factors influencing holiday choice. There are extremely complex processes at work. Global models pick out the broad relationships with temperature. But the results suggest that the intricacies of the climate relationships differ even within countries. Micro-analyses using individual tourist behaviour provide the most detail, but lack the temporal perspective. Ideally, to understand the influence of climate more clearly we would have data differentiating between pre-booked and spontaneous trips, between destination type (coastal, urban, winter sport regions), information on the difference between the climate at the target destination and the climate of the source region, and knowledge of when trips were planned or booked.[13]

4. CONCLUSIONS

The relationship between climate change and tourism is multifaceted and complex. The existing studies have but started to unveil these complexities, by means of often very heterogeneous approaches and scarcely comparable studies. A comprehensive, coherent quantitative message cannot yet be drawn from the existing studies.

The broad qualitative message emerging from the literature is clear, however: climate change will affect tourism, and the consequences for the economy might be wide and pervasive, given the importance of the industry.

The empirical example we have presented illustrates how complex the relationship between climate and tourism demand can be even in a simple framework where weather and its extremes are the only explanatory factors taken into account: it is not just temperature that counts, but also the expectations about future temperature levels (with different impacts according to the month and the region under scrutiny); not just the presence of weather extremes, but also the expectations about their future occurrence.

There is much more that needs to be explored. As far as extreme weather events are concerned, the range of events to be taken into consideration should be expanded to include the impacts of increased occurrence of storms, heat waves and drought, with particular attention to the likely increase in their geographical and temporal variability.

Other gaps in the literature can be pinpointed by looking at our survey of the main strands of the literature on tourism and climate change. Our survey has disregarded the issue of adaptive behaviour. In a sense, all destination choice studies are about adaptation: changing holiday destination is a form of adaptation on the part of the tourist. However, there is shortage of detailed information on adaptive behaviour, which could be obtained, for instance, by means of survey analysis. We need better knowledge about which aspects of climate tourists are sensitive to: pleasant weather is attractive, but what about its predictability? Can lack of weather predictability be compensated by the availability of alternative activities? The relative importance of spatial and temporal substitution is unknown. Tourists may react to adverse weather conditions not only by changing their planned destination, but also by revising their planning, by means of last-minute changes, or by changing their booking patterns, taking shorter holidays more frequently or at different times of the year. They might try to reduce the risk associated with the reduced predictability of climate by relying more on travel insurance that can make cancellation cheaper.

On the supply side, firms in the tourism sector can be very adaptive too. They may limit the damages to their business by, for instance, installing air-conditioning appliances, by building swimming pools or other architectural improvements, by building artificial snow plants in mountain resorts, and, to a certain extent, by insuring themselves against the occurrence of extreme events. Gradual climate change does not pose a particular threat to such a versatile sector. The limits of adaptability of course may be reached if climate change threatens the very existence of the only reason that may attract tourists in a given area: if an atoll becomes submerged, there is no more scope for adaptation there.

We also have disregarded studies about the role of mitigation policies (e.g. Piga, 2003). There is a growing interest in the impact of carbon reduction policies, which can have a direct impact on tourism (e.g. an aviation carbon tax) and in general in the impact of carbon taxes on the operation of the tourism industry. Mitigation measures may have interactions with the adaptive behaviour of firms in the tourist sector: air conditioning runs on electricity, which may be targeted by a carbon tax.

Also, the interactions among various climate impacts on tourist areas need to be assessed. Tourists might be deterred not only by unbearable weather conditions, but also because the nice sandy beaches that used to be the pride of a resort are no longer there due to sea-level rise and coastal erosion, or because the unique ecosystem of a destination has been compromised, or because, by travelling in that area, catching some tropical disease has become more likely. On the other hand, the position of some resorts will be strengthened as their competitors disappear (e.g. atolls and skiing on natural snow).

The research on climate change and tourism is still far from having covered all the angles of the relationship between climate change and tourism. Results to date indicate that further research would be fruitful and worthwhile.

NOTES

1. The top ten origins for total tourist numbers generate almost 3 billion tourists per year. See Bigano et al. (2004b).
2. World Tourism Organization (http://www.world-tourism.org/facts/tmt.html).
3. The analysis presented in section 3 differs from the one in Agnew and Palutikof (2001) in that it restricts its geographical focus to Italy and pays more attention to extreme weather events.
4. See Galeotti et al. (2004).
5. T is the time trend variable, while t is the time index of each observation.
6. Random variables are independent and identically distributed (i.i.d.) if their probability distributions are all mutually independent and if each variable has the same probability distribution as any of the others.
7. The WISE project was carried out in 1997–99. The time series for the relevant variables covers the last half of the 1990s.

8. Source: ISTAT (*Statistiche del turismo, Annuario statistico di commercio interno e del turismo, Bollettino mensile*, various issues).
9. Source: ISTAT (*Statistiche Meteorologiche*, 1964–91).
10. These results are not reported in Table 6.2.
11. See Agnew and Palutikof (2001) for a more detailed comparison of international results.
12. Both the study on the UK and the study on the Netherlands include quadratic temperature terms. The global optimal temperature has been derived within the study on the Netherlands. See Agnew and Palutikof (2001).
13. See Agnew and Palutikof (1999, 2001).

REFERENCES

Abegg, B. (1996), *Klimaänderung und Tourismus – Klimafolgenforschung am Beispiel des Wintertourismus in den Schweizer Alpen*, Zurich, Switzerland: vdf Hochschuleverlag an der ETH.

Agnew, M.D. and J.P. Palutikof (1999), Background document to the WISE Workshop on 'Economic and Social Impacts of Climate Extremes. Risks and Benefits', 14–16 October, Amsterdam.

Agnew, M.D. and J.P. Palutikof (2001), 'Climate impacts on the demand for tourism', in A. Matzarakis and C. de Freitas (eds), *International Society of Biometeorology Proceedings of the First International Workshop on Climate, Tourism and Recreation*, available at http://www.mif.uni-freiburg.de/isb/ws/report.htm

Amelung, B. and D. Viner (2004), 'The vulnerability to climate change of the Mediterranean as a tourist destination', in B. Amelung, K. Blazejczyk, A. Matzarakis and D.Viner (eds), *Climate Change and Tourism: Assessment and Coping Strategies,* Dordrecht: Kluwer Academic Publishers.

Beerli, A. and J.D. Martin (2004), 'Tourists' characteristics and the perceived image of tourist destinations: a quantitative analysis – a case study of Lanzarote, Spain', *Tourism Management*, 25(5), 623–36.

Berritella, M., A. Bigano, R. Roson and R.S.J. Tol (2004), 'A general equilibrium analysis of climate change impacts on tourism', Research Unit Sustainability and Global Change Working Paper FNU-49, Hamburg University and Centre for Marine and Atmospheric Science, Hamburg, Germany.

Bigano, A., J.M. Hamilton and R.S.J. Tol (2004a), 'The impact of climate on holiday destination choice', FNU-55, Hamburg University and Centre for Marine and Atmospheric Science, Hamburg.

Bigano, A., J.M. Hamilton, M. Lau, R.S.J. Tol and Y. Zhou (2004b), 'A global database of domestic and international tourist numbers at national and subnational level', FNU-54, Hamburg University and Centre for Marine and Atmospheric Science, Hamburg.

de Freitas, C.R. (1990), 'Recreation climate assessment', *International Journal of Climatology*, 10, 89–103.

de Freitas, C.R. (2001), 'Theory, concepts and methods in tourism climate research', in A. Matzarakis and C. de Freitas (eds), *International Society of Biometeorology Proceedings of the First International Workshop on Climate, Tourism and Recreation*, available at http://www.mif.uni-freiburg.de/isb/ws/ report.htm

Divisekera, S. (2003), 'A model of demand for international tourism', *Annals of Tourism Research*, 30(1), 31–49.

Elsasser, H. and R. Bürki (2002), 'Climate change as a threat to tourism in the Alps', *Climate Research*, **20**, 253–57.

Englin, J. and K. Moeltner (2004), 'The value of snowfall to skiers and boarders', *Environmental and Resource Economics*, **29**(1), 123–36.

EUROSTAT (1997), Demographic statistics.

Gable, F.J. (1997), 'Climate change impacts on Caribbean coastal areas and tourism', *Journal of Coastal Research*, **27**, 49–70.

Galeotti, M., A. Goria, P. Mombrini and E. Spantidaki (2004), 'Weather impacts on natural, social and economic systems (WISE) – part I: sectoral analysis of climate impacts in Italy', Fondazione Eni Enrico Mattei Note di Lavoro no. 31.04.

Gallarza, M.G., I.G. Saura and H.C. Garcia (2002), 'Destination image: towards a conceptual framework', *Annals of Tourism Research*, **29**(1), 56–78.

Gössling, S., M. Bredberg, A. Randow, P. Svensson and E. Swedlin (2004), 'Tourist perceptions of climate change: a study of international tourists in Zanzibar', *Climatic Change*, submitted.

Hamilton, J.M. (2003), 'Climate and the destination choice of German tourists', Research Unit Sustainability and Global Change Working Paper FNU-15 (revised), Centre for Marine and Climate Research, Hamburg University, Germany.

Hamilton, J.M., D.J. Maddison and R.S.J. Tol (2003), 'Climate change and international tourism: a simulation study', Research Unit Sustainability and Global Change Working Paper FNU-31, Centre for Marine and Climate Research, Hamburg University, Germany.

Hamilton, J.M., D.J. Maddison and R.S.J. Tol (2004), 'The effects of climate change on international tourism', Research Unit Sustainability and Global Change Working Paper FNU-36, Centre for Marine and Climate Research, Hamburg University, Germany.

Harrison, S.J., S.J. Winterbottom and C. Shephard (1999), 'The potential effects of climate change on the Scottish tourist industry', *Tourism Management*, **20**, 203–11.

Hu, Y. and J.R.B. Ritchie (1993), 'Measuring destination attractiveness: a contextual approach', *Journal of Travel Research*, **32**(2), 25–34.

ISTAT, National Institute of Statistics, *Annuario statistico di commercio interno e del turismo* [Annual Statistics of Internal Commerce and Tourism], 1961–82.

ISTAT, National Institute of Statistics, *Bollettino mensile* [Monthly Bulletin], 1992–96.

ISTAT, National Institute of Statistics, *Statistiche del turismo* [Statistics on Tourism], 1983–95.

ISTAT, National Institute of Statistics, *Statistiche meteorologiche* [Meteorological Statistics], 1964–91.

ISTAT, National Institute of Statistics, *Statistiche del turismo* [Tourism Statistics], 1976–96.

Kozak, M. (2002), 'Comparative analysis of tourist motivations by nationality and destinations', *Tourism Management*, **23**(3), 221–32.

Kromp-Kolb, H. and H. Formayer (2001), 'Klimaänderung und mögliche Auswirkungen auf den Wintertourismus in Salzburg', Universität für Bodenkultur, Vienna, Austria.

Krupp, C. (1997), *Klimaänderungen und die Folgen: eine exemplarische Fallstudie über die Möglichkeiten und Grenzen einer interdisziplinären Klimafolgenforschung*, Berlin, Germany: edition Sigma.

Lancaster, K.J. (1966), 'A new approach to consumer theory', *Journal of Political Economy*, **74**, 132–57.

Lanza, A., P. Temple and G. Urga (2003), 'The implications of tourism specialization in the long term: an econometric analysis for 13 OECD economies', *Tourism Management*, **24**(3), 315–21.

Lim, C. (1995), 'Review of international tourism demand models', *Annals of Tourism Research*, **24**(4), 835–49.

Lise, W. and R.S.J. Tol (2002), 'Impact of climate on tourism demand', *Climatic Change*, **55**(4), 429–49.

Lohmann, M. (2001), 'Coastal resorts and climate change', in A. Lockwood and S. Medlik (eds), *Tourism and Hospitality in the 21st Century*, Oxford: Butterworth-Heinemann, pp. 284–95.

Lohmann, M. and E. Kaim (1999), 'Weather and holiday destination preferences, image attitude and experience', *The Tourist Review*, **2**, 54–64.

Loomis, J.B. and J. Crespi (1999), 'Estimated effects of climate change on selected outdoor recreation activities in the United States', in R. Mendelsohn and J.E. Neumann (eds), *The Impact of Climate Change on the United States Economy*, Cambridge: Cambridge University Press, pp. 289–314.

Lyssiotou, P. (2000), 'Dynamic analysis of British demand for tourism abroad', *Empirical Economics*, **15**, 421–36.

Maddison, D. (2001), 'In search of warmer climates? The impact of climate change on flows of British tourists', in D. Maddison (ed.), *The Amenity Value of the Global Climate*, London: Earthscan, pp. 53–76.

Matzarakis, A. (2002), 'Examples of climate and tourism research for tourism demands', in *Proceedings of the 15th Conference on Biometeorology and Aerobiology joint with the International Congress on Biometeorology*, 27 October to 1 November, Kansas City, Missouri, pp. 391–2, available at http://www.mif.uni-freiburg.de/matzarakis/publication.htm

Mendelsohn, R. and M. Markowski (1999), 'The impact of climate change on outdoor recreation', in R. Mendelsohn and J.E.Neumann (eds), *The Impact of Climate Change on the United States Economy*, Cambridge: Cambridge University Press, pp. 267–88.

Morley, C.L. (1992), 'A microeconomic theory of international tourism demand', *Annals of Tourism Research*, **19**, 250–67.

Nicholls, R.J. and F.M.J. Hoozemans (1996), 'The Mediterranean: vulnerability to coastal implications of climate change', *Ocean and Coastal Management*, **31**, 105–32.

Parker, P. (2000), *Physioeconomics: The Basis for Long-Run Economic Growth*, Cambridge, MA: The MIT Press.

Perry, A. (2000), 'Impacts of climate change on tourism in the Mediterranean: adaptive responses', *Nota di Lavoro* 35.2000, Fondazione Eni Enrico Mattei, Milan, Italy.

Piga, C.A.G. (2003), 'Pigouvian taxation in tourism', *Environmental and Resource Economics*, **26**, 343–59.

Pike, S. (2002), 'Destination image analysis – a review of 142 papers from 1973 to 2000', *Tourism Management*, **23**, 541–9.

Richardson, R.B. and J.B. Loomis (2004), 'Adaptive recreation planning and climate change: a contingent visitation approach', *Ecological Economics*, **50**(1–2), 83–99.

Scott, D. and G. McBoyle (2001), 'Using a "Tourism Climate Index" to examine the implications of climate change for climate as a tourism resource', in

A. Matzarakis and C. de Freitas (eds), *International Society of Biometeorology Proceedings of the First International Workshop on Climate, Tourism and Recreation*, available at http://www.mif.uni-freiburg.de/isb/ws/report.htm

Scott, D., G. McBoyle, B. Mills and G. Wall (2001), 'Assessing the vulnerability of the alpine skiing industry in Lakelands Tourism Region of Ontario, Canada to climate variability and change', in A. Matzarakis and C. de Freitas (eds), *International Society of Biometeorology Proceedings of the First International Workshop on Climate, Tourism and Recreation*, available at http://www.mif.uni-freiburg.de/isb/ws/report.htm

Seddighi, H.R. and A.L. Theocharous (2002), 'A model of tourism destination choices: a theoretical and empirical analysis', *Tourism Management*, **23**(5), 475–87.

Shoemaker, S. (1994), 'Segmenting the U.S. travel market according to benefits realized', *Journal of Travel Research*, **32**(3), 8–21.

Smith, J.B., H.-J. Schellnhuber, M.M.Q. Mirza, S. Fankhauser, R. Leemans, E. Lin, L. Ogallo, B. Pittock, R.G. Richels, C. Rosenzweig, R.S.J. Tol, J.P. Weyant and G.W. Yohe (2001), 'Vulnerability to climate change and reasons for concern: a synthesis', in J.J. McCarthy, O.F. Canziani, N.A. Leary, D.J. Dokken and K.S. White (eds), *Climate Change 2001: Impacts, Adaptation, and Vulnerability*, Cambridge: Cambridge University Press, pp. 913–67.

Tol, R.S.J. (2000), 'Screening exercise', in R.S.J. Tol (ed.), *Weather Impacts on Natural, Social and Economic Systems in the Netherlands*, Amsterdam: Institute for Environmental Studies R00–02, Vrije Universiteit.

Viner, D. and M. Agnew (1999), 'Climate change and its impacts on tourism', report prepared for WWF-UK, Godalming, UK.

Wall, G. (1998), 'Implications of global climate change for tourism and recreation in wetland areas', *Climatic Change*, **40**, 371–89.

Witt, S.F. and C.A. Witt (1995), 'Forecasting tourism demand: a review of empirical research', *International Journal of Forecasting*, **11**, 447–75.

WTO (2003), *Yearbook of Tourism Statistics*, Madrid, Spain: World Tourism Organization.

7. Sustainable tourism and economic instruments: international experience and the case of Hvar, Croatia[1]

Tim Taylor, Maja Fredotovic, Daria Povh and Anil Markandya

INTRODUCTION

Tourism activities often have a significant environmental impact on a tourist destination, including congestion and pollution. These environmental concerns have led to moves towards the development of sustainable tourism in recent years, particularly as the numbers of tourists and the distances they are travelling has increased. Such developments have included the use of ecolabelling, for example, the use of 'ecotourism', and the taxing of tourists in order to raise the revenues to correct the environmental damage caused. This chapter examines the latter of these two measures, first from an international perspective and then from the local case of Hvar, Croatia.

DEFINING SUSTAINABLE TOURISM

There are a number of definitions of sustainable tourism. The distinctions arise due to differences in the definition of sustainability, and this obviously impacts on how certain sectors can be seen to be making progress towards sustainability. Sustainable tourism may be defined as 'the optimal use of natural and cultural resources for national development on an equitable and self sustaining basis to provide a unique visitor experience and an improved quality of life through partnership among government, the private sector and communities' (OECS website, undated). Others have considered sustaining tourist numbers to be the objective. Whatever the case, it is clear that tourism has important economic, social and environmental implications that should not be overlooked in evaluating the impacts of the tourist industry on a region. The main aim of this chapter is to examine the potential implications for the use of tourist eco-taxes, taking the quality of life of the community as the objective, through examining the economic impact of such measures, as well as their impact on the quality of the environment and tourist enjoyment. This approach enables an integrated assessment of the current and future implications of tourism on the environment.

DEFINITION OF ECO-TAXES

Tourists face a number of taxes, including departure taxes, value added taxes and room taxes. The question as to what distinguishes an eco-tax from these other techniques is important. Here we will define an 'eco-tax' in its broadest sense as one that is placed on a good or service to internalize some, or all, of the external costs of the activity undertaken or one that is hypothecated to the use of environmental protection. For a recent review of the application of environmental or eco-taxes in developing countries see Markandya et al. (2002).

Tourist eco-taxes, therefore, are defined as being those that are raised on tourists for environmental purposes. They may or may not have a direct impact on the incentives provided to the tourist to pollute, but must, in any event, be used for environmental purposes. An example is the tourist eco-charge in Hvar, Croatia that is discussed later in this chapter. In that case, the charge is levied not on the volume of pollution but on the number of days spent in Hvar. This charge is then hypothecated, that is, it is earmarked for use in environmental protection.

ANALYTICAL FRAMEWORK

We can define the demand for a tourist site as follows:

$$Q_t = f(p_t, e_t, d, c, x),$$

where
Q_t is the quantity of tourist days spent in a region in time t;
p_t is the price of staying in the tourist region in time t (including taxes);
e_t is the level of environmental quality in time t in the region;
d is the distance travelled;
c represents the climate of a region; and
x represents all other factors.

The first derivative of Q_t with respect to p_t provides us with the key information to calculate the price elasticity of demand for a tourist area. This will be determined by a number of factors, including the availability of substitute sites and behavioural aspects of the consumer. As the price of visiting a given region increases, so there is a demand response to that price change. This shows us one impact of the imposition of an eco-tax on the tourist economy.

Another impact, however, is shown by the change in environmental quality that may be attributed to the eco-tax, or actions taken using the revenues of such a tax. It has been shown in the literature that there is a positive relationship between demand for a site and the level of environmental quality (see, for example, Milhalic, 2000). This has led to the rise of so-called ecotourism in some regions. In the case of a tourist eco-charge, these two aspects may to a certain extent work in opposite directions, and the aggregate impact on tourist revenues will depend on the relative strengths of each impact. This is shown in a stylized form in Figure 7.1.

In the initial position, the equilibrium is given by PQ, where supply and demand intersect. With the application of a uniform tourist eco-tax of t, the equilibrium moves to P_1Q_1 as the price per day of the trip increases. However, the improvement in the level of environmental quality leads to

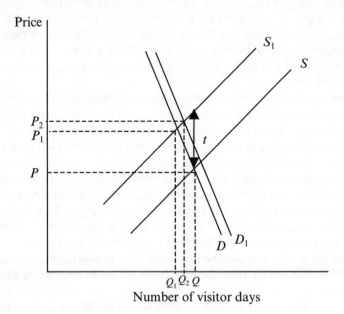

Figure 7.1   Theoretical impact of tourist eco-tax

an increase in the level of demand to D_1. The equilibrium position is P_2Q_2 – which in this case represents a slight reduction in tourist numbers from the initial equilibrium. The relative strength of the price effect and the environmental quality effect is what this chapter will attempt to determine.

In terms of the impact of a change in price on the level of demand for tourism, a number of studies have shown that demand for tourism is inelastic. This means that as the price of a trip rises, one would expect to see a less than proportionate reduction in the quantity of tourist days. In a meta-analysis of 44 studies, Crouch and Shaw (1992) found that the average price elasticity of demand was −0.39, suggesting that a 1 per cent increase in price would lead to a 0.39 per cent reduction in the numbers of tourists. This is similar to the findings of Vanegas and Croes (2000) for US tourists in Aruba, where the price elasticity was found to be −0.56 in the short run,[2] indicating that a 1 per cent increase in price will lead to a 0.56 per cent reduction in tourist demand. In other studies by Hiemstra and Ismail (1992, 1993) the elasticity was found to be –0.44. This is important, as it suggests that the demand for tourism will not be greatly affected by tourist eco-taxes, which make up a relatively small part of the total cost of a trip – and hence the economy will not suffer greatly, if at all, from such a measure. Whilst this is the case for marginal taxes, it should be noted that it is important not to levy such a large tax that it has significant competitiveness aspects.

Another important aspect is the price elasticity of supply, which indicates the degree to which the tax will be passed on to consumers. Hiemstra and Ismail (1993) found that the supply elasticity for hotel rooms was 2.86, indicating that approximately $6 of every $7 of a hotel tax is passed on to the tourist (Dixon et al., 2001). Thus there is a very small impact on the tourist industry.

In terms of the increase in demand due to an improvement in the environment, the growth of ecotourism suggests that environmental quality may form an important part of the consumer's consumption decision. The issue of information arises in this context, whereby it is difficult to re-establish a reputation for good environmental quality once this is lost (Dixon et al., 2001). Certification schemes and proactive environmental management may play a role in improving environmental quality (as the tourism industry changes behaviour to meet certification standards) and access to information on the quality of the environment. Certification schemes include the EU's blue flag scheme, which has been extended to a number of countries.

The time aspect may also be important. In the short term, the stock of pollutants may mean that the reduction of environmental damage or improvement in environmental quality is less than would otherwise be the case, thus reducing the positive environmental quality impact in the near term. However, in the longer term improvements in environmental quality should lead to increased tourist numbers (unless actions are taken, e.g. through increased eco-taxes to mitigate the impacts of congestion).

We now review some of the main environmental damages associated with tourism, before presenting an overview of some of the policy measures that have been taken to mitigate such impacts.

ENVIRONMENTAL DAMAGE AND TOURISM

The linkages between tourism and environmental damage have been reviewed in a number of publications (see Davies and Cahill, 2000 for the US case). This section will examine a number of key impacts of tourism on the environment.

Congestion[3]

Congestion costs have not, to date, been assessed in any serious empirical way. The demand functions for tourism have been estimated (e.g. Crouch and Shaw, 1992), but such demand functions do not look at how the willingness to pay (WTP) for a visit is a function of the number of visitors. In terms of Figure 7.2, the WTP for a group of identical visitors, OP, assuming that some critical number is not exceeded, is given as OB. The marginal cost per visit is OC. Each visitor will compare that marginal cost with the WTP as given by the line ZZ^*. This results in a number of visitors equal to OV. However, the marginal visitor creates congestion effects on all other visitors, resulting in an additional or marginal value as depicted by the line ZZ^{**}, which is below ZZ^*. The socially optimal number of visitors is OW, but the free access equilibrium will result in a number equal to OV. The potential pool of visitors is OP.

The literature does show that tourists perceive crowding as being a negative externality. Hillary et al. (2001) in a study based in Australia found that in assessing visitor perception of environmental quality this was the most common factor highlighted as an issue, with tourist tracks and consequent soil quality being the next most important aspect.

The literature on tourism does not contain serious estimates of the value of this congestion effect. To be sure, there are estimates of the price demand elasticity of visits to sites using the travel cost method, but these estimates do not separate out the decline in the WTP due to the fact that people with a lower WTP are visiting the site (a factor we have eliminated in Figure 7.1), and the fact that the WTP of any one visitor declines with the number of visitors. If we are to develop tools for sustainable tourism it is precisely these kinds of data and analysis that are needed.

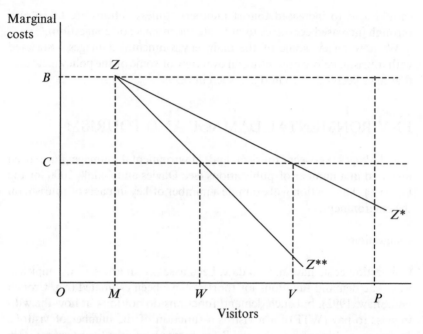

Figure 7.2   Congestion costs of tourism

The impacts of tourist-generated traffic congestion on local communities were studied by Lindbergh and Johnson (1997) for the case of Oregon. They found that households were willing to pay $110 to $186 annually on average to get rid of such congestion. This indicates that there may be significant side-benefits to local communities of reducing congestion by tourists.

Congestion not only has an impact on tourist benefits; it also may have a significant environmental impact in terms of increased pollution. In the case of Hvar, as discussed in the case study below, high densities of tourists lead to extreme pressures on wastewater treatment, on the deposition of litter and on land-based pollution such as emissions from vehicles. Such costs need to be considered when levying a tourist eco-charge.

The potential for the levying of charges for congestion at tourist attractions has been raised in the past in Wanhill (1980). Wanhill identifies difficulties of administration, implementation and equity in levying charges based on congestion, yet draws the following positive advantages for such charges:

- the amenity appropriates the surplus caused by excess demand for the attractions;

- it should encourage efficient use of the attraction and the correct allocation of resources;
- the revenue provided could be used to diversify or rationalize the operation of the amenity; and
- a booking or quota system may include those who are not prepared to pay the price of congestion and exclude those who are.

Increased Pollution Loads in Water and Air

Pollution loads in water and air are clearly an issue of some concern to local authorities and national governments. There may be impacts on health – through incidence of asthma or water-borne diseases. Water pollutants may raise costs for extraction of drinking water from freshwater sources. In the empirical literature, some work has been carried out to estimate the impacts of such pollution arising from tourism. These impacts include:

- Increased air pollution:
  - 33 to 44 per cent increase in traffic in peak season in Sochi, Russia (Lukashina et al., 1996);
  - increased emissions from airplanes: increased emission of pollutants such as NO_x, carbon monoxide and particulate matter, among others. However, these have been shown to be very small in relation to total emissions in the US case, with less than 0.2 per cent of total CO emissions being due to tourist-related air travel, though they are increasing in importance (Davies and Cahill, 2000);
  - air emissions from energy use.
- Increased water pollution:
  - impact of cruise ships and recreational vessels on the marine environment may be significant due to dumping of waste at sea. This includes solid waste and the dumping of bilge tanks at sea (Patullo, 2000; Davies and Cahill, 2000);
  - tourism may place a significant burden on wastewater management facilities (Kamp, 1998).

Water Use

Water is an important resource in a number of areas in the world. This is true for the Mediterranean region among others, and the issue of water resource management is growing increasingly important with increased risk of drought due to changes in climate and the pollution of groundwater and surface water sources. It has been estimated that the average tourist in Spain uses 440 litres of water per day (up to 880 when one includes swimming pools and golf courses) compared to the average Spanish resident consumption of 250 litres (WWF, undated).

Waste

Tourists have been shown to generate a more than proportionate quantity of waste, both solid and liquid. A recent World Bank study by Dixon et al. (2001) found that in St Lucia tourists generate approximately twice the amount of solid waste that residents generate. The total level of waste generated by tourists may be less than that of local residents, due to the time scale of the tourist season. However, the waste generated may have important impacts as waste is generated in areas where it is likely to affect environmental quality and the concentration of tourist-generated waste around the peak season means that it is likely to cause more damage to the tourist industry (Dixon et al., 2001).

Degradation of Cultural Heritage

The impact of tourism on the cultural heritage of a nation or region has been the subject of some debate in the literature. It is possible that, if properly managed, tourism may provide positive effects on local communities, with increased community pride, sense of identity, support for the economy of the community and increased employment opportunities. However, where inadequate care is taken, tourism may result in problems of cultural commodification, higher living costs, displacement, increased crime, undermining of traditional ways of life and pollution (Jamieson, 2000). Cultural considerations must be taken into account in the promotion of sustainable tourism. Fears about the negative impact of tourism on culture have been the driving force behind the tourism policy of Bhutan, as highlighted below.

Ecological Impacts

Tourism may have diverse impacts on the ecological system within a country. Such impacts are difficult to measure, as presented by Hughes (2002) in evaluating environmental indicators for the case of the impact of tourism on coral reefs. Dixon et al. (2001) note that 'the simple presence of tourists can have adverse environmental impacts in some particularly sensitive ecological systems'.

Tourist development may, if left unregulated, have significant impacts on wetlands and forest habitat. Davies and Cahill (2000) give examples of the impact of infrastructure development, with Jamaica having lost 700 acres of wetlands due to tourist development since the 1960s (Bacon, 1987).

For the Mediterranean, WWF (undated) suggests that over 500 plants are threatened with extinction and face pressure from tourism development in some overbuilt destinations. The impact is not limited to flora, with monkseal populations being threatened and sea turtles having their nesting grounds disturbed.

Positive Impacts of Tourism

It is important to note that tourism does not only have negative impacts on an area or region; it may also have significant benefits in terms of development and preservation of heritage sites. The positive economic impact of tourism may provide needed funds for preserving the environment or cultural heritage. This is clearly above and beyond the economic impacts of tourism, which may be important for development.

INTERNATIONAL EXPERIENCE WITH TOURIST ECO-TAXES

A number of countries have experimented with tourist charges, and the contribution that tourists make to the tax revenues of visited countries is increasing. This section focuses specifically on those taxes instigated for environmental purposes.

The impact of an eco-tax on the competitiveness of a region as a tourist destination may be important to the government in deciding on the implementation of such charges. This section will look at the charge schemes that exist to date.

Balearic Islands, Spain

The Balearic Islands are an important tourist destination located off the coast of Spain. In 2001 just over 10 million tourists visited the islands, with 1.5 million from Spain and the rest largely made up of British and German tourists (Government of the Balearics, 2002). This level of tourism has created great pressure on the infrastructure and environment of the Balearics. In terms of the environment, the following have been the major impacts:

- pressure on water resources led to the level of underground water falling by 90 metres from 1975 to 1999;

- production of domestic waste is double the national average of Spain; and
- increased use of energy: in Majorca electricity consumption rose by 37 per cent between 1993 and 1998.

The Balearic Islands introduced an eco-tax on tourism to raise revenues for a 'Tourist Areas Restoration Fund'. This eco-tax consisted of a system of charges based on length of stay in tourist accommodation. The tax excluded those under 12 and those coming under a social programme. Rates of the tax are shown in Table 7.1. The rates of the tourist eco-tax in the Balearics ranged from €0.5 per day for low-rating hotels and apartments up to €2 per day for high-rating hotels and apartments. The tax was paid by the visitor to the hotel.

The 'Tourist Areas Restoration Fund' was established in 1999. The aims of this fund are described in Box 7.1, with the general aim being to promote the sustainable development of the tourism industry and to enhance the competitiveness of the Balearics.

The eco-tax was abandoned in early 2003 as a result of a change in government and pressure from the tourism industry. The tax was successful in raising revenues, and anecdotal evidence of a shift in tourists to other

Table 7.1 Tourist eco-tax in the Balearics

Accommodation	Rate (euros/day)
5 star hotels and aparthotels	2
4 star hotels and aparthotels	1
3 star hotels and aparthotels	1
2 star hotels and aparthotels	0.5
1 star hotels and aparthotels	0.5
4 key tourist apartments	2
3 key tourist apartments	1
2 key tourist apartments	1
1 key tourist apartments	0.5
Holiday tourist homes	1
Property rental with complementary services	1
Camping sites or tourist camps	0.75
Rural hotels	1
Interior hotels	1
Agritourism	0.25

Source: Ecotaxa web site.

BOX 7.1   AIMS OF TOURIST AREAS
RESTORATION FUND

- Redesign and restore tourist areas
- Recuperate resources and open and rural spaces
- Revalue heritage features with social, cultural and tourist relevance
- Revitalize agriculture as a financially competitive activity

Source: Ecotaxa web site.

---

resorts was reported – though tourist arrivals from the UK, a major market, increased (Templeton, 2003).

Bhutan

Bhutan has strict rules on tourism and charges a large minimum tariff for staying in the country of €179 (low season) to €217 (high season) per night for a member of a tour party of more than three persons, through one of 33 official tour operators.[4] There is an additional supplement of €43 per night for a single person and €33 per night per person for couples. This charge was levied and other restrictions placed on tourism in the light of the government's view that 'tourism must be environmentally and ecologically friendly, socially and culturally acceptable and economically viable' (Government of Bhutan, undated). Since 1974 strict controls have been placed on tourism, with Bhutan aiming for low-volume, high-value tourism. The impacts of these controls, combined with other measures to protect the environment (including bans on the export of raw timber), have been to reduce the social and environmental impact of tourism in Bhutan. There have been some potential costs associated with this programme, however, in terms of economic development – with some Bhutanese suggesting the programme has gone too far (US DOE, 2001). The Bhutanese case is not a tax as such, but it has had impacts on visitor numbers – which are also limited by the seasonal nature of tourism in Bhutan – and it has had a positive impact on the profits of tour operators (Dorji, 2001).

Dominica

Tourism is an important part of the Dominican economy, with total visitors numbering 309 086 in 1998, contributing €46.3 million (Government of Dominica, 1999). Over three-quarters of tourists to Dominica arrive by

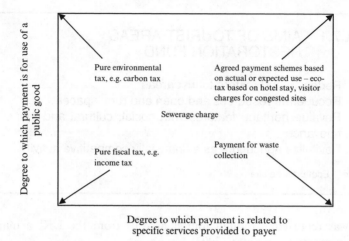

Figure 7.3   Tourist eco-tax experience

cruise ships and significant environmental problems have arisen as a result of the discharge of wastes. As a consequence, Dominica has an environmental levy of €1.62 per head on departure, to pay for a waste management scheme funded by the World Bank. Difficulties were experienced in establishing this charge, with cruise ships threatening to boycott the island. However, it has been instigated (Patullo, 2000) without the proposed boycott materializing.

Conclusions

From the above it can be seen that examples of 'environmental taxes' range from those that are taxes in the sense that they are payments not based on the costs of supplying a particular service, to those that are really charges for services provided. For example, in the case of waste collection charges (as in Dominica), the payment is a charge for a service and provides for environmental protection. Of course tourists should not be subsidized in the provision of such services, but all too often this is the case. Pure charges, such as those in the Balearics case, provide for environmental protection based on visitor usage. We can thus distinguish between these charges, and Figure 7.3 provides a mechanism for this.

CASE STUDY OF HVAR

We now turn to examine the potential for the application of a tourist eco-tax in Hvar, Croatia.

The town of Hvar is located in the west part of the island of Hvar, one of the islands of Middle Dalmatia. It is situated to the South of Split and is the largest island in Croatia. Hvar has 4224 residents (2001). In the summer months it is a popular tourist destination for Croatian nationals and increasingly for European holiday makers. The increase in tourist numbers has led to a range of environmental problems, ranging from pressures on wastewater services to increased littering and congestion in the town of Hvar.

The coastline and the landscape are, along with cultural monuments, the most valuable natural resources and form part of the tourist attraction to the area. Under the Law on Nature Protection, the islands of Pakleni otoci and the small island of Galešnik (at the entrance to the port of Hvar) are treated as protected landscape areas. Under the Law on the Protection of Cultural Heritage, the urban areas of the town of Hvar and rural areas of Velo Grablje, Malo Grablje and Zarače have the status of protected areas. Furthermore, there are a number of archaeological sites in the area: the hydroarchaeological site Palmižana, the *villa rustica* in Soline, a site at Vira, and a fort at Lompić in the Gračišće Bay. In addition, there are 73 protected cultural monuments within the historical city centre of the town of Hvar (including the Arsenal and Theatre, the City Fortress and Wally, the Cathedral and cemetery, numerous palaces etc.) and 23 more of them outside the town centre.

As stated above, tourism is becoming increasingly important in the Hvar economy. It currently contributes directly to one-third of the employment in the town. The development of tourism in Hvar dates back prior to the development of mass tourism in other parts of Europe. During the 1960s and 1970s, a number of large tourist facilities were constructed. These developments were functional but not aesthetically pleasing. Tourism development has been accompanied by an expansion in residential property, and developments have not been properly planned. As a consequence there are a range of infrastructure problems, including a lack of parking facilities, narrow roads and waste and wastewater management problems.

Tourism declined in the 1990s as a consequence of the civil war in Croatia and neighbouring Bosnia and Herzegovina. War was not the sole cause of the lack of growth, however, as the supply of tourist accommodation and infrastructure also restricted development.

Recently, the construction of accommodation and catering facilities has been recorded in previously non-inhabited bays (e.g. Milna and Velo Zarače) and also on the Pakleni otoci. These are illegal, without building permits, and are harmful to the environment and landscape. Similar construction has been recorded in the bays on the northern part of Hvar. Valuable resources of the land and sea have been damaged in the process.

Table 7.2   Accommodation in the town of Hvar

Type of accommodation	Category	Number of beds
Hotels	***	932
	**	1363
Private accommodation	***	3770
	**	2730
Total number of beds		8795

Source: Hvar Tourist Office.

The current official accommodation capacity in the town of Hvar is 8795 beds, as shown in Table 7.2. In addition to the data below it is estimated that 2000 additional, unregistered beds are made available in the peak season.

Tourism and Environment in Hvar

Tourism has a significant impact on the state of the environment in Hvar. It places a large burden on wastewater services, on waste collection and on other services provided by the municipality. In the peak season, the ratio of tourists to locals is three to one, which is indicative of the significant burden of peak loads on wastewater and other facilities.

Tourist-related litter is an issue on the island. In addition, other discharges from boats pollute the water and coastline.

It would be wrong to categorize Hvar as heavily polluted, but in the peak season some negative impacts of tourism can reduce the enjoyment of the town and the surrounding area. The likely growth of tourist volume indicates that resources are needed to create an environment in which tourism can develop sustainably. One mechanism that has been identified that could contribute significantly to mitigating the environmental effect of tourism is a tourist eco-charge. The following sections outline the proposed charge.

Proposed Tourist Eco-charge

Tourists produce serious pressure on the natural resources and the infrastructure in the town of Hvar and the surrounding area. Thus, according to the polluter pays principle, tourists should contribute towards the remediation of environmental damage caused by their activities. It should be noted that tourism is also considered to be the main potential source of economic development of the area in the future, and hence it is important that actions bear in mind responses of tourists and also contribute towards the sustainable development of the island as a tourist destination.

The proposed instrument is earmarked, its main purpose being to reduce/prevent pollution of the coast and coastal sea originating from the land-based sources (and pollution in general).

This economic instrument was defined as a 'tourist eco-charge' for a number of reasons. First, it is earmarked for environmental improvement. Second, it could not be described as a 'tax' in Croatia because it is collected and controlled at the local level whereas, in the Croatian case, 'taxes' go to the state budget, and it would be quite unlikely that it would be transferred back to the local budget for environmental purposes. It has to be the revenue of the local authority budget to ensure that revenues are spent on environmental remediation and also to deal with the specific issues facing Hvar. The problem of Hvar is local in nature, and therefore should be solved at the local level.

The charge is aimed at tourists. The term 'tourist' refers to anyone outside his/her place of residence. However, it was rather difficult to decide how to design the charge so as to address all the tourists in the area, due to several problems.

Tourists come to the island of Hvar by sea. They usually take the ferry and come through the ports of Sućuraj or Stari Grad (located outside of the area under study). Some come directly to Hvar town by ferry, though there is no car ferry connecting Hvar town with the mainland. A large number of the tourists come through organized tours, though many others are not on package deals, especially during the peak season.

Nautical tourism is also important in Hvar. Some of these tourists visit Hvar town, others do not – remaining on their boats in the Adriatic.

These were just some of the issues that had to be taken into account when designing the tourist eco-charge. The point is that 'the tourist' had to be defined so as to ensure relatively easy enforcement as well as the possibility to charge the majority of tourists.

It is impossible to impose a charge upon arrival or departure, since the people move freely and the area under study encompasses just a part of the island of Hvar. Also it is not feasible to include the charge in the price of the ferry ticket (or similar) owing to strong opposition from the ferry operators. Moreover, the procedure of transferring the revenues to the local authorities would be extremely difficult, if not impossible, under existing Croatian law.

Another set of issues regarded the possibility of charging the tourists while they are within the territorial limits of the area under study. Future enforcement procedure and measures also limit the way a tourist eco-charge can be collected. For example, to include the charge in the bills for drink and food, or in the price of the transfers from the town to the Pakleni islands, would face significant implementation problems, particularly as the competitiveness of some of the economic agents in the area would be affected, and not all of the tourists would be charged. The 'grey economy' in Croatia is also an issue, as many sales are not recorded in official documentation and so taxation of goods is difficult to enforce.

Following the polluter pays principle, since there is a link between length of stay and consequential impact on the environment, it seems right to relate the charge to the length of the stay within the area under study. Payment of the charge in any of the ways described above does not provide this opportunity, though a tourist eco-charge on accommodation would mean that there would be a link between the payment and the length of stay.

The Level of the Tourist Eco-charge

There were several key factors that had to be taken into account during the design of proposals for the tourist eco-charge for the town of Hvar.

First, the main problems occur in the peak season (20 July–20 August), when the number of tourists is three times the number of local population (16 000 altogether). Interviews with hotel management, the Tourist Office director and local government officials revealed that it was their mutual intent to reduce the number of tourists in the peak season. This was driven by the fact that visitors in this season are not tourists of 'high quality', according to their expenditures as well as their accommodation requirements. It was also a stated aim to prolong the season. Currently the season lasts from June until the end of September. Therefore it seemed reasonable to differentiate the tourist eco-charge for various times of the year.

Furthermore, the interviewed people pointed out that the number of tourists during the period October to May is very low, and the majority of the accommodation facilities are closed. Therefore there is no, or rather low, pressure on natural resources and infrastructure caused by the tourists during that time of the year. It was therefore decided that the tourist eco-charge should not be imposed during that time of the year. This can also be considered as another incentive for the prolongation of the season. Of course, this policy can be changed over time if necessary.

The next point to consider is the already existing sojourn fee, which is also differentiated: based on the attractiveness of the area and the time of the year, it goes from 2 to 7 kuna.[5] Due to the fact that the area under study is one of the most attractive areas in Croatia, this fee is set at 7 kuna in the peak season, 5.5 kuna during the season (except the peak season), down to 4.5 kuna at other times of the year. The fee is calculated on the basis of person-nights.

In discussing the level of the tourist eco-charge, the hotel management was especially concerned about the competitiveness of the destination. This was underlined by the fact that the majority of the hotel guests come through tour operators, and the charge had to be included in the price of the destination. Bearing in mind the prices of the 'tourist packages' in the world market, as well as the costs of the hotel company in Hvar, and in Croatia in general, the profit rate of the hotel is already rather low. So any additional burden (such as a tourist eco-charge) would have a significant impact on the hotel profit rate. From that point of view, the charge has to be rather low.

The hotel's ability to pay is important to the successful implementation of the charge. If the charge is included in the room price, it has to be transferred from the hotel company to the local authority. The hotel company can make the payment only after being paid by the tour operator in the case of package holidays. The experience with the sojourn fee shows that the payments are delayed, sometimes by a whole year or so. Thus, if the total amount to pay due to the tourist eco-charge is very high and there are low penalties for failure to pay, payments will be delayed. Taking into account that approximately 70 per cent of registered tourists are accommodated in hotels, it would mean that the great majority of the revenues from the tourist eco-charge would not be paid in time, and the tourists would not be able to experience the results of the charge, which would affect the effectiveness of implementation.

Despite all these problems, the hotel company strongly supported the idea of the tourist eco-charge. The reason for this is quite simple. The low prices that the company achieves on the world tourist market are partly due to the fact that the tourist attraction of the town is quite poor, despite the natural and historic resources available. Thus, bearing in mind the long-term development perspective, the hotel company is willing to give up a part of its already small profit, provided it has a strong guarantee that the money will be spent on the improvement of the environmental conditions in the town and surrounding area. This will eventually result in the better reputation of the area as a tourist destination. Furthermore, it will also enhance its chance of attracting guests of 'higher quality', who spend relatively more per day.

Taking into account all the above, as well as the opinions of the hotel management and Tourist Office, it was concluded that the tourist eco-charge should not exceed the level of the sojourn fee.

There was a request for immediate actions that would result in improved environmental quality in the area under study, particularly in respect of the land-based sources of pollution. The request is to be understood from the standpoint of tourists, since the tourist eco-charge seems justified only if the tourists can see the results of their payments. Considering the present pollution problems (caused by both land-based activities and seagoing vessels), it was agreed to concentrate on the cleaning of the shores and shallow sea both in the town and surrounding beaches as well as along the Pakleni islands. Calculations showed (taking into account the overall costs of the process and the enforcement of the charge on the one hand, and assuming the same number of tourists) that the charge should not be lower than 1.5–2.0 kuna. However, this level of charge would be sufficient only for cleaning purposes, while the other land-based sources, and pollution in general, would not be addressed at all. Therefore, three alternative levels of the tourist eco-charge were proposed, as shown in Table 7.3.

Obviously, the proposed levels of the tourist eco-charge are quite low, even in the peak season, when compared to those that have been implemented internationally. However, they can be raised in the future, according to the improved environmental quality of the destination and the changing nature of the tourist market.

Willingness to Pay for the Environment and Survey of Visitors

To estimate the willingness to pay for environmental improvement, a limited survey[6] was conducted in the town of Hvar. This survey, aimed at tourists, was translated into a number of languages and was conducted over the period May–July 2002. A total of 290 responses were received, of which 26 completed surveys were rejected on the basis that those interviewed were locals. The survey included some basic biographical detail on the respondents, a view as to their environmental preferences and an assessment of their willingness to pay – the question asked is presented below. The respondent profile is shown in Table 7.4. Both the age and length of stay varied widely across the sample. Residents of the island of Hvar were excluded, along with Croatian nationals reporting a length of

Table 7.3   Proposed levels of the tourist eco-charge (kuna)

Scenarios	Time of year			
	10 June – 20 July	20 July – 20 August	20 August – 30 September	Other
Scenario I	1.5	2.0	1.5	–
Scenario II	2.0	3.0	2.0	–
Scenario III	3.0	4.0	3.0	–

Table 7.4 Descriptive statistics of respondents

Country	Average age (years)	Respondents		Occupation (% respondents)					Average stay (days)
		Count	as % total	Student	Employee	Freelance	Manager	Other	
Austria	42.7	3	1.15	0.00	66.67	33.33	0.00	0.00	6.3
Bosnia–Herzegovina	19.0	1	0.38	100.00	0.00	0.00	0.00	0.00	13.0
Croatia	31.8	118	45.21	28.81	36.44	14.41	12.71	7.63	11.9
Czech Rep.	36.0	3	1.15	0.00	33.33	33.33	33.33	0.00	22.0
France	33.9	14	5.36	21.43	21.43	28.57	28.57	0.00	9.1
Germany	43.5	11	4.21	9.09	54.55	9.09	9.09	18.18	8.9
Ireland	24.3	7	2.68	42.86	0.00	14.29	42.86	0.00	5.9
Italy	33.0	66	25.29	33.33	25.76	21.21	7.58	12.12	12.2
Poland	25.5	2	0.77	50.00	50.00	0.00	0.00	0.00	120.0
Slovakia	43.0	1	0.38	0.00	0.00	0.00	100.00	0.00	14.0
Slovenia	30.3	22	8.43	50.00	45.45	0.00	4.55	0.00	8.5
Sweden	44.0	1	0.38	0.00	0.00	100.00	0.00	0.00	6.0
Switzerland	27.0	2	0.77	50.00	0.00	50.00	0.00	0.00	10.0
UK	32.8	6	2.30	0.00	50.00	33.33	0.00	16.67	3.7
USA	35.8	4	1.53	0.00	50.00	25.00	25.00	0.00	8.8
Total	32.6	261	100.00	29.50	33.72	16.86	12.26	7.66	11.9

stay over 30 days. It should be noted that the respondents from Poland are not typical, in that they were both young and stayed for long durations. The total number of respondents was 261, with an average age of 32.6 years and a length of stay of 11.9 days.

Visitor perceptions of the environment are described in Table 7.5. The most important aspects in attracting visitors to the island and town of Hvar were the sea (88 per cent), the historic nature of the town (82 per cent), the islands (62 per cent) and the landscape (54 per cent). In terms of environmental priorities identified, the most significant were litter, waste collection, cleaner beaches, cleaner coastal sea and marine traffic. This shows that the general perception of the tourists of the environmental stresses on Hvar is similar to those identified above, providing evidence that the tourists are environmentally aware.

The willingness to pay for environmental improvement in Hvar was assessed using a combination of an open-ended (OE) question and a dichotomous choice (DC) around a payment of 7 kuna (1 euro). The open-ended question used to elicit the willingness to pay for environmental improvement was 'What sum of money (in HRK) would you agree to set aside a day for the improvement of the environment in the town and coastal area of Hvar, including the Islands of Pakleni otoci?' A full version of the questionnaire is included as an Appendix to this chapter. Of the completed accepted responses, 171 were open-ended questionnaires.

In terms of the dichotomous choice (DC) question posed, the question was 'Would you be willing to pay 7 HRK (1 euro) a day for improvement of the environment in the town and coastal area of Hvar, including the Islands of Pakleni otoci?' Seven kuna was chosen on the basis of the tax in

Table 7.5   Perceptions of the environment

Most appealing (%)		Priorities (average, 4 = most important, 1 = least)	
Sea	88.12	Waste collection	2.70
Historic town	82.38	Clean beach	2.67
Pakleni otoci islands	62.45	Coastal water	2.67
Landscape	53.64	Litter	2.55
Beaches	37.93	Marine traffic	2.11
Hospitality	36.78	Traffic and parking	2.00
Adventures	29.89	Flowers	1.92
Food	28.35	Woods	1.91
Cultural events	24.14	Parks	1.89
Parks	17.24	Water supply	1.75
Sports	9.58		

place in the Balearics at that time. For the purposes of the pooled analysis of the use of these results alongside the OE, if a respondent responded that they were willing to pay at least 7 kuna, then the value taken was 7 kuna; correspondingly in the one case where the respondent replied to the dichotomous choice question that they were unwilling to pay 7 kuna, a willingness to pay of zero was set. This is clearly an underestimate of the true willingness to pay, but it provides a useful approximation of the willingness to pay for the purposes of calculating a tourist eco-charge. Of the total completed responses, 93 were dichotomous choice.

For the pooled dataset, the mean willingness to pay estimated was 4.56 kuna, or approximately 65 euro cents per day. The mean willingness to pay for a non-Croatian visitor was 4.77 kuna, or 68 euro cents per day, whilst the same figure for a Croatian visitor was 4.31 kuna or 61 euro cents per day. Separate regressions were carried out on the OE and pooled datasets to determine the factors that influenced willingness to pay. Variables included as explanatory factors were age, average per capita income of the country from which the visitor came, length of stay, whether they were specially attracted to the beaches and whether they were specially drawn to Hvar because of the quality of the sea. The results are given below for the OE and pooled data.

Open-ended: Regression Results

The results from the OLS regression of the results of the OE question are shown as Table 7.6 below. All the signs on the coefficients are as one would expect, apart from income, which is insignificant (probably due to the use of country-wide average data for this variable). Willingness to pay rises when respondents are in Hvar to enjoy the beach and sea (though the latter is not highly significant) – and as these are the major areas that the eco-tax would improve this is to be expected. WTP is strongly negatively correlated with length of stay and weakly negatively correlated to the age of respondent.

Pooled Data: Regression Results

A simple regression was carried out to assess the determinants of the willingness to pay expressed. Table 7.7 reports the results of this analysis. Income was approximated using per capita GNI taken from the World Development Indicators. The other variables which could be used to approximate income, including type of job, were considered but turned out to be insignificant. The overall explanatory power of the regression is not high, with an R-squared of 0.035, but the results show some interesting linkages.

Table 7.6   OE regression results

Ordinary least squares estimation

Department variable is WTP
172 observations used for estimation from 1 to 172

Regressor	Coefficient	Standard error	t-ratio [prob.]
CONSTANT	3.4758	0.73674	4.7179 [0.000]
AGE	−0.015339	0.014679	−1.0449 [0.298]
GNI	−0.3984E-5	0.1927E-4	−0.20672 [0.836]
LENGTH	−0.015728	0.0085528	−1.8390 [0.068]
BEACHES	0.56202	0.35317	1.5914 [0.113]
SEA	0.47433	0.50581	0.93775 [0.350]
R-squared	0.052290	R-bar-squared	0.023745
S.E. of regression	2.2128	F-stat. F(5, 166)	1.8318 [0.109]
Mean of dependent variable	3.3605	S.D. of dependent variable	2.2395
Residual sum of squares	812.8045	Equation log-likelihood	−377.6151
Akaike info. criterion	−383.6151	Schwarz Bayesian criterion	−393.0576
DW-statistic	1.8528		

As can be seen from Table 7.7, age was insignificant in determining willingness to pay, but income, length of stay and whether the islands (location of the main beaches) were the main attraction were all significant to varying degrees. The signs are as one would expect, with 'GNI' and 'Islands' showing a positive sign. 'GNI' can be expected to have a positive sign, given that environmental quality is given a higher value by those with higher incomes; that is, previous studies have shown a positive income elasticity of demand for environmental quality. 'Islands' reflects the nature of the visit, with beach and marine tourism forming the most important part of the stay. The islands are sensitive to pollution, both by litter and by marine pollution. 'Length' shows a negative sign, reflecting a lower willingness to pay among those who would have to pay more. A variable to analyse the influence of whether the respondent was national or not was constructed, but turned out to be insignificant.

From the above analysis, we can conclude that tourists would be willing to contribute towards improving the environment, and that significant revenues could be obtained from tourists for this purpose. The proposed eco-charge for tourists in Hvar would seem to be viable from an economic

Table 7.7   Regression results: WTP in kuna

Ordinary least squares estimation

Dependent variable is WTP
264 observations used for estimation from 1 to 264

Regressor	Coefficient	Standard error	t-ratio [prob.]
CONSTANT	4.3994	0.56275	7.8176 [0.000]
AGE	−0.013694	0.013134	−1.0427[0.298]
GNI	−0.2896E-4	0.1773E-4	1.6336 [0.104]
LENGTH	−0.014995	0.0090599	−1.6551 [0.099]
ISLANDS	0.64986	0.32602	1.9933 [0.047]
R-squared	0.035496	R-bar-squared	0.020600
S.E. of regression	2.5141	F-stat F(4, 259)	2.3830 [0.052]
Mean of dependent variable	4.5492	S.D. of dependent variable	2.5404
Residual sum of squares	1637.1	Equation log-likelihood	−615.4653
Akaike info. criterion	−620.4653	Schwarz Bayesian criterion	−629.4052
DW-statistic	1.9267		

point of view, though political and legal barriers have risen to restrict the application of tourist eco-charges in Hvar at present.

CONCLUSIONS

Tourism has been shown to have significant impacts on the environment, through a number of impact pathways. Economic instruments, such as tourist eco-charges, present one possible means of addressing the negative aspects of tourism, both through changing behaviour and by providing funds for environmental improvement. Such charges have been applied in a number of countries, including the Balearic Islands, Bhutan and Dominica.

This chapter presents the case for economic instruments in the Croatian town of Hvar, which faces ever-increasing environmental pressures from tourists in the peak season in particular. Stakeholder analysis has shown that there is general support for a tourist eco-charge in Hvar and a pre-liminary willingness-to-pay study shows a willingness to pay for environmental improvement of approximately €0.65 per day, higher than the proposed charge. This charge would be earmarked for use on improving the environment.

Barriers to the implementation of this charge still exist, notably from the political and legal standpoint. However, actions are being taken at present to remove these barriers and it is anticipated that a charge may be in place in the near future.

NOTES

1. This study forms part of the UNEP PAP–RAC project 'Sustainability of SAP: Development of Economic Instruments for the Sustainable Implementation of the Strategic Action Programme to address marine pollution from land-based activities in the Mediterranean (SAP MED)'. The authors would like thank UNEP for their funding, the PAP–RAC in Split and participants in the wider project for comments. Thanks also to participants at the 2003 International Conference on Tourism and Sustainable Economic Development: Micro and Macro Economic Issues, Sardinia, for useful comments.
2. Vanegas and Croes (2000) also report a long-run price elasticity of −4.38, indicating a very high long-run response to a change in price. It must be noted that this is the most elastic response they reported, with the range going from −1.07 to −4.38 depending on the equation system. The average elasticity found was −0.29, not including long-run and short-run effects. Thus, overall, the analysis of Aruba suggests an inelastic response to a price change.
3. This section is based on Markandya (2000).
4. Additional charges are raised depending on services provided.
5. 7 kuna are equal to approximately €1 at the current rate of exchange.
6. It should be noted that the survey was not a full CVM survey as is usually applied in the literature on valuation of the environment. Due to budgetary and logistical reasons only a few questions could be asked to survey participants. As such, results from this survey should be treated with care.

REFERENCES

Bacon, Peter R. (1987), 'Use of Wetlands for Tourism in the Insular Caribbean', *Annals of Tourism Research*, **14**, 104–17, cited in Davis and Cahill (2000).

Crouch, G.I. and R.N. Shaw (1992), 'International Tourism: A Meta-analytical Integration of Research Findings', in P. Johnson and B. Thomas (eds), *Choice and Demand in Tourism*, London: Mansell.

Davies, T. and S. Cahill (2000), *Environmental Implications of the Tourism Industry*, discussion paper 00–24, Resources for the Future, Washington, DC, available online from http://www.rff.org.

Dixon, J., K. Hamilton, S. Pagiola and L. Segnestam (2001), *Tourism and the Environment in the Caribbean: An Economic Framework*, Environment Department Paper No. 80, The World Bank, Washington, DC.

Dorji, T. (2001), 'Sustainability of Tourism in Bhutan', *Journal of Bhutan Studies* **3**(1), available online at http://www.bhutanstudies.com/.

Ecotaxa web site, available online at http://www.ecotaxa.org.

Government of Bhutan (undated), *Tourism in Bhutan*, Department of Tourism web site, Government of Bhutan, available online at http://www.tourism.gov.bt/index.html.

Government of Dominica (1999), *Country Profile*, available online at http://www.ndcdominica.dm/invest/countryprofile.doc.

Government of the Balearics (2002), *Tourism Statistics*, available online at http://www.visitbalears.com/turisme/estudis/ct/pu/readfile/55.

Hiemstra, Stephen J. and Joseph A. Ismail (1992), 'Analyses of Room Taxes Levied on the Lodging Industry', *Journal of Travel Research*, **31**(1), 42–9.

Hiemstra, Stephen J. and Joseph A. Ismail (1993), 'Incidence of the Impacts of Room Taxes on the Lodging Industry', *Journal of Travel Research*, **31**(4), 22–6.

Hillary, M., B. Nancarrow, G. Griffin and G. Syme (2001), 'Tourist Perception of Environmental Impact', *Annals of Tourism Research*, **28**(4), 853–67.

Hughes, G. (2002), 'Environmental Indicators', *Annals of Tourism Research*, **29**(2), 457–77.

Jamieson, W. (2000), 'The Challenges of Sustainable Community Cultural Heritage Tourism', paper presented at UNESCO Conference/Workshop on Culture, Heritage Management and Tourism, Bhaktapur, April.

Kamp, H. (1998), 'Position Paper of the German NGO Forum on Environment and Development on the Environmental and Social Responsibility of Tourism in the Context of Sustainable Development', paper presented to the 7th meeting of the Commission for Sustainable Development, New York.

Lindbergh, K. and R. Johnson (1997), 'The Economic Values of Tourism's Social Impacts', *Annals of Tourism Research*, **24**(1), 90–116.

Lukashina, N., M. Amirkhanov, V. Anisimov and A. Trunev (1996), 'Tourism and Environmental Degradation in Sochi, Russia', *Annals of Tourism Research*, **23**(3), 654–65.

Markandya, A. (2000), 'Economic Instruments for Sustainable Tourism Development', in A. Fossati and G. Panella (eds), *Tourism and Sustainable Economic Development*, Boston, MA, Dordrecht and London: Kluwer Academic Publishers.

Markandya, A., P. Harou, L. Bellu and V. Cistulli (2002), *Environmental Economics for Sustainable Growth: A Handbook for Practitioners*, Cheltenham, UK: Edward Elgar.

Milhalic, T. (2000), 'Environmental Management of a Tourist Destination: A Factor of Tourism Competitiveness', *Tourism Management*, **21**, 65–78.

Organization of Eastern Caribbean States (OECS) (undated), cited by Jamaica Sustainable Development Network Sustainable Tourism page, available online at http://www.jsdnp.org.jm/susTourism.htm.

Patullo, P. (2000), 'The Problems of Two Aspects of Intensive Tourism (Cruise and All Inclusives) in the Caribbean', in *Calpe 2000: Linking the Fragments of Paradise, Proceedings of an International Conference on Environmental Conservation in Small Territories*, Government of Gibraltar and UK Overseas Territories Conservation Forum, available online at http://www.ukotcf.org.

Templeton, T. (2003), 'A Kick in the Balearics for Eco-tax', *The Observer*, Sunday, 8 June.

US DOE (2001), *Bhutan Country Brief*, US Department of Energy, January, available online at http://www.eia.doe.gov/emeu/cabs/bhutan.html.

Vanegas, M. and R. Croes (2000), 'Evaluation of Demand: US Tourists to Aruba', *Annals of Tourism Research*, **27**(4), 946–63.

Wanhill, S. (1980), 'Charging for Congestion at Tourist Attractions', *International Journal of Tourism Management*, September, 168–74. Reprinted in C. Tisdell (2000), *The Economics of Tourism II*, Cheltenham, UK: Edward Elgar.

WWF (undated), *Tourism Threats in the Mediterranean*, WWF background paper, available online at http://www.panda.org.

APPENDIX: QUESTIONNAIRE IN ENGLISH

QUESTIONNAIRE ON THE ENVIRONMENTAL CONDITIONS IN THE TOWN AND COASTAL SEA OF HVAR

The town of Hvar has initiated, in co-operation with PAP/RAC of MAP-UNEP, the preparation of a pilot project to improve the quality of the environment in the town and its coastal sea. To that end, you are kindly requested to fill in this questionnaire, which would greatly help to identify and solve the main environmental problems of the town and its coastal sea. Please, read the questionnaire carefully and respond to it frankly. Thank you.

Country of origin: _____   *Age:* _____

Occupation: _____

Duration of your stay in Hvar: _____

What is most appealing for you in Hvar (please, mark as many answers as you want):

Historical town	☐	Sea	☐
The islands of Pakleni otoci	☐	Adventures in the island	☐
Sport activities	☐	Food	☐
Beaches	☐	Parks	☐
Cultural events	☐	Landscape	☐
Other: _____		Hospitality	☐

What are your priorities with regards to the improvement of the environment in Hvar and the Islands of Pakleni otoci (please, mark the priority rank: 1 – the highest priority, 2 – medium priority, 3 – low priority, 4 – no priority):

Cleaner beaches	_____	Litter in general	_____
Cleaner coastal sea	_____	Waste collection	_____
Parks in the town	_____	Marine traffic	_____
Clean woods around the town	_____	Traffic and parking	_____
More flowers in the town	_____	Water supply	_____
Other: _____			

What sum of money (in HRK) would you agree to set aside a day for the improvement of the environment in the town and coastal area of Hvar, including the Islands of Pakleni otoci?

_____ **HRK**

ATTENTION: **Hvar eco-lottery** *is organised aiming to promote ecological ideas and activities in Hvar.* **Eco-lottery** *takes place at the* **Hvar eco-corner** *in front of the Tourist Office in the centre of the town. Results of the* **Hvar eco-lottery** *are announced every Thursday at 9:00 p.m. at the* **Hvar eco-corner**. *If you wish to participate in the* **Hvar eco-lottery**, *please, enter your name at the bottom of the questionnaire form, throw the filled-in questionnaire in one of eco-lottery boxes (at the hotel or Hvar eco-corner) and drop by the Hvar eco-corner to see, if you were lucky and won one of the typical* **Hvar eco-prizes**. *Thank you and good luck! Please, enter your name:_____*

8. Tourism and sustainable development: lessons from recent World Bank experience

Anil Markandya, Tim Taylor and Suzette Pedroso

1. INTRODUCTION

The purpose of this chapter is to look at how the World Bank has treated tourism in its development strategy and in its lending and other activities. Until recently, tourism was not a major focus of World Bank efforts, though an increased recognition of this sector as a driver for economic growth and sustainable development has led to its inclusion in a number of projects. World Bank strategies are starting to include sustainable tourism development as an objective, but progress is slow and tourism has been targeted in some Country Assistance Strategies (CAS) and Poverty Reduction Strategy Papers (PRSPs).

The chapter is structured as follows. Section 2 reviews the findings of the research on the key linkages between tourism and development and looks at the relevance of this to the World Bank and its operations. Section 3 reports on the Bank lending that has been supportive of tourism (directly or indirectly), through financial and technical assistance for infrastructure investment, management of tourism facilities and sites and general community development. Fifty-nine projects have been looked at, which cover the last five years (1997–2002). Section 4 examines those projects that have had at least some funding from GEF (Global Environment Facility) sources as well as the Bank. These are projects involving protection of global public goods, such as biodiversity, where the case for some tourism is frequently made on the grounds that such use of the resource can provide some of the much-needed financial flows essential to ensure conservation in the long run. There were 193 such projects between 1992 and 2003, covering biodiversity protection, international waters and 'multiple objectives' – that is, more than one of the global public goods whose protection comes under the mandate of the GEF. Section 5 concludes the paper.

2.   LINKAGES BETWEEN TOURISM AND SUSTAINABLE DEVELOPMENT

There are three major linkages between tourism and sustainable development: economic, social and environmental. A typology of the impacts of World Bank tourism projects and the projects' impacts on sustainable development is given in Figure 8.1. World Bank projects have focused on a number of sectors, including transport, health and cultural heritage. These sectors have impacts on, and are likewise affected by, tourism development. Figure 8.1 presents the impacts as positive (+) or negative (−) and shows the main linkages identified in the literature on this subject, where the direction

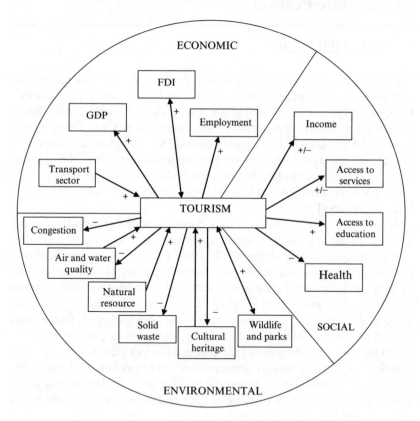

Note: + indicates positive influence (i.e. improvement), − indicates a negative influence (i.e. deterioration, exacerbation).

Figure 8.1   Linkages between World Bank projects and sustainable development

of influence is indicated by arrows. In this section, we report on the key issues in each set of linkages and some of the Bank work relating to them.

Economic

Tourism is growing in importance for many of the Bank's client countries. Between 1995 and 2000, tourism receipts, measured in US dollars, have grown at 6 per cent per annum in Africa, 7 to 14 per cent in Central and South America, 6 per cent in the Middle East and 7 per cent in South Asia. Only in East Asia and the Pacific has growth (at 2 per cent) been significantly below the world average of 3.1 per cent. Even in Eastern Europe, which was experiencing significant transition problems over this period, tourism receipts grew at 2.8 per cent per annum. A summary of tourism receipts by region is given in Table 8.1.

Tables 8.2 and 8.3 show tourism receipts as a percentage of GDP in a selection of countries. As can be seen from the tables, tourism is more important in middle-income and low-income countries as a share of GDP than it is in high-income countries (i.e. 2.25 per cent in the former against 1.33 per cent in the latter). Of course, within each group there are large variations, with some island economies deriving as much as 99 per cent of GDP directly from tourism.

The potential economic benefits and costs of increased tourism in Figure 8.1 are:

- increased foreign exchange earnings from hotels, restaurants and tourism-related groups such as guiding and the informal sector;
- increased employment, particularly for women;
- increased access to foreign direct investment;
- revenues from under-exploited natural resources and possibilities for differential taxation of tourists;
- increased GDP, both direct and as a result of the multiplier effects of tourism revenues, particularly to the informal sector. Typical figures are in the range of 2 to 3 – that is, each dollar spent by a tourist creates between 2 and 3 dollars of output in an economy with surplus resources.

The economic benefits have to be weighed, however, against the costs that may arise:

- inflationary pressures due to tourist demand;
- costs of infrastructure development;
- leakage to international investors or corporations.

Table 8.1   Tourism receipts by region

	International tourism receipts (US$ bn)			Average growth 1995–2000
	1990	1995	2000	
World	263.4	406.5	474.4	3.1
Africa	5.3	8.1	10.9	6.0
North Africa	2.3	2.7	3.7	5.9
West Africa	0.6	0.7	1.1	9.7
Central Africa	0.1	0.1	0.1	6.6
East Africa	1.1	1.9	2.6	6.0
Southern Africa	1.2	2.6	3.4	5.0
Americas	69.2	99.6	132.8	5.9
North America	54.8	77.5	101.0	5.5
Caribbean	8.7	12.2	16.8	6.7
Central America	0.7	1.6	3.1	14.2
South America	4.9	8.4	11.8	7.0
East Asia and Pacific	39.2	73.7	81.4	2.0
Northeast Asia	17.6	33.5	41.1	4.1
Southeast Asia	14.5	27.9	26.5	−1.1
Oceania	7.9	12.2	13.8	2.1
Europe	143.2	212.9	233.0	1.8
Northern Europe	24.7	32.6	34.6	1.2
Western Europe	63.2	82.0	80.7	−0.3
Central/Eastern Europe	4.8	22.7	26.1	2.8
Southern Europe	44.6	65.8	78.2	3.5
East Mediterranean Europe	5.9	9.7	13.3	6.6
Middle East	4.4	8.7	11.5	5.8
South Asia	2.0	3.5	4.9	7.2

Source: World Tourism Organization.

There is, of course, a substantial literature on the economic impacts of tourism, as can be seen in many of the other chapters in this volume. Here we focus only on work that has been done specially in the Bank, and related to the Bank projects.

In recent Bank work, Christie and Crompton (2001) reviewed the tourism potential in Africa and concluded that tourism could have a significant impact on economic growth in the continent. Presently Africa has less than 4 per cent of world tourists and less than 2 per cent of overall tourist receipts, according to the WTO (World Tourism Organization). Hence there is considerable potential for growth. The paper notes that 'if African countries can better cater to consumer preferences in originating

Table 8.2   Tourism receipts as percentage of GDP

Country/region	GDP US$ trillion (2001)	Tourism receipts US$ bn (2000)	Tourism receipts as share of GDP (%)
High income	25.3	336.4	2.25
Developing countries	6.2	139.3	1.33
Middle-income DCs	5.1	122.8	2.41

Selected developing countries			
Country	GDP US$ bn (2001)	Tourism receipts US$ mn (2000)	Tourism receipts as share of GDP (%)
Azerbaijan	5.3	63.0	1.19
Cayman Islands	1.0	447.9	44.70
Colombia	83.2	1000.0	1.20
Congo DR	4.9	6.0	0.12
Ghana	5.0	386.0	7.72
India	457.0	3200.0	0.70
Oman	19.8	120.0	0.61
Seychelles	0.6	115.3	19.36

Source: Based on World Development Indicators.

markets, tourism could have a strong impact on economic growth'. Policies to encourage tourism would include those aimed at enhancing public health and safety, air policy, human resource development, institutional capacity building and environmental protection. With such policies, they forecast growth of tourism in Africa at a rate of over 5 per cent in the decade 2000–2010, with the industry accounting for over 11 per cent of GDP by the end of the period.

Christie and Crompton (2001) also reviewed projects on tourism supported by the IFC (the private sector arm of the World Bank Group). The assessment showed that hotel-related projects yielded a real *ex post* economic rate of return of 12 per cent, which is acceptable but not as high as the private sector demands in developing countries due to the risky nature of investments and the shortage of capital. Moreover, it is important to note that the return on hotel investment derives largely from the additional direct expenditures of visitors outside the hotel complex. Table 8.4 shows typical estimates of additional expenditures based on the IFC projects.

Table 8.3 Tourism receipts as percentage of GNP, exports and per capita

Country	Percentage of GNP	Country	Percentage of exports	Country	Per capita (US$)
Maldives	99.1	Antigua and Barbuda	83.3	Antigua and Barbuda	4062
Antigua and Barbuda	83.3	St Lucia	63.4	Austria	1877
St Lucia	45.9	Maldives	57.4	Barbados	1788
Seychelles	31.0	Barbados	56.3	St Kitts and Nevis	1595
Barbados	27.4	Dominican Republic	48.6	Malta	1578
Jamaica	26.7	Seychelles	43.2	St Lucia	1333
St Vincent & Grenadines	24.9	St Vincent & Grenadines	41.5	Switzerland	1109
Belize	24.4	Belize	38.0	Denmark	728
Malta	21.8	Grenada	38.0	Spain	567
Grenada	18.1	Jamaica	37.0	Belize	540
Gambia, The	15.3	Dominica	25.8	Maldives	496
Fiji	14.8	Egypt	25.2	Iceland	496
Vanuatu	14.3	Fiji	24.3	St Vincent & Grenadines	495
Dominican Republic	13.9	Gambia, The	24.0	Ireland	463

Source: IFC/World Bank/MIGA (2000).

230

Table 8.4   Outside-hotel expenditure in selected countries

Country	Other expenditure as % of in-hotel expenditure
Barbados	82
Cyprus	100–130
Jamaica	61
Kenya – city	50
Kenya – safari	113–188
Tunisia	57

Source: IFC.

These additional expenditures give rise to multiplier effects, which are realized if the region in question has surplus economic resources. Typically this is the case, but it is not always so. Hence in calculating the multiplier effects, caution is needed to make sure that the additional expenditure is not simply shifting resources from one use to another. However, Christie and Crompton (2001) suggest that the multiplier effects of tourism spending on total output and on employment are significant. Tourism has significant impacts on a number of industries, notably transport, food, construction, handicrafts and financial services. It also offers opportunities for SME (small to medium enterprise) involvement.

In terms of employment, the average number of employees per hotel room in developing countries is estimated at two, depending on the type of hotel and the local skill base. These jobs are generally considered 'good jobs' as they have good working conditions (compared to other industries) and relatively good pay.

A major factor that determines the scale of local benefits from tourism projects is 'leakage', which can be defined as the proportion of monies invested or earned in the tourism sector that end up overseas. The level of 'leakage' of tourism investment and earnings is an issue that has been given some attention in Bank work and in the wider literature on the linkage between tourism and sustainable development. Christie and Crompton (2001) identify a number of causes of leakage in their review of tourism in Africa, including:

- types of tourism facilities developed and costs of marketing and promotion;
- demand patterns and volumes of tourists;
- extent of local ownership, management and employment in the accommodation and services sector;
- availability of free transfer of profits;

- import restrictions and duties on imports;
- prior existence of infrastructure, particularly capital intensive (e.g. airports) or technology intensive (telecoms);
- level of development of industries and sectors linked to tourism that can supply materials needed at construction stage and for operation of facilities.

A number of studies have calculated the leakage rates of tourist expenditure, and a recent IFC study found that leakage is quite significant for some countries. For underdeveloped countries, particularly islands, the leakage rate is 55 per cent (i.e. only 45 per cent of foreign exchange earnings from tourism remain in the country), while for other countries, including Mexico, Thailand, Turkey and the Dominican Republic, the leakage rate is less than 15 per cent.

Social

The main social impacts of tourism are divided into those affecting poverty and those affecting gender.

Poverty
Tourism may have a number of impacts on poverty, depending on the type of tourism and the underlying conditions in the area affected. Increased tourism may have positive impacts on poverty reduction through the following pathways:

- increased employment, with consequential increase in incomes;
- positive environmental changes;
- increased access to services such as water supply and sanitation as an ancillary benefit of tourism development projects;
- increased access to education.

Negative impacts on poverty may include:

- impact of price changes on real incomes;
- reduced access to water and energy due to tourist demand;
- negative environmental impacts, including reduced access to conservation areas;
- impacts on health.

Some of the Bank's work in support of National Poverty Reduction Strategies (PRSPs) has identified the importance of tourism as a source of positive as well as potentially negative environment/poverty linkages, for the same reasons as given above (World Bank, 2002a, 2003). In practice, PRSPs mention the possible role of tourism in providing additional income, which makes a case for some conservation expenditures on that basis. However, the extent to which the benefits are quantified is small, and detailed assessment of the impacts of such programmes on the poor is rare (see sections 3 and 4). The World Bank *Sourcebook on Poverty Reduction Strategies* (World Bank, 2002b) does not include tourism policies. Furthermore, tourism has not been identified as a major source of poverty reduction through environmental management. It is interesting, for example, that a major report that links poverty and environmental management and was prepared by the World Bank, DFID, the EC and UNDP for the World Summit on Sustainable Development (DFID, 2002) does not include tourism as a policy option for reducing poverty and improving the environment. Possibly this reflects some misgivings about the linkages between these two objectives, but it probably also reflects the fact that the links are complex and need to be examined in detail at the micro level before designing a project or programme relating to tourism.

Studies outside the Bank (e.g. IIED, 2001) have also looked at the impacts of tourism on poverty, and their work points to the following measures as important in ensuring that tourism projects are pro-poor:

- Include local communities in planning and decision making when tourist facilities are being developed – i.e. carry out proper strategic assessments of the proposed developments.
- Ensure a high level of local inputs in service provision to tourists and minimize leakage, subject to maintaining the required level of services for the tourists.
- Ensure that an alternative livelihood is provided where tourism is based on reduced access to local common resources (e.g. parks) for the local population. Often the argument is made that the tourist facility will provide alternative employment, but this rarely makes up for the losses for all individuals.

Gender
The impact of tourism development on women was highlighted by Hemmati (1999), who analyses employment patterns across countries and finds that the tourism sector is a particularly important employer of women, with the percentage of women working in this sector normally higher than that in other economic sectors. However, jobs occupied by women follow the 'gender pyramid' found in other sectors – women tend to be in occupations with low career development prospects and managerial

positions are male-dominated. This study suggests that gender and tourism issues should not be separated from mainstream policy making.

Environment

Much work has focused on the environmental impacts of tourism. In a recent study for the World Bank, Dixon et al. (2001) reviewed the impacts on the environment of tourism in the Caribbean, identifying direct and indirect impacts and the threats to specific resources. Tourism is a particular threat to environmental quality owing to its location and timing. The location is often in environmentally sensitive areas, and the loading of wastewater becomes problematic during significant peak periods, especially in developing countries. It is important to note that poorly managed tourism development may not only have a detrimental impact on the environment, but also on economic and social conditions.

The linkages between tourism and environmental damage have been reviewed in a number of publications (see Davies and Cahill, 2000 for the US case). The main linkages include:

- congestion – impacts of tourist numbers on both enjoyment of tourism destination and on environmental quality, with services such as wastewater being potentially overloaded in peak season;
- increased pollution loads in both water and air;
- use of resources – particularly freshwater and energy resources;
- solid waste generation;
- degradation of cultural heritage;
- ecological impacts;
- impacts of induced settlement; and
- positive impacts as a means of generating revenues to preserve the environment.

For a more detailed review of these linkages see Taylor et al. (2003).

3.   RECENT BANK WORK ON TOURISM AND SUSTAINABLE DEVELOPMENT

In this section we review all IBRD and IDA lending operations at the World Bank, excluding those in which there was a GEF component.[1] The latter are assessed separately in section 4. The procedure involved going through all projects and selecting those in which the appraisal, supervision and completion documents included 'tourism' or related words. Documents examined for this chapter included Project Appraisal Documents, Implementation Completion Reports and Project Information Documents. The period covered was 1997–2002. During this period, new Bank lending amounted to $129 billion, covering 1555 projects. Of these, projects with some tourism component added up to 59 in the non-GEF category, amounting to $2.7 billion, and 40 in the GEF category, amounting to $1.4 billion. In total, therefore, projects with some tourism component accounted for $4.1 billion, or 3 per cent of total lending.

IBRD/IDA Grants and Loans and Impact on Tourism

Tourism may play a number of roles in terms of World Bank projects and programmes. These can be broadly summarized in three main categories:

- Type I – projects where tourism is central to the project both in terms of investments and outcomes
- Type II – projects where tourism is not the main focus of the investment but where tourism outcomes are significant
- Type III – projects where tourism is seen to be a minor ancillary benefit of the project

Table 8.5 presents a summary of the projects reviewed by type of project and by region. The table shows how the projects are unevenly spread across the regions, with many more awarded in Africa and Latin America/ Caribbean. This may be due to the pattern of the Bank's lending in general. Type III programmes (with tourism as an indirect outcome of the programme) accounted for 46 per cent of those monitored. The Africa and East Asia regions both had more Type II than Type I, whereas the LAC, MENA and ECA had more Type I than Type II. A number of reasons can be given for this, but it is likely to be due to regional characteristics; for

Table 8.5 Summary table: types of project

Regions	Type I	Type II	Type III	Total
Africa	3	5	10	18
East Asia	0	3	4	7
ECA	3	2	2	7
LAC	5	3	8	16
MENA	6	2	2	10
SAS	0	0	1	1
Total	17	15	27	59

example, regions with a more highly developed tourist base may be awarded more Type II than Type I programmes. This would be because tourism is an established part of national income/development and so can be part of a wider scheme, whereas in places with a less developed tourist industry, a specific programme aimed at tourism is likely to be given more importance.

The Bank has, on the whole, avoided Type I projects, with the main financer of direct tourist infrastructure being the IFC. However, the recognition of the importance of tourism as a driver for economic development has led to some projects that fund direct tourism actions, where these projects are generally infrastructure- or biodiversity-related. Such projects include the Abu Soma Development Project in Egypt, which provided for direct expenditure in the tourism sector.

Type II projects include major infrastructure development projects and some biodiversity actions which, whilst not funding investment directly in the tourist sector, are expected to yield significant tourism benefits to the recipient of the loan. These may be the major driving force behind the investment programme. Examples of Type II projects include the Hubei Xiaogan–Xiangfan Highway Project, where transport is the major sector receiving investment but expected tourism benefits in terms of increasing access to sites are the main economic benefits anticipated from the project.

Type III projects are those where some small economic benefit can be expected from the project, but where tourism is not the major beneficiary from the investment. Such projects include the HIV/AIDS project in Cameroon, and various roads/transportation projects (e.g. projects in China, India, Madagascar, Mexico).

Key Findings

The review of the above projects has produced the following key findings:

1. In terms of infrastructure, transport is a key sector in the facilitation of the development of tourism, as shown in a number of projects, including those in China and in Belize. Access to sites of particular historical, natural or cultural interest clearly has a significant influence on the development of tourism in an area. Air transport is a particular issue in the development of tourism in some developing countries, with access being restricted by expensive air flights or a lack of infrastructure. Restrictions on visas may also prove to be a barrier to travel to some countries, and this barrier was successfully addressed in the recent project in Madagascar.
2. Cultural heritage and tourism clearly have significant interlinkages, and this may increase in the future since the interest in ethno-tourism

is growing. A number of projects have provided support in the form of better management of sites, including protection against damage, provision of supporting infrastructure, and marketing and promotion. The review indicates that these have been successful in most cases. It should be noted also that tourism can harm cultural heritage if steps are not taken to mitigate the negative impacts of tourism on historical sites and potentially on the homogenization of culture, particularly in areas where indigenous populations interact with large numbers of tourists. Steps have been taken to prevent such negative impacts in the reviewed Bank projects, and social impact assessments ensure that such impacts on the cultural integrity of a tourist destination are mitigated.

3. In terms of health, one ongoing Bank project for HIV/AIDS in Cameroon addresses the tourism sector as a priority sector. Tourism can facilitate the spread of diseases, including STDs and HIV/AIDS, and the HIV/AIDS project attempts to mitigate the negative impact of increased tourism on health. The recent SARS epidemic also highlights the impact that health can have on tourism.

4. Very few of the projects investigated have quantified the impacts on tourism to any significant degree. Of the 59 projects investigated, only eight presented any real quantified estimates of the impacts of these projects on tourism. The nature of the eight projects is interesting, in that they are – as one would expect – Type I (five of the eight) and Type II (three of the eight) projects. However, it is noticeable that these do not represent the majority of Type I and II projects, which means that there is need for further work at the Bank on the expected economic, environmental and social benefits and costs of tourism-related projects, particularly where these are a major focus of the project.

5. The quantitative data for the eight projects that is available is given in Table 8.6. The following key findings are noted.

    (a)   The most complete assessment of tourism impacts was carried out for the Abu Soma tourism development project in Egypt, where the full set of economic, environmental and social impacts was quantified. The project showed the benefits that can result from investment in tourism-related infrastructure. These are not especially high in economic terms (a rate of return of 10.3 per cent is not spectacular, but in line with other Bank investments in tourism-related infrastructure – see Christie and Crompton, 2001). However, the indirect benefits, such as creation of jobs in the region, are not measured in the rate of return but are important and need to be taken into account.

Table 8.6 Non-GEF Bank projects with quantitative information on tourism

Project	Loan $ mn	Main components	Impacts		
			Economic	Environmental	Social
Abu Soma tourism development project, Egypt. Project Type I	62.5	Tourism policy development Financial support for infrastructure in major tourist areas Environmental management of Red Sea	Arrivals increased by 20 000 p.a. FE earnings increased by $1.7 p.a. Private sector investment in tourism increased by $352 mn Economic rate of return *ex post* estimated at 10.3%	EIA carried out and negative impacts mitigated	Primary jobs in tourism increased by 20 000 Total jobs created: approximately 44 000
Belize City infrastructure project. Project Type II	20.0	Transport improvement, flood control and wastewater treatment Tourism benefits arise from increased day visits and stopovers as a consequence of improved transit and environment	Annual benefits from tourism estimated at: $1.5 mn in years 2–3, $3 mn in years 4–5, $5 mn in year 6 of project and $7.1 mn after year 7. ERR was 33.1% *ex ante*	Decrease in air and water pollution, flood protection Reduction of water-borne diseases by 80%	Improvements of infrastructure, water and electricity These are expected to provide benefits to all sections

Wastewater disposal in tourism centres in Dominican Republic. Project Type II	5.0	Provide sewerage services to one region to mitigate negative impact of tourism and to improve bathing water quality	NVP of $4.3 mn at 12% discount rate. Benefits estimated using WTP for improved coastal water quality	Improvement in coastal water quality achieved	Job creation noted but not quantified
Community development and culture project, FRY Macedonia. Project Type I	5.0	Established cultural centres in pilot sites. Only about $0.5 mn was for tourism	2% annual growth in visitors. Economic benefit estimated at $1.3 mn. *Ex ante* IRR = 18%	EA carried out and mitigation plan implemented	
Sustainable coastal tourism, Honduras. Project Type I	5.0	Management of tourism along north coast by strengthening local capacity to manage. TA to include HIV/AIDS prevention Restoration of cultural site at historic centre of Turjilo Small business training to develop business opportunities (handicrafts, tour operations etc.)	Increase in growth of tourism from 4% up to 8% p.a. Increased revenue from marine and coastal parks Increased revenue from taxes paid by tourists. Increased incomes generated by tourist spending Annual benefits range from $2.7 mn to $38.4 mn depending on assumptions related to increase in tourism	EA carried out Piloted innovative ways to enhance capacity for EA of tourism-related impacts	Social assessment conducted and design reflects findings Small employment gain estimated

Table 8.6 (continued)

Project	Loan $ mn	Main components	Impacts		
			Economic	Environmental	Social
Cultural Heritage and Tourism Development Project, Lebanon. Project Type I	31.50	Investment in a number of historic sites, including Tyre and Tripoli, to protect and manage them	Anticipated increase in number of visitors between 6% and 17% depending on site Anticipated revenues per visitor to rise by between 37% and 65%	EA conducted and management plan designed	Improved quality of life from urban upgrading for all Cultural areas are presently areas of neglect and project will uplift them
Structural Adjustment Project, Madagascar. Project Type II	60.8*	Simplify procedures for tourist visas. Privatization of airline to facilitate cheaper flights	No. of visitors and FE earnings both went up, up 69% from 1997 to 2001 but amount due to project not clear		Social development was a key objective of loan
Cultural Heritage Project, Tunisia. Project Type I	17.0	Assist government to develop its cultural heritage and increase revenues by marketing, site development etc.	IRRs esitmated at between 17% and 70% *ex ante*	EA conducted and design reflects findings	Social assessment undertaken and project design reflects need to conserve tradition and local culture

Notes: * Wide package of reforms; most funds are not for tourism-related expenditures.

(b) The relatively small projects (around $5 million or even less), which invest in providing technical assistance and improving facilities or establishing small businesses to supply tourism services, can have significant, greater benefits than the larger projects such as the one in Egypt. The projects in the Dominican Republic, Macedonia and Honduras are all examples of these small projects.

(c) Projects that support worthwhile and important cultural sites can have a very high return. Although not fully quantified, the data available indicate that the returns can be impressive.

(d) Quantification is not easy and some of the numbers provided have to be taken with a grain of salt. The basis for the estimation is often no more than guesswork, and the error bounds on the estimates are large, although this is not always acknowledged. In the one case where it is acknowledged (e.g. the sustainable coastal tourism project in Honduras), we see quite how wide the range of benefits can be. This underscores the need for more effort in improving the estimation of benefits. Only two or three projects have used state-of-the-art tools for the valuation of tourism benefits.

4. PROJECTS WITH A GEF COMPONENT

The projects considered for this section concentrate on the environmental and natural resources management theme. Also, these projects are at least partly supported by the Global Environment Facility (GEF) as facilitator and funding mechanism for integrating global concerns into the development process, and by the World Bank as the implementing agency for the GEF. From the fiscal years 1992 to 2003, on average, the Bank approved 15 projects and provided GEF grants worth $138 million annually. Some of the funds served as complements to Bank lending and other co-financing resources, mainly in the areas of conservation and sustainable use of biodiversity and the promotion of energy efficiency and renewable energy development.

All information about the projects was obtained from the World Bank–GEF projects database (http://www-esd.worldbank.org/gef/fullProjects.cfm), which provides the following:

● country and region
● project name
● focal area (e.g. biodiversity)
● operational programme (e.g. coastal, marine, and freshwater ecosystems)

- Amount of grants from GEF, IDA and IBRD (in US$ mn)
- World Bank documents and reports (e.g. Project Appraisal Document).

The total number of projects evaluated is 193, and the areas considered are biodiversity, international waters and multi-focal areas. Figure 8.2 shows the project portfolio as represented by each focal area. The majority of the projects are centred on biodiversity (80 per cent), followed by international waters (12 per cent) and multi-focal (8 per cent).

Figure 8.3 shows each region's share of projects, which are classified by focal area. Most of the projects on biodiversity, international waters and multi-focal areas were implemented in the Latin America and Caribbean Region (LCR), Europe and Central Asia (ECA) and Africa (AFR), respectively.

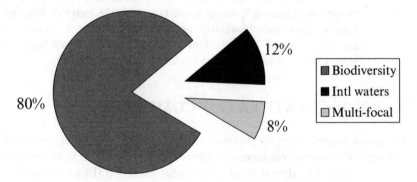

Figure 8.2   Percentage shares of focal areas in the evaluated WB–GEF project portfolio

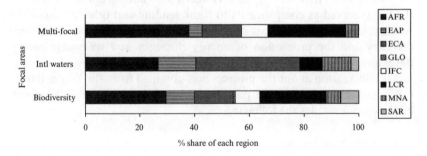

Note: GLO: Global; MNA: Middle East and North Africa; SAR: South Asia.

Figure 8.3   Regions' percentage share of World Bank–GEF projects by focal area

Table 8.7   Treatment of tourism by focal area (no. of projects)

Treatment of tourism	Not mentioned	Mentioned briefly	Highlighted	Highlighted and quantified	No information available	Total
Biodiversity	22	20	40	8	45	135
International waters	11	14	6	0	6	37
Multi-focal	8	4	2	0	7	21
Total	41	38	48	8	58	193

Source: World Bank–GEF database.

The available World Bank documents and reports for each of the 193 projects were examined to determine whether a project has included tourism or eco-tourism as one of its components. Table 8.7 shows the treatment of tourism in the projects, which is classified as:

● not mentioned – when there is no reference to the tourism potential;
● mentioned briefly – when tourism potential is mentioned in passing;
● highlighted – when the key role of tourism is emphasized in the project;
● highlighted and quantified – when tourism is emphasized as a project component and when (expected) benefits from tourism are quantified;
● no information available – in cases where there are no available documents/ reports.

Most of the projects for international waters somehow mention tourism, while most of the multi-focal projects did not mention the tourism's potential. Based on the available documents on biodiversity-related projects, the majority of the projects highlighted the opportunities for tourism. Only the biodiversity theme has projects where benefits from tourism were calculated (e.g. expected revenues from entrance fees to protected areas). However, the percentage of these projects is significantly small relative to those biodiversity projects that fall in the other classifications, and even more so relative to the total number of projects. Out of the 193 projects evaluated, a total of 94 projects have mentioned tourism (though emphasis on the activity differed) and of the 94, only eight projects have quantified the tourism benefits. The subsequent subsections will provide some details about these eight projects.

An Overview of the Eight World Bank–GEF Projects

A more in-depth examination was made of the eight World Bank–GEF projects, which have both highlighted and quantified the benefits of tourism. In particular, the following aspects were evaluated: (a) how the benefits from tourism were measured; and (b) how these benefits were taken into account in the calculation of the project's overall benefits. Table 8.8 summarizes the results, from which the following are the key findings:

1. In a number of cases quantitative information on tourism is included but it is only background information (to emphasize the need for biodiversity conservation efforts) and is not directly relevant to the evaluation of the project. This is the case, for example, for the eco-tourism industry in Costa Rica and the tourism values of coral reefs in Indonesia.
2. Developing nature-based tourism is highlighted as a significant component of the projects in Burkina Faso, Honduras, Peru, South Africa and Uganda. Revenues from tourism were calculated for Honduras and Uganda but not for the other countries. Furthermore, the data were not presented as a separate entry in the calculation of benefits from the project and the basis of the estimates was not always made clear.
3. Costa Rica's Biodiversity Resources Development Project compared the benefits and costs of two scenarios: 'without the project' and 'with the project'. The revenues from tourism were included in the calculation and showed that in terms of revenue it would play an important part (about half of all additional revenues). However, the total increase in income from the project is modest, and the justification for the investment has to be in terms of other benefits that do not generate income flows. Another shortcoming of the benefit–cost analysis made in the project is that only non-discounted annual figures were provided.

5. SUMMARY AND CONCLUSIONS

This study has examined the role of tourism in the World Bank development strategy and has looked at its lending activities in an attempt to estimate the impacts on sustainable development of Bank actions. In terms of development strategy, tourism has not played an important role in the recent past, although there are some signs that it is now seen as more important, especially in the context of the sustainable use of natural resources and the growing importance of the sector as a share of GDP, source of foreign exchange etc. Of the 1500 or so new projects in the Bank

Table 8.8 *World Bank–GEF projects with quantitative information on tourism*

Project	Description	Link to tourism	Quantification
Costa Rica eco-markets	The project focuses on initiating efforts to increase forest conservation by providing market-based incentives to forest owners in the buffer zones and other areas connected to the natural parks and reserves, and by strengthening the institutional capacity of the stakeholders	There is no explicit linkage made between forest conservation and tourism in the documents; however, tourism can benefit from the project's activities since this industry is primarily nature-based	Quantitative information provided in documents on the importance of tourism to Costa Rica but not directly relevant to the project
Second Coral Reef Rehabilitation and Management Program Project – Indonesia	Arrest degradation of coral reefs in the country	Annual tourism value of coral reefs has been estimated at US$3000/km^2 for low-potential areas and US$500 000/km^2 for high-potential areas	The project emphasizes establishing sustainable coastal management by the community. Tourism benefits are mentioned only to support the awareness and institutional capacity of the concerned coastal communities in managing their resource. Tourism or eco-tourism is not a component of any of the project's activities
Partnership for Natural Ecosystem Management Project	PAGEN seeks to implement the National Natural Ecosystem Management Program by addressing biodiversity conservation in the protected	Tourism is identified as a source of revenue for the management of conservation areas	In 1999, $300 000, or 0.07% of national fiscal base came from tourism fees. Tourism is highlighted as an additional source of revenue but the additional amount is not

Table 8.8 (continued)

Project	Description	Link to tourism	Quantification
(PAGEN) – Burkina Faso	areas through: strengthening the capacity of the Forestry Dept. staff, concessionaires and private operators; studies/workshops to support sector reforms, economic and financial analysis of protected areas; and financial, advisory and technical support		quantified for the duration of the project
Biodiversity in Priority Areas Project – Honduras	Aims to contribute to bio-diversity conservation in core areas, and its more sustainable use in the buffer zones of the Mesoamerican Biological Corridor, through capacity building of parks management. It also fosters the development of local communities, as well as the use of the National System of Protected Areas as a destination for eco-tourists who are expected to generate significant benefits for the Honduran economy over the medium to long term	Nature-based tourism is promoted by strengthening the local capacity to manage the protected areas and by venturing on eco-tourism marketing (i.e. radio advertising)	Project provides financial projections of revenues from entrance fees, based on assumptions of growth in visitor numbers and increase in fee rates. Reason why numbers will increase as much as indicated and whether they will be willing to pay the increased fees is not provided. If correct, however, the increases would provide a major justification for the initial investment of $20 mn

Project	Objectives	Tourism component	Notes
Participatory Management of Protected Areas Project – Peru	The project's objectives are: (a) to ensure biodiversity conservation by strengthening the capacity and involvement of the communities and the private sector to sustainably manage the protected areas and (b) to obtain sustainability for the financing of recurrent costs. It has three components: (1) participatory protected area management; (2) institutional development; and (3) project area financing, administration, monitoring and evaluation, and information dissemination	A subcomponent of participatory protected area management is the development of sustainable economic activities, one of which is wildlife management for tourism development and use of tourism services (e.g. research, educational awareness)	Presently 9% of protected area expenditures are covered by fees but the project estimates a deficit of \$2.95 mn annually. Although one of the activities identified for the project is to develop tourism, the recommendations did not include measures to exploit tourism's potential as a revenue generator
The Greater Addo Elephant National Park Project – South Africa (AENP)	Because AENP is threatened by ecosystem degradation and loss of natural resources, the aim of the project is to increase the area under conservation within the current AENP into the Greater AENP (including terrestrial and marine ecosystems)	One major component of the project is economic development, where the sub-components focus on eco-tourism: i.e. (a) marketing and product development, and (b) concessions and partnership, where the private sector will be encouraged to invest in eco-tourism facilities	The project documents do not specify the share of tourism revenues from the national fiscal returns. Also, there is no estimate of potential benefits from tourism that will arise from the project (i.e. *ex post* quantified benefits)
Bwindi Impenetrable National Park	Project will support a long-term conservation of the biodiversity of both BINP and MGNP	Tourism is one the sources of revenue from the parks, which will help in the sustainable	A gorilla tourism plan was prepared and projected earnings of US$321 000 to US$1 348 000 p.a.

Table 8.8 (continued)

Project	Description	Link to tourism	Quantification
(BINP) and Mgahinga Gorilla National Park Conservation (MGNP) – Uganda	directly and indirectly. The direct support is from incremental grant funds for park management and related research activities. Local communities dependent on the parks' forest resources would have limited access when both parks are established. The indirect support is from grants to help local community groups develop economic activities that will make available alternative means of livelihood; for example, beekeeping, agro-forestry and eco-tourism	management	from tracking fees in 1996. However, the MGNP did not open that year because of security considerations but is expected to benefit to yield similar revenues in the future. Financial flows were projected from 1995 to 2024, but did not include eco-tourism. Nonetheless, it can be noted that the estimated annual earnings from the gorilla tracking fees alone, which is US$834 500 on average, is about 67 % higher than the annual total expenditures from other sources
Biodiversity Resources Development Project – Costa Rica	Undertake biodiversity inventory-related activities in the Conservation Areas and strengthen the institutional capacity at the National Biodiversity Institute (INBio)	Tourism is one source of revenue for the Conservation Areas	Income from tourism is expected to go up by $70000 p.a. but the basis of the estimate is not provided. Tourism revenue is about half of the increase in income resulting from the project amounting to $1.1 mn. Estimates provided are only for one year

in the last five years, about 6 per cent in terms of number and 3 per cent in terms of value had some tourism dimension.

The Bank can and has supported tourism in a number of ways. In terms of lending there are direct Bank operations that have invested in infrastructure where a key benefit is the facilitation of tourism development. There are others that have tried to mitigate the negative impacts of tourism – e.g. the spread of diseases such as HIV/AIDS. In terms of strategic and policy advice, it has provided support for developments in the sector that are environmentally and socially sustainable and that help reduce poverty – the main mission of the Bank's development strategy. The chapter has looked at how future projects and programmes can be designed with these objectives in mind. One important observation is how small a role tourism has been given so far in the poverty reduction strategies that the Bank has been espousing. Much more can be done in this regard.

In looking at the actual operations of the Bank, the assessment was divided into two: projects that focus on economic development through infrastructure provision; and projects that address the problem of global public goods such as international waters and biodiversity. In the first group, of the 1500 or so projects that were appraised between 1997 and 2002, about 56 mentioned tourism as an issue of some importance and of these 32 had tourism as a central or significant feature. Only eight of these 32, however, provided any real quantification of the benefits of tourism, which points to the fact that analysis of the impacts of this sector needs to be strengthened. A careful look at these eight has revealed that infrastructure investment can provide benefits from tourism, with the larger projects yielding internal rates of return of around 10–12 per cent. Smaller projects, however, investing in improving facilities and providing technical assistance, have yielded higher returns. Cultural site development and promotion have also yielded large benefits. In terms of environmental impacts the projects have generally followed good practice, and ensured that negative environmental impacts are avoided or, if inevitable, mitigated. Social impacts, however, have been studied in less detail.

The GEF-related projects show that a majority of the biodiversity-related projects mention eco-tourism as an important source of revenue for the protection and sustainable management of the facility, but of the 94 projects that do state this, only eight carry out any kind of detailed quantitative analysis of the income to be derived from eco-tourism. These studies reveal that the role of such tourism can be important in the sustainable management of the resource, but it is not always the key or most important source of revenue. Additional income from other sources is often needed.

Given the combination of a stated importance of eco-tourism and a limited quantification of its impacts, there is danger that too much will be expected from this source. This needs to be avoided by careful assessment of what can be achieved.[2] Everyone thinks their sites are special but fails to take account of the fact that this sector is one of intense competition and limits to market growth need to be considered. The impact of increased incomes on demand for environmental quality in terms of tourist destination also needs to be considered.

In addition to the above, there was inadequate consideration of mechanisms to remove barriers to tourism development in some projects reviewed. A number of constraints have been identified in Bank work, including the following:

(i)   poor and expensive transportation;
(ii) difficult operating environment for tourist industry;
(iii) weak promotional activity;
(iv) difficulties of preserving cultural heritage.

Of these, point (iv) has gained most attention in the projects surveyed as part of this study. Cultural heritage has been given a high level of importance, owing to the intergenerational issues involved in its preservation, and because of international actions including the UNESCO World Heritage sites initiative. Issues of transportation have gained some attention, particularly in terms of road transport in areas with tourism (e.g. the Hubei Xiaogan–Xiangfan Highway Project in China). However, issues of air transportation have largely been overlooked and such issues are important for the development of an economically viable tourism sector. The difficult operating environment for tourism and the lack of promotional activity has hardly been covered in Bank projects to date, though some efforts have been made in terms of national park promotion as part of GEF projects. These issues are important, as they are precursors to the development of a tourism industry and if neglected may pose significant problems for the long-term sustainability of tourism as a driver for economic growth.

NOTES

1. The coverage did not include IFC projects, which were not accessible through the same database. IFC is the private sector arm of the Bank group. IBRD is the part of the Bank that makes standard bank loans and IDA is the part that makes concessional loans to low-income countries.
2. It is important to be realistic. One project (subsequently dropped) estimated a sustained growth of 20 per cent per annum over 15 years, which was clearly infeasible. If unrealistic expectations of the gains from eco-tourism are presented to the communities involved, this may harm the longer-term sustainability of project gains and also the longer-term economic development of the community.

REFERENCES

Christie, I. and D. Crompton (2001), 'Tourism in Africa', Africa Working Paper Series Number 12, Washington, DC: World Bank.

Davies, T. and S. Cahill (2000), 'Environmental Implications of the Tourist Industry', Discussion Paper 00–14. Resources for the Future. Available online at http:// www.rff.org/CFDOCS/disc_papers/PDF_files/0014.pdf

DFID (2002), *Linking Poverty Reduction and Environmental Management: Policy Challenges and Opportunities*, London: DFID.

Dixon, J. et al. (2001), *Tourism and the Environment in the Caribbean: An Economic Framework*, Washington, DC: World Bank.

Hemmati, M. (ed.) (1999), *Gender and Tourism: Women's Employment and Participation in Tourism. Summary of UNED UK's Project Report*, UNED forum.

IFC/World Bank/MIGA (2000), *Tourism and Global Development*, Washington, DC: World Bank.

IIED (2001), 'Pro-poor Tourism: Harnessing the World's Largest Industry for the World's Poor', paper prepared for World Summit on Sustainable Development, May.

Taylor, T., M. Fredotovic, D. Povh and A. Markandya (2003), 'Sustainable Tourism and Economic Instruments: The Case of Hvar, Croatia', Working Paper, Centre for Public Economics, University of Bath.

World Bank (2000), *Environment Matters: An Annual Review of the Bank's Environmental Work*, Washington, DC: World Bank.

World Bank (2002a), *Financing for Sustainability: Generating Public Sector Resources: A Framework for Public Sector Financing of Environmentally Sustainable Development in Developing Countries*, Washington, DC: World Bank.

World Bank (2002b), *A Sourcebook for Poverty Reduction Strategies*, 2 vols, Washington, DC: World Bank.

World Bank (2003), *Poverty Reduction Strategies and Environmental Sustainability: An Assessment of the Alignment with Millennium Development Goal No.7*, Washington, DC: World Bank.

World Bank–GEF Projects Database (undated), accessed at http://www-esd.worldbank.org/gef/fullProjects.cfm

9. Using data envelopment analysis to evaluate environmentally conscious tourism management[1]

Valentina Bosetti, Mariaester Cassinelli and Alessandro Lanza

INTRODUCTION

Decisions taken within the framework of tourism management may have important impacts on the environment that may have in turn feedback effects on the tourism responses. More generally, tourism management practices that are environmentally focused may be reactive, e.g. responding to environmental regulations, or proactive, e.g. effective in order to be competitive with other tourist locations and to satisfy consumers' preferences.

To develop tools which support policy evaluation and decision making processes may be of critical importance in order to account for all the different and often correlated features of the local management of the tourism industry.

In order to give guidelines, to correct inefficient management directions and to promote the positive effect of competition between municipalities, the use of performance indicators will prove fundamental. Thus, finding a way to produce simple indicators summarizing different elements which characterize management strategies is crucial to the formation of policy mechanisms. Indeed, as Hart emphasizes, an indicator is 'something that helps you to understand where you are, which way you are going and how far you are from where you want to be' (Hart, 1997, p. 67).

However, although indicators have a growing resonance in politics, it is often easier to formulate them in theory rather than in practice. In addition to difficulties commonly encountered in selecting good indicators, there might be some additional problems specific to the tourism sector. Indeed, data on tourist areas are often incomplete and, in particular, in relation to measures of the tourism impact on the original ecosystem, for it is frequently impossible to disentangle the portion of the impact due to the indigenous population from the one directly deriving from the presence of tourism masses (Cammarota et al., 2001; Miller, 2001).

The focus of this chapter is the valuation of the efficiency of the management of tourist municipalities located on the coasts of Italy. The analysed data set is composed of 194 municipalities. For each of them, the analysis takes into consideration a set of factors (inputs and outputs) that are considered relevant when valuing the performance of a management strategy, as regards both economic and environmental factors.

One major problem in measuring the efficiency of public organizations whose policies have market as well as non-market effects is that traditional economic measures, such as benefit–cost ratio or net present value, are difficult to apply. Moreover, measurements are often incommensurable; therefore assigning weights to different factors becomes crucial. In this chapter, in order to overcome these difficulties, data envelopment analysis (DEA) is applied. Indeed, DEA is a methodology that has been developed and successfully applied in order to deal with multiple and non-commensurable input and output problems.

The chapter is organized as follows. Section 1 provides the background of the decision environment, specifically dealing with the issue of the importance of managing tourism in a sustainable way and the use of DEA. In section 2 a brief description of DEA methodology is given, while in section 3 the data set, the developed model and the performed analysis are described. Section 4 is a description of the main results and section 5 concludes with a summary of the main findings, along with final remarks and future extensions.

1. THE DECISION ENVIRONMENT

The tourism industry is a sector of fundamental importance for the Italian economy (6.7 per cent of GDP in 1997) and its relevance is undoubtedly growing considering that the tourism flow has increased by 18.6 per cent during the period 1990–97.[2] Further, 33.8 per cent of tourists visit the coastal areas of Italy, with a resulting intense pressure on local ecosystems. As in more general cases, the Italian tourism industry has two main effects on the sustainable management of environmental resources, which work in opposite directions:

1. Negative impacts due to anthropization of natural areas, increased pollution of air (mainly due to increased traffic) and of water, abnormal production of waste, and increased burning of forests.
2. Positive impacts due to the increased demand for high environmental

standards, which is becoming essential in order for a tourist area to be competitive with other locations.

Hence the necessity to assess the performance of the tourism management of Italian municipalities not only in respect of economic considerations but also under the environmental sustainability paradigm. In particular, the assessment procedure proposed would be even more useful if it allowed us not only to estimate how efficient is the *status quo*, but also how potential improvements could be made.

Relevant insights can be derived by applying data envelopment analysis, which is an approach first proposed in Charnes et al. (1979) in order to measure the relative efficiency of generally defined decision making units transforming multiple inputs into multiple outputs. DEA has been applied to evaluate the relative performance not only of public organizations, such as the study on medical services in Nyman and Bricker (1989) and that on educational institutions in Charnes et al. (1981), but also of private organizations such as banks, see for example Charnes et al. (1990). A thorough review of DEA theory and applications can be found in Charnes et al. (1993). In 1986 DEA was first applied to the hospitality industry (see Banker and Morey, 1986), specifically to the restaurant section. Corporate travel management has been analysed in Bell and Morey (1995), while the hotel sector has been analysed in several works; see for example Morey and Dittman (1997) and Anderson et al. (2000). However, the relative performance of municipalities' tourism management has not been analysed to date.

2. METHODOLOGY

DEA is a multivariate technique for monitoring productivity and providing some insights into possible ways to improve the *status quo*, when inefficient. In particular, DEA is a non-parametric technique; that is, it can compare input/output data making no prior assumptions about the probability distribution under study. The origin of non-parametric programming methodology, in respect of relative efficiency measurement, lies in the work of Charnes (Charnes et al., 1978, 1979, 1981). Although DEA is based on the concept of efficiency that is near to the idea of a classical production function, the latter is typically determined by a specific equation, while DEA is generated from the data set of observed operative units (Decision Making Units or DMUs). The DEA efficiency score of any DMU is derived from the comparison with the other DMUs that are included in the analysis, considering the maximum score of unity (or 100 per cent) as a benchmark. The score is independent of the units in which outputs and inputs are measured, and this allows for greater flexibility in the choice of inputs and outputs to be included in the study.

An important assumption of DEA is that all DMUs face the same unspecified technology and operational characteristics, which defines the set of their production possibilities.

The idea of measuring the efficiency of DMUs with multiple inputs and outputs is specified as a linear fractional programming model. A commonly accepted measure of efficiency is given by the ratio of the weighted sum of outputs over the weighted sum of inputs. It is, however, necessary to assess a common set of weights and this may raise some problems. With DEA methodology each DMU can freely assess its own set of weights, which can be inferred through the process of maximizing the efficiency. Given a set of N DMUs, each producing J outputs from a set of I inputs, let us denote by y_{jn} and x_{in} the vectors representing the quantities of outputs and inputs relative to the mth DMU, respectively. The efficiency of the mth DMU can thus be calculated as:

$$e_m = \frac{\sum_{j=1}^{J} u_j y_{jm}}{\sum_{i=1}^{I} v_i x_{im}}, \qquad \begin{bmatrix} j = 1, \ldots, J \\ i = 1, \ldots, I \end{bmatrix} \tag{9.1}$$

where u_j and v_i are two vectors of weights that DMU m uses in order to measure the relative importance of the consumed and the produced factors. As mentioned, the set of weights, in DEA, is not given, but is calculated through the DMU's maximization problem, stated below for the mth DMU:

$$\max e_m$$

s.t.

$$\frac{\sum_{j=1}^{J} u_j y_{jn}}{\sum_{i=1}^{I} v_i x_{in}} \leq 1 \quad \forall n = 1, \ldots, m, \ldots, N \tag{9.2}$$

$$0 \leq u_j \leq 1$$
$$0 \leq v_i \leq 1$$

To simplify computations it is possible to scale the input prices so that the cost of the DMU ms inputs equals 1, thus transforming the problem set in (9.2) into the ordinary linear programming problem stated below:

$$\max h_m = \sum_{j=1}^{J} u_j y_{jm}$$

s.t.

$$\sum_{i=1}^{I} v_i x_{im} = 1$$

$$\sum_{j=1}^{J} u_j y_{jn} - \sum_{i=1}^{I} v_i x_{in} \leq 0 \quad \forall n = 1, \ldots, m, \ldots, N \qquad (9.3)$$

$$\varepsilon \leq u_j \leq 1, \, \varepsilon \leq v_i \leq 1, \, \varepsilon \in \mathfrak{R}^+$$

In addition to the linearization, a further constraint is imposed on weights that have to be strictly positive, in order to avoid the possibility that some inputs or outputs may be ignored in the process of determination of the efficiency of each DMU.

If the solution to the maximization problem gives a value of efficiency equal to 1, the corresponding DMU is considered to be efficient or non-dominated; if the efficiency value is below 1, then the corresponding DMU is dominated, and therefore does not lie on the efficiency frontier, which is defined by the efficient DMUs.

Let us consider a simple example of five DMUs (tourism management units), denoted by A, B, C, D and E in Figure 9.1, each using different combinations of two inputs, say labour and number of beds, required to produce a given output quantity, say number of tourists (data are summarized in

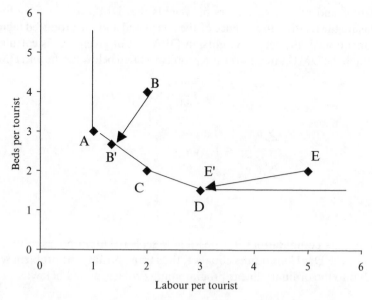

Figure 9.1   An example of efficient frontier with five DMUs

Table 9.1   Example data

DMUs	Labour	Beds	Tourists	Labour per tourist	Beds per tourist
A	200	600	200	1	3
B	600	1200	300	2	4
C	200	200	100	2	2
D	600	300	200	3	1.5
E	500	200	100	5	2

Table 9.1). In order to facilitate comparisons, the input level must be converted to those needed by each DMU to 'produce' one tourist.

The data plotted in Figure 9.1 are abstracted from differences in size. A kinked frontier is drawn from A to C to D and the frontier envelops all the data points and approximates a smooth efficiency frontier using information available from the data only. DMUs (municipalities) on the efficient frontier of our simple example are assumed to be operating at best practice (i.e. efficiency score equal to 1), whereas, management units B and D are considered to be less efficient. DEA compares B with the artificially constructed municipality B', which is a linear combination of A and C. Municipalities A and C are said to be the 'peer group members' of B and the distance BB' is a measure of the efficiency of B. Compared with its benchmark B', municipality B is inefficient because it produces the same level of output but at higher costs.

As for every linear programming problem, there is a dual formulation of the first formulation of the maximization problem outlined in (9.3), which has an identical solution. While the primal problem can be interpreted as an output-oriented formulation (for a given level of input, DMUs maximizing output are preferred), the dual problem can be interpreted as an input-oriented formulation (for a given level of output, DMUs minimizing input are preferred).

The model presented above does not take into consideration scale effect. However, when DMUs are not all operating at an optimal scale, as frequently happens in the case of tourism management, it becomes necessary to extend the basic model as presented in (9.3) in order to account for variable returns to scale. In the present work, the extension of the constant return to scale DEA model to account for the variable returns to scale situation suggested by Banker et al. (1984) has been applied.

Finally, in order to perform dynamic analysis, thus producing not only a static picture of efficiency, but also considering the evolution of efficiency of each municipality, the window approach first put forward by Charnes et al. (1978) has been used. The DEA is performed over time using a similar moving-average procedure, where a municipality in each different period is treated as if it were a 'different' municipality. In other words, a municipality's performance in a particular period is contrasted with its performance in other periods in addition to performance of the other municipalities.

3.   DATA, MODELS AND ANALYSIS PERFORMED

In our analysis, the DMU represents a municipality producing the tourism good given two different inputs. The first is the cost of managing tourism infrastructures and, more generally, of the production of tourism services. The second is the environmental cost deriving from the increased number of people depending on the same environmental endowment.

Data used in the analysis are from ISTAT,[3] ANCITEL[4] and ARPA.[5] Table 9.2 summarizes the inputs and outputs specification that has been considered for each municipality.

Data collected relate to the years 2000/2001. On the input side, management and environmental costs have to be captured. The number of beds is considered as an approximation for management expenses and is computed by adding up the number of beds in hotels, camping sites, registered holiday houses and other accommodation. In the south of Italy there is a very high percentage of second houses rented to tourists which are not registered as holiday houses. Indeed, the actual tourism flows are not clearly known for those areas and for this reason the analysis has been performed solely on municipalities located in northern and central Italy, restricting the DMU sample from the original 194 to 70 municipalities.

As an indicator of environmental costs, data on yearly tons of solid waste produced in each municipality have been collected. Italian tourism is extremely seasonal. Indeed, 23 per cent of annual visitors are concentrated in August, when tourism in Italian seaside resorts is included, but

Table 9.2   Inputs and outputs specification in the model (sources in parentheses)

Input
Number of beds: Proxy for management costs (ISTAT)
Solid waste: Proxy for environmental costs (ARPA)

Output
Rate of use: Proxy for profit from tourism (ANCITEL)
        Tourism presences/number of beds

---

the phenomenon is even more intense when resorts located in the southern regions are taken into account (over 30 per cent of visitors are concentrated in August). Therefore, an indicator of the temporal distribution of waste production would be extremely helpful in defining the severity of environmental costs due to tourism. However, per-month data on municipal waste production are not yet available. Hence, for the purposes of the present study we rely on a yearly aggregated indicator.

On the output side, an indicator measuring the rate of use of existing beds has been used as a general approximation of profit deriving from the tourist industry. As mentioned above, the presence of a well-developed tourism industry may represent an incentive for environmental protection. While in the present study we consider such environmental benefit implicitly as part of the tourism profit indicator, in a future extension it would be desirable to consider it separately.

As far as models are concerned, in the present study output-oriented models have been preferred to input-oriented ones, as they are more suited to issues considered relevant for management purposes and they help to address the germane questions, given the nature of input and output indicators. In particular, the number of beds has been modelled as an uncontrollable input, while the quantity of solid waste (the environmental cost) has been considered as a controllable input. Indeed, in order to augment the efficiency of an inefficient municipality, the most direct policy lever is to introduce constraints on the uncontrolled deployment of environmental resources, rather than restricting the dimension of the tourism business. It is arguable that policy actions undertaken in order to control for inefficiency should not be to the detriment of the tourism industry itself.

Variable returns to scale models have been mainly considered given the presence of regional or local budget constraints, imperfect competition, constraints on finance and so on, which may cause one or more DMUs not to operate at optimal scale. However, an analysis using a constant returns to scale DEA model has also been conducted on the same data set in order to disentangle the inefficiency component due to 'pure' technical inefficiency from that due to 'scale' inefficiency.

As mentioned, following some preliminary tests, the main analysis was performed on a subsample of the original data set. Indeed, municipalities belonging to regions located in the south of Italy and on the islands (Sicily and Sardinia) have been excluded from the analysis because of the lack of reliability of information concerning the effective number of beds. Thus the set of DMUs which will be referred to as the data set does not included municipalities belonging to the mentioned areas.

First, an output-oriented variable returns to scale model has been used to compute the relative static efficiency of 70 Italian municipalities, for the years 2000 and 2001. For comparative purposes the same data set has been analysed through an input-oriented analysis.

However, the repeated application of DEA through the two years' data sets produces little more than a continuum of static results. In reality the behaviour underlying the production processes is likely to be dynamic because tourism management may take much more than one time period to adjust the output levels given the input factors. Furthermore, environmental costs have a multi-period dimension since they generate effects which are generally visible in future periods.

Consequently, it appears more interesting to get an idea of how the efficiency of such municipalities is performing over time, rather than giving a static picture. Thus, an input-oriented variable returns to scale model has been used to compute the dynamic efficiency of the group of municipalities over the years 2000/2001.

4.   RESULTS

The main results and findings of the static and the dynamic analysis are given below.

The input-oriented static analysis performed over the data set produces a ranking of the considered municipalities (in Table 9.3 we give the efficiency scores for the first 20 municipalities, the whole data set ranking being too large to be shown here), where 100 is the maximum level of efficiency and 0 is the minimum.

Data can be presented in several ways. One possible *ex post* transformation is to compute the average efficiency score for each region, as shown in Table 9.4.

In Table 9.5, we then represent the first 20 scoring municipalities in the output-oriented static analysis. This ranking differs slightly from the previous one because the procedure used here gives greater importance to higher rate of use rather than to lower costs. The analysis, for each municipality, specifies not only the relative efficiency scores, but also potential improvements in the case of scores lower than 100. Let us concentrate on a specific example, the case of Deiva Marina, Liguria. As shown in Figure 9.2 for Deiva Marina, the efficiency score is 46.27 per cent, the main potential improvements falling within the category of the environmental domain. Indeed, the main lever to increase efficiency would be a decreased quantity of yearly produced waste, which is an input with both economic and environmental costs. The information about the relative efficiency score, but also concerning potential improvements in case of inefficiency, is calculated from the comparison with the member/s of the peer group (as shown in

Table 9.3   First 20 scoring municipalities in the input-oriented static analysis, 2001

Municipality	Efficiency score
Rio nell'Elba	100
Riva Ligure	100
Vernazza	100
Santo Stefano al Mare	99.57
Portofino	83.8
Bonassola	69.01
Riomaggiore	66.84
Cervo	60.36
Deiva Marina	46.27
Isola del Giglio	45.04
Monterosso al Mare	44.92
Moneglia	43.85
Marciana Marina	42.38
Rio Marina	39.29
Noli	37.77
Sirolo	30.71
Laigueglia	29.07
Camogli	28.85
Marciana	28.24
Ospedaletti	27.94
Portovenere	27.28

Table 9.4   Average score of Italian regions, 2001

Italian regions	Average efficiency score
Liguria	33.63
Toscana	19.42
Lazio	15.09
Marche	9.13
Veneto	5.52
Emilia Romagna	2.27

Figure 9.3 in the case of Deiva Marina, Liguria, the peer group is composed by Vernazza, Liguria). Indeed, in order to find the projection of Deiva Marina on the efficiency frontier, that is, to compute the virtual DMU which represents Deiva Marina but managed fully efficiently, it is necessary to compare it with a peer group belonging to the efficiency frontier. However, the members of the peer group do not necessarily belong to

Table 9.5   First 20 scoring municipalities in the output-oriented static analysis, 2001

Municipality	Efficiency score
Rio nell'Elba	100
Riva Ligure	100
Vernazza	100
Santo Stefano al Mare	99.5
Camogli	56.93
Portofino	30.4
Santa Margherita Ligure	27.54
Ospedaletti	27.4
Monte Argentario	23.84
Rapallo	23.69
Portovenere	19.9
Bonassola	19.09
Taggia	17.34
San Remo	16.1
Monterosso al Mare	14.98
Noli	14.6
Andora	13.4
Celle Ligure	12.99
Follonica	12.54
Bordighera	11.09
Forte dei Marmi	10.81

the same geographical area where the inefficient DMU is located, but may be in a very different area. The information concerning municipalities composing the peer group may be valuable in promoting the exchange of management guidelines between areas which are dispersed, with mutual benefit.

As mentioned in the previous section, a static analysis has also been performed using a constant returns to scale model, in order to capture separately 'scale' inefficiency and 'technological' inefficiency. Indeed, while the constant returns to scale model captures both sources of inefficiency, the variable returns to scale model captures exclusively 'technological' inefficiency. When comparing results from both studies (see Figure 9.4) it becomes clear that scale inefficiency has a much greater effect on the performance scores of inefficient municipalities.

The necessity to capture dynamic trends in the efficiency levels has naturally led to the designing of the second type of analysis, which is performed on the same data set, but in a dynamic framework. Again, the analysis produces a ranking for each of the three subgroups of the considered municipalities (in Table 9.6 the first 20 municipalities are presented). However, now

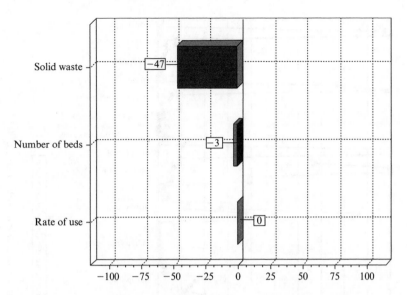

*Figure 9.2   Deiva Marina (Liguria), efficiency score 2001: 46.27.
Suggested improvements*

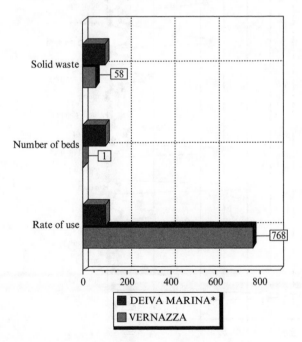

Figure 9.3   Deiva Marina's peer group (Vernazza, Liguria)

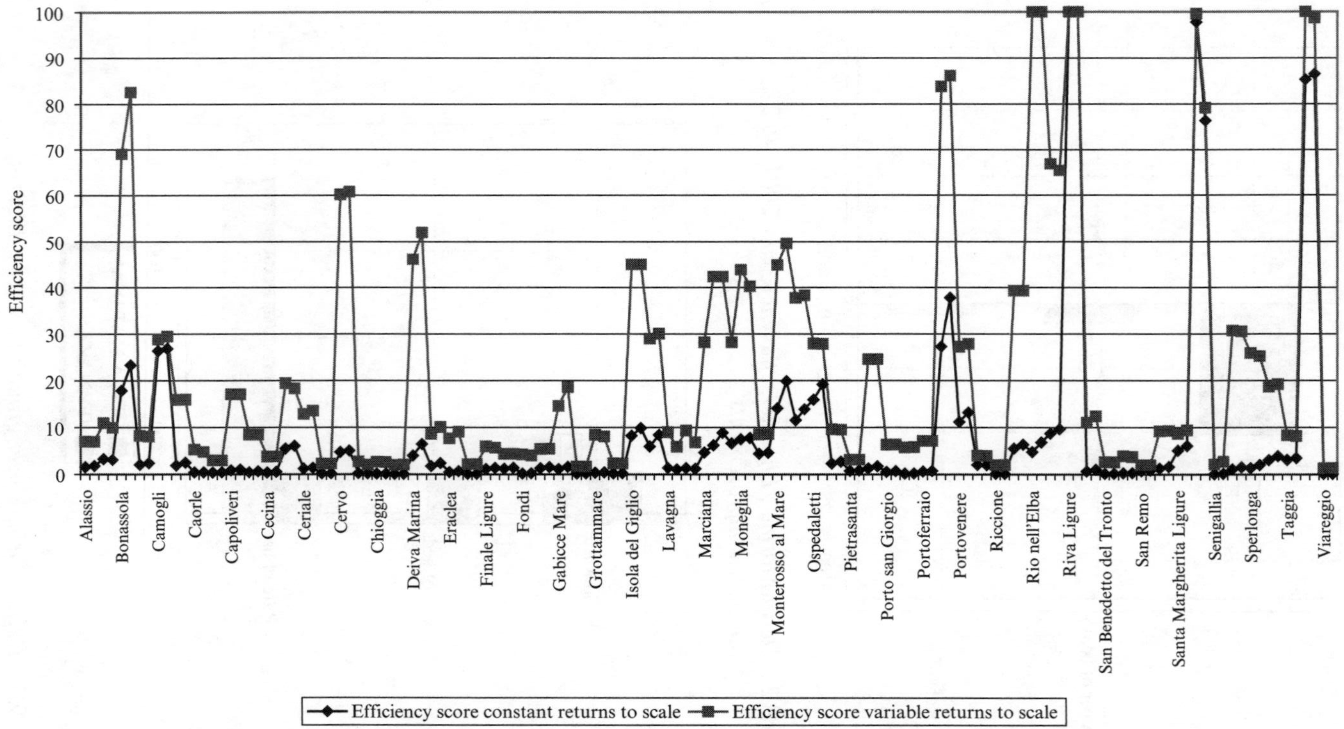

Figure 9.4   Input-oriented, constant returns to scale versus variable returns to scale model (Italy, 2001)

Table 9.6 First 20 scoring municipalities in dynamic analysis results

Municipality (DMU)	Efficiency score
Vernazza	100
Riva Ligure	100
Riva Ligure*	100
Santo Stefano al Mare	99.5
Vernazza*	98.28
Santo Stefano al Mare*	76.86
Rio nell'Elba	70.37
Camogli	52.77
Camogli*	51.7
Portofino*	42.4
Ospedaletti*	30.59
Portofino	30.4
Santa Margherita Ligure*	28.4
Bonassola*	25.95
Santa Margherita Ligure	25.53
Ospedaletti	25.4
Monte Argentario*	23.29
Monte Argentario	22.1
Rapallo	21.96
Rapallo*	21.72

Note: *Data for 2001; otherwise for 2000.

each municipality performance in 2001 is compared to other municipalities' performances as well as to its own performance in the year 2000. In the case of Vernazza, for example, there appears to be a worsening in the efficiency from year 2000 to year 2001, whereas the contrary happens for the case of Portofino, which appears to improve its efficiency score over time.

Finally, general information on aggregated potential improvements is summarized in Figure 9.5. This information could be valuable when considering different potential investment and different formulation of guidelines in the direction of improving the tourism industry from a national government perspective.

5. FINAL REMARKS

Data envelopment analysis can be effectively applied in assessing the economic and environmental performance of tourism management. It can be

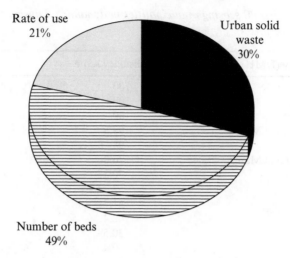

Figure 9.5   Total potential improvements. Input-oriented, variable returns to scale model

even more useful for countries such as Italy, where the tourism industry has both increasing economic relevance and a growing impact on the environment. As discussed in the present chapter, DEA produces relative efficiency indices for each considered municipality and also gives useful information concerning which lever is likely to be more effective in moving to higher levels of efficiency.

Although the present study does provide important insights on the issue of sustainable tourism management, there are some important further steps that should be considered:

- to analyse in detail the relative efficiency of specific services for tourists, such as natural areas, beaches, etc.;
- to extend the data set in order to include southern Italian regions and, furthermore, other European tourist resorts;
- to extend the study to a greater number of time periods in order to get a better picture of trends and dynamic processes;
- to make *ex post* analysis of the efficiency scores in order to understand how they relate to other important economic factors, such as income and, above all, geographic position, through regression analysis. Indeed, flows of tourists are very non-homogeneous through the peninsula, both in quantity (e.g. only 19.2 per cent of tourism flow relates to southern regions) and quality (e.g. just 13 per cent of foreign tourists go to southern regions).

Finally, data on tourism flow are scarce and incomplete (in particular data concerning southern Italian regions), and this kind of study will largely benefit from more accurate data collection. In the meantime, such studies may represent an incentive for municipalities to promote data collection processes.

NOTES

1. Assistance from Carmine Pappalardo (ISAE), Paola Morelli (ISTAT) and Luca Fazzalari (Legambiente) is gratefully acknowledged.
2. For general information and statistics on tourism in Italy, see ISTAT (1997).
3. ISTAT – National Institute of Statistics. Tourism statistics for years 2000/2001.
4. ANCITEL S.p.A. – Society of Services of the National Association of Italian Municipalities.
5. ARPA – Italian Regional Agencies for the Environment.

REFERENCES

Anderson, R.I., Fok, R. and Scott, J. (2000), 'Hotel industry efficiency: an advanced linear programming examination', *American Business Review*, January, 40–48.

Banker, R.D. and Morey, R.C. (1986), 'Efficiency analysis for exogenously fixed inputs and outputs', *Operations Research*, **34** (4), 513–21.

Banker, R.D., Charnes, A. and Cooper, W.W. (1984), 'Some models for estimating technical and scale inefficiencies in data envelopment analysis', *Management Science*, **30** (9), 1078–92.

Bell, R.A. and Morey, R.C. (1995), 'Increasing the efficiency of corporate travel management though macro benchmarking', *Journal of Travel Research*, **33** (3), 11–21.

Cammarrota, M., Costantino, C. and Fängström, I. (2001), Joint final report of the sector infrastructure project. Tourism. European Statistical Laboratory.

Charnes, A., Cooper, W.W. and Rhodes, E. (1978), 'Measuring efficiency of decision making units', *European Journal of Operational Research*, **2** (6), 429–44.

Charnes, A., Cooper, W.W. and Rhodes, E. (1979), 'Measuring efficiency of decision making units', *European Journal of Operational Research*, **3** (4), 339.

Charnes, A., Cooper, W.W. and Rhodes, E. (1981), 'Evaluating program and managerial efficiency: an application of data envelopment analysis to follow through', *Management Science*, **27** (6), 668–96.

Charnes, A., Clark, T., Cooper, W.W. and Golany, B. (1985), 'A development study of data envelopment analysis in measuring the efficiency of maintenance units in the U.S. Air force', *Annals of Operations Research*, **2**, 95–112.

Charnes, A., Cooper, W.W., Huang, Z. and Sun, D. (1990), 'Polyhedral cone-ratio DEA models with an illustrative application to large commercial banks', *Journal of Econometrics*, **46** (1/2), 73–91.

Charnes, A., Cooper, W.W., Lewin, A.Y. and Seiford, L.M. (1993), *Data Envelopment Analysis: theory, methodology and application*, Boston: Kluwer Academic Publishers.

Hart, S. (1997), 'Strategies for a sustainable world', *Harvard Business Review*, Jan.–Feb., 67–76.

ISTAT (1997), 'I viaggi in Italia e all'estero nel 1997', www.istat.it.

Miller, G. (2001), 'The development of indicators for sustainable tourism: results of a Delphi survey of tourism researchers', *Tourism Management*, **22**, 351–62.

Morey, R.C. and Dittman, D.A. (1997), 'An aid in selecting the brand, size and other strategic choices for a hotel', *Journal of Hospitality and Tourism Research*, **21** (1), 71–99.

Nyman, J.A. and Bricker, D.L. (1989), 'Profit incentives and technical efficiency in the production of nursing home care,' *Review of Economics and Statistics*, **71** (4), 586–94.

10. A tale of two tourism paradises: Puerto Plata and Punta Cana – the determinants of room price in the Dominican Republic using a hedonic function approach

Giovanni Ruta and Suzette Pedroso*

1. INTRODUCTION

The objective of this chapter is to estimate the effect of different variables on room price in tourist areas in the Dominican Republic (DR). It has been generally argued that environmental quality matters for the tourism industry as environmental goods and services are among the main inputs in the tourism production function. The government is currently designing a plan that will set the rules and guide tourism development over the next 10–15 years. A major challenge of the plan is to make the best use of the lessons learned during the past 30 years of tourism development in the DR.

The data have been collected through a hotel survey, carried out by Horwath, Sotero Peralta Consulting, a leading firm in tourism industry analysis in the DR. The data set is composed of 83 observations, taken from hotels in tourist areas along the Dominican Republic coast. DR coasts can be divided in seven 'macro' areas but our analysis will emphasize two of them, which have been characterized by substantial tourism development: Puerto Plata and the Altagracia provinces are the main all-inclusive resort poles in the DR. Development has differed widely in the two areas, giving rise to a spectrum of challenges which manifest themselves in different ways in each zone. Our analysis identifies key areas of concern and provides insight into policy issues.

2.   THE TOURISM INDUSTRY IN THE DOMINICAN REPUBLIC

Bordered by 1389 km of coasts, the Dominican Republic presents a very rich composition of coastal and marine ecosystems ranging from sandy beaches, rocky coasts, estuaries, mangroves, marine prairies and coral reefs. Geographically, the country's coast can be divided into seven macro areas:[1]

- The north-west (Montecristi) – characterized by coral reefs and estuaries, one of the most important areas from the ecological viewpoint. Tourism development has not occurred in this area, which conserves its natural state. Main threats are the pollution of the Yaque del Norte river, which carries sediments and pollutants from the agricultural areas upstream.
- The north (Puerto Plata, Sosua, Cabarete) – characterized by rocky coasts, sandy beaches, mangrove ecosystems and wetlands and coral reefs. Most of the coast has seen rapid tourism development and is threatened by high loads of organic pollutants originating from urban areas along the coast and previously by the sugar cane plantations.
- The north-east (Samaná peninsula) – characterized by sandy beaches (a small portion of which is of coral origins) interrupted by rocky coasts and coral reefs. The south of the peninsula is characterized by an estuary (Yuna river), whose natural sedimentation caused a former island to become the current peninsula. The country's highest production of prawns takes place in this area. The southern part of the peninsula forms the Haitises National Park, with estuaries and small portions of coral reefs. This is an area with high tourism and eco-tourism potential, given the diversity and proximity of ecosystems.
- The east (Bávaro – Punta Cana) – dominated by coral reefs, this area is predominantly characterized by white sands very attractive for the tourism industry. The coast continues with cliffs of coral origin. This part of the island was formed by coral deposition, which makes it very different from the rest of the country, which is mainly of volcanic origins. The only relevant economic activity in the area is tourism.
- The south-east (La Romana–Bayahibe) – characterized by sandy beaches (the ones in the Parque Nacional del Este are in their natural state) and cliffs. The area is very important for tourism development and with a high potential for the cruise industry.
- The capital area (Boca Chica, Juan Dolio, Guayacanes and Santo Domingo) – characterized by artificial beaches – has been heavily transformed by tourism development (being the first tourism pole in the country) and other economic activities such as ports, yacht

Table 10.1   Coastal areas and economic activities in the Dominican Republic (areas included in the study are in bold)

Area	Tourism development	Coral	Mangroves	Fisheries	Urban development	Zone in this study
North-west	Low	YES	High	Low	Very low	Not included
North	**High**	**Partially**	**Medium**	**High**	**High**	**Zone 1**
North-east	Medium	Partially	High	High	Low	Not included
East	**High**	**YES**	**Medium**	**Low**	**Low**	**Zone 2**
South-east	High	YES	Low	Low	High	Not included
Capital district	**High**	**Partially**	**Low**	**Low**	**Very high**	**Zone 3**
South	Very low	YES	Medium	Low	Very low	Not included

marinas and commercial activities associated with urban areas. White sandy beaches, of high aesthetic value, originated from a small coral reef formation.

- The south – characterized by rocky coasts – interrupted by small beaches formed by the sedimentation of the various rivers. The area west of the Parque Nacional Jaragua is lower in altitude and has a coral reef origin. It is characterized by white sandy beaches and for this reason the area has a very high tourism potential, so far untapped.

Table 10.1 and Figure 10.1 summarize and give a description 'at a glance' of the coastal areas in the country, while identifying the areas subject to analysis in this chapter.

3.   TOURISM DEVELOPMENT AND THE COST OF DEGRADATION

Stylized facts about the tourism industry in the Dominican Republic are:

- The tourism industry has been growing faster than the rest of the economy in the past ten years. Between 1995 and 2000, the tourism component of GDP grew by 12 per cent every year, compared to 8 per cent for the rest of the economy.

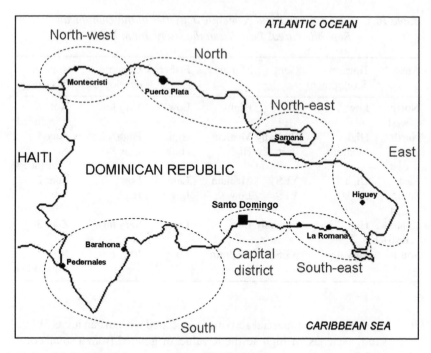

Figure 10.1   The Dominican Republic coasts

- The tourism industry is a very important economic sector. In 2000 the tourism component of GDP accounted for nearly 8 per cent of total GDP; tourism revenues represented 40 per cent of GDP and three times the flow of foreign direct investments (FDI).
- Ownership in the tourism industry is segmented: small hotels (i.e. fewer than 50 rooms) belong to individuals; larger hotels (i.e. more than 100 rooms) belong to corporations.

The Dominican tourism industry faces a series of environmental challenges, including the availability of water services (sewerage and drinking water) and the lack of disposal of solid waste. Booming urban development around tourist poles is affecting the aesthetic qualities of tourism centres. Another source of environmental degradation may arise in the future due to the unsustainable exploitation of underground water, especially in the east. While no systematic information has been collected on marine water quality and on the state of coastal and marine ecosystems (mangroves and wetlands, coral reefs), degradation is probably causing serious losses in the services provided by such ecosystems. Table 10.2 provides an overview of

Table 10.2   Sources of environmental stress in the tourism industry

Source of damage	Type of damage
Damage caused by tourism sector to itself	Superficial, underground and coastal water pollution Congestion of beaches Over-exploitation of aquifers Degradation of ecosystems (i.e. coral reef eutrophication)
Damage caused by other economic sectors (agriculture, industry and cities)	Uncontrolled landfills Solid waste accumulation Superficial and underground water pollution Landscape degradation Air pollution Noise

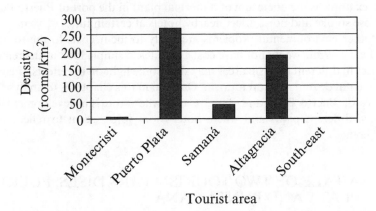

Tourist area

Figure 10.2   Density of selected tourist areas

the main environmental problems affecting the tourism sector classified by source.

Some of the environmental challenges faced by tourism are caused by tourism itself. In particular, water services are facing increasing demand and water resources are expected to receive growing pressure from tourism development. Congestion in tourism areas is also increasing. Evidence suggests that growth in certain tourism poles has been very high, posing threats to the sustainability of the industry itself. Figure 10.2 compares densities across tourism areas. The province of Puerto Plata, in the north, is by far the most congested province (in rooms per square kilometre), followed by the province of Altagracia, in the east.

Other sources of degradation arise from agriculture, industry and the booming growth in urban areas. Urbanization is a major pressure on the tourism resource base. The rapid growth in the tourism sector has had the effect of increasing the urban population in the vicinity of tourism centres. The growth of cities has been, in many cases, unplanned, and evidence shows that the process is affecting the tourism industry itself. A recent survey of hotel operators (Banco Central de la Republica Dominicana, 2002) shows that the problem is particularly acute on the north coast and is a growing problem in Samaná, where more than 55 per cent of hotels surveyed consider slums as a limiting factor to development. Water pollution caused by nearby activities has incurred the need to increase hotels' expenditure on beach clean-up (Playa Dorada has recently started to deal with the accumulation of solid waste on the beach) and on occasion has caused closure.

Industrial activities in coastal areas are linked to the generation of electricity and port operations with high potential impacts for tourist areas. An example is the operation of a thermal plant in the port of Puerto Plata, whose smoke and noise affect nearby hotels at certain times of year.

Other environmental problems are likely to incur costs to the tourism industry. While we do not have cost estimates, a simple look at the relative prices in different tourism areas may shed some light on the effects of environmental degradation on tourism. Our aim in this chapter is to analyse the cases of Puerto Plata and Punta Cana, where tourism development has taken different paths and where hotel room prices seem to reflect such differences.

4. A TALE OF TWO TOURISM PARADISES: PUERTO PLATA AND PUNTA CANA

Puerto Plata (on the north coast) and Punta Cana (on the east coast) constitute a good comparative case study of development patterns the tourism industry can take. The relative endowments of natural and manmade resources are very different on the two sites. The Puerto Plata area, located north of the city of Santiago, has enjoyed good transport infrastructure since it was first conceived as a tourism pole, and has benefited from the wave of public and private investment following the 1971 tourism incentive law. On the other hand Punta Cana, in the 'far east' of the country, was developed in the late 1980s, in an area with very little or no infrastructure. Currently these locations have, respectively, 16 000 and 18 000 hotel rooms and are the two main tourism poles in the country.

Compliance with environmental norms has been strikingly different. A recent survey (Banco Central de la Republica Dominicana, 2002)

Table 10.3   Puerto Plata and Punta Cana – basic comparison

Location	% of hotels without treatment plants in the area	% of hotels disposing of wastewater underground in the area	Density (rooms/km^2)
Puerto Plata	75	73	269
Bavaro–Punta Cana	23	37	167

highlights that, in Puerto Plata, 75 per cent of hotels (mostly small) do not have a treatment plant and 73 per cent use the soil as a receptor body. In Bavaro–Punta Cana the numbers are respectively 23 per cent and 37 per cent. Densities (measured as the number of rooms per square kilometre) are also different: Puerto Plata has 269 rooms/km^2 versus Punta Cana's 167 rooms/km^2. Table 10.3 summarizes this information. Information on room or hotel price would certainly allow us to analyse how far these differences are captured by markets and reflected in tourist preferences.

Our objective is to identify key determinants of room price and compare them across coastal zones in the DR. The country's tourism strategy has traditionally been based on meeting demand through 'all-inclusive' service packages. Attention to environmental aspects has been limited until recent years, when fast urban growth and congestion have affected the 'sun, sand, sea' development paradigm.

Let us consider the approach of a typical private agent who wants to invest in a tourism project. People choose to invest in an area of coast that has sun, sand and sea; easy access to an international airport; and good infrastructure such as roads, water service and sanitation facilities. These preferences are reflected in the value of the land on which the hotel is placed and are reflected in the room price. Other factors boost the demand for rooms, hence their unit price. Examples of these are facilities such as golf courses, tennis courts, swimming pools, cable TV, spas, casinos, and so on. The variables likely to affect room price can be divided into four qualitatively distinct groups: (1) hotel services, which are those variables that affect directly visitors' well-being; (2) location variables, which determine how accessible are amenities outside the hotel such as shopping malls and urban centres; (3) environmental variables, which affect the quality of the area near the hotel, such as the smell from treatment facilities or nearby landfills,[2] the quality of the beach, the quality of water; and (4) infrastructure service variables, such as the existence of treatment plants and municipal water connections.

In general, the 'hedonic' price method requires that the following questions be answered positively:

- Do environmental and infrastructure variables systematically affect room prices?
- Is knowledge of this relationship sufficient to predict changes in room prices from changes in the level of the environmental and infrastructure variables?
- Do changes in room prices adequately reflect changes in social welfare?

The hedonic price method typically entails a two-step estimation as suggested by Rosen (1974). In the first step, an implicit price for environmental quality is calculated. Theoretically, the implicit price overestimates the benefits from improving the environmental characteristics. This would thus justify a second step, in which a new regression is used to calculate the welfare change from a marginal change in environmental quality. Empirical evidence suggests that the extent of overestimation is sometimes negligible (e.g. Brookshire et al., 1982). Moreover, data limitations and other sources of error may be too great, given the small size of our sample, to justify the additional effort of carrying out the second-step estimation. For this reason, our estimation is limited to the first stage, yet allows us to obtain important information on the impact of certain variables in room prices.

5.   EMPIRICAL FRAMEWORK

The price of the ith room, '*ROOMPRICE*', is a function of the different characteristics and amenities of the hotel:

$$ROOMPRICE = f(SERVICES_i, LOCATION_i, ENVQUAL_i, INFRASTR_i)$$

Following Freeman (1992), we used a semilog specification: that is, we ran a regression of the logarithm of room price on the level of hotel services, location, environmental and infrastructure characteristics. The dependent variable is room price in logarithm terms, and it refers to the standard room daily rate in double occupancy. Thus the sample provides prices for a homogeneous type of room. At the same time, explanatory variables refer essentially to hotel characteristics, rather than room characteristics. It is fairly safe to assume that by including the star classification of the hotel, our model is capturing differences in room characteristics across hotels. Table 10.4 provides a list of the grouped explanatory variables with a suggested sign.

Table 10.4   Variable description and expected signs

Variable	Description	Expected sign	Type of variable
LOGHIGH	Log of double room price during high season		Dependent variable
LOGLOW	Log of double room price during low season		Dependent variable
C	Constant		
STAR	Hotel star grading	Positive	Hotel services
YEAR	Year hotel was built	Positive / negative	
AQUA	Hotel has an aqua park (dummy)	Positive	
CASINO	Hotel has a casino (dummy)	Positive	
DISCO	Hotel has a disco (dummy)	Positive	
GOLF	Hotel has a golf course (dummy)	Positive	
SPA	Hotel has a spa (dummy)	Positive	
TENNIS	Hotel has at least one tennis court (dummy)	Positive	
ZONE1	Hotel on north coast (dummy)	Positive / negative	Location
ZONE2	Hotel on east coast (dummy)	Positive / negative	
ZONE3	Hotel on south-east coast (dummy)	Positive / negative	
ROOMDENS	Number of rooms per km^2 of beach	Negative	
AIRPORTKM	Distance from airport (km)	Negative	
BEACHKM	Distance from beach (km)	Negative	
CITYKM	Distance from closest urban centre (km)	Positive / negative	
POPDENSITY	Population density in the region	Negative	
GARBAGE	Garbage is collected every day or more frequently (dummy)	Positive / negative	Environmental quality
SMELL	It is possible to notice smell of effluents and solid waste (dummy)	Negative	
WASTEBEACH	It is possible to observe occasional accumulation of solid waste on the beach (dummy)	Negative	

Table 10.4   (continued)

Variable	Description	Expected sign	Type of variable
SEWTREAT	Hotel has a sewage treatment plant (dummy)	Positive	Water infrastructure
WATERMUN	Hotel is connected to municipal water service (dummy)	Positive	

Hotel services variables include the star grading of the hotel and a series of dummies regarding the availability of aqua park, casino, discotheque, golf course, spa and tennis courts. Location variables provide information both on the geographic location of the hotel with respect to the country (zone variables) and on the distance from key services and amenities such as airport, urban centres and beach. A series of 'ZONE' dummies identifies hotels by the coast they are located on. Most of our analysis will focus on comparing hotels in Puerto Plata (ZONE1) and Punta Cana (ZONE2). Environmental variables include the frequency of the solid waste collection service, the existence of smell from effluents and solid waste, and the accumulation of rubbish on the beach. Information on site-specific environmental quality is not available and the environmental variables used have been obtained by questioning the hotel administrators directly. These are discrete variables, where 1 means that the environmental problem is actually being observed and 0 means that there is no evidence of the environmental problem. Finally, infrastructure variables refer to the existence of municipal water connections and a treatment plant for the hotels observed.

Table 10.4 also indicates what sign we expect to obtain from the estimation. Ambiguity is indicated for CITYKM and GARBAGE. Being close to an urban centre may explain higher room prices because of the vicinity to services and amenities of urban areas. But urban areas are also a source of pollution and coastal degradation that may well mean fewer tourists. Daily garbage collection may be linked positively to price as it implies higher quality of service (in many places waste is collected once a week). However, this variable may also be capturing the relative cleanliness of the area (so higher collection frequencies may also mean more dirt).

Infrastructure variables are expected to impact positively on hotel prices. The recent Central Bank survey of the hotel industry in the DR asked hotel operators to report on the state of infrastructure. The survey also served as an opinion poll to ask how different factors affected the tourism industry in the country. In the DR, only 10–15 per cent of smaller hotels (with fewer than 50 rooms) have a water treatment plant. Most small hotels depend on the municipal, and often inefficient, coverage. On the other hand, about 90–100 per cent of the larger hotels (more than 100 rooms) have claimed to have water treatment plants. Our model tests the hypothesis that the availability of treatment plants allows a higher room price, everything else being constant. The availability of treatment plants is also important for environmental reasons. A total of 59 per cent of wastewater from DR tourist facilities is infiltrated in the subsoil (and only 10 per cent goes to sewerage systems). With regard to drinking water, most of the smaller hotels use the municipal system. Larger hotels are much less dependent on municipalities and use aquifer resources. Figure 10.3 shows the sources of drinking water for hotels according to their size. Large resorts depend heavily on aquifer resources, especially in the east, characterized by relatively little precipitation, fewer and distant water bodies and the limestone composition of the area. Availability of water in the future may pose a threat to tourism development: a recent survey showed that nearly 50 per cent of hotel operators consider the lack of water infrastructure a limiting factor to development. Our model tests the hypothesis that the availability of municipal water is positively linked to room price.

A questionnaire specifically designed for this study was applied by Horwath, Sotero Peralta Consulting to gather the data for the analysis. The data set is composed of 83 observations, taken from hotels in tourist areas along the DR coast. Data collected refer to the following coastal areas: Puerto Plata (ZONE1), Punta Cana (ZONE2) and the south-east (ZONE3).

Data were collected using a telephone survey. A typical shortcoming of telephone surveys of this type is that hotels usually tend to hide the true

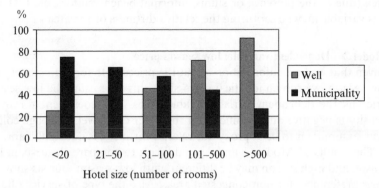

Figure 10.3   Sources of drinking water by hotel size

price of the room for various reasons, such as marketing, competition and fiscal. Our comparative advantage, however, is that the survey was administered by a Dominican consulting company specialized in monitoring the tourism industry. Their database contains accurate hotel-specific information on room prices for different types of rooms and for different times of year. The consulting company also counts with credibility and trust among hotel operators.

6.   RESULTS

Five model specifications are presented in this chapter. Models 1 to 3 make use of observations from all zones, while Models 4 and 5 utilize observations only for Zone 1 and Zone 2, respectively. The estimation method used in the following five model specifications is ordinary least squares (OLS).

Regression results for each of the specifications are presented below. Note that bold figures identify parameters that are statistically significant at the 10 per cent level.

6.1   Regression Utilizing Observations from all Zones

Model 1   Dependent variable: high season price
The results of the first regression are presented in Table 10.5. The coefficient for GARBEVERY1[3] is negative, while conventional wisdom would typically suggest a positive relationship between garbage collection frequency and room price. The negative coefficient may imply that garbage needs to be collected every day because of the high production of garbage in the area (due to the presence of slums, informal beach vendors, etc.). Hence this variable may be capturing the relative dirtiness of the area.

Model 2   Dependent variable: low season price
Given that we have information about the prices both for high season and low season, we run an identical regression, this time using the low season price as the dependent variable (Table 10.6). The coefficient for room density is negative and significant at the 5 per cent level. Garbage collection, assuming it to be a 'proxy' for relative dirtiness, is not significant.

The results of Models 1 and 2 are difficult to compare. Tourists in low season and high season may be different, with low-season tourists showing clear preferences for non-congested areas. Also the type of service offered may be different in different seasons.

Table 10.5   Regression-1 results

Variable	Coefficient	Std error	*t*-statistic	Prob.
C	−16.59560	20.57721	−0.806504	0.4265
ZONE1	**0.606015**	**0.230059**	**2.634173**	**0.0134**
ZONE2	0.558709	0.330301	1.691515	0.1015
AIRPORTKM	**−0.018337**	**0.005129**	**−3.575358**	**0.0012**
DISTKM	**−0.000372**	**0.000204**	**−1.825781**	**0.0782**
DISTURBANKM	0.005568	0.004450	1.251194	0.2209
POPDENSITY	−0.000736	0.001239	−0.593926	0.5572
ROOMDENSITY	−0.002257	0.001544	−1.461881	0.1545
STAR	**0.330712**	**0.146156**	**2.262732**	**0.0313**
YEAR	0.010530	0.010435	1.009072	0.3213
AQUAPARK	0.096129	0.183088	0.525045	0.6035
CASINO	**0.452520**	**0.156752**	**2.886844**	**0.0073**
DISCO	−0.234264	0.194029	−1.207365	0.2370
GOLF	−0.193345	0.171235	−1.129118	0.2681
SPA	0.268347	0.181786	1.476166	0.1507
TENNIS	0.231997	0.266839	0.869430	0.3918
GARBEVERY1	**−1.180330**	**0.678043**	**−1.740789**	**0.0923**
SMELL	**−1.178291**	**0.548826**	**−2.146931**	**0.0403**
SWASTEBEACH	−0.066512	0.173256	−0.383895	0.7039
SEWTREAT	−0.207572	0.157697	−1.316267	0.1984
WATERMUN	0.136885	0.191745	0.713893	0.4810

R-squared	0.739331	Mean dependent var.	4.140059
Adjusted R-squared	0.559559	S.D. dependent var.	0.570761
S.E. of regression	0.378790	Akaike info. criterion	1.191601
Sum squared resid.	4.160966	Schwarz criterion	1.994651
Log likelihood	−8.790031	F-statistic	4.112602
Durbin–Watson stat.	2.412859	Prob. (F-statistic)	0.000291

Notes:
Sample (adjusted): 182.
Included observations: 50.
Excluded observations: 32 after adjusting endpoints.

Model 3   Dependent variable: low season price; omitted service variables
Using Model 2, where the low season price was used as the dependent variable, we performed an F-test on the service variables of the hotel (i.e. aquapark, golf, tennis, etc.) (Table 10.7). This test aims to determine whether they are redundant, given that the STAR grading variable may have already captured the effect of these variables. The null hypothesis states that the coefficient estimate of each service variable is equal to zero: $\hat{C}_i = 0$; $i = 11, 12, 13, 14, 15, 16$. The test accepted the null hypothesis. Therefore a

Table 10.6   Regression-2 results

Variable	Coefficient	Std error	*t*-statistic	Prob.
C	−13.52369	19.21826	−0.703689	0.4872
ZONE1	**0.427830**	**0.228793**	**1.869948**	**0.0716**
ZONE2	**0.708582**	**0.320837**	**2.208540**	**0.0353**
AIRPORTKM	**−0.013473**	**0.004760**	**−2.830715**	**0.0084**
DISTKM	−0.000321	0.000198	−1.626696	0.1146
DISTURBANKM	0.003773	0.004344	0.868557	0.3922
POPDENSITY	−0.001069	0.001210	−0.883068	0.3845
ROOMDENSITY	**−0.003041**	**0.001465**	**−2.075138**	**0.0470**
STAR	0.256115	0.159126	1.609507	0.1183
YEAR	0.008776	0.009753	0.899798	0.3756
AQUAPARK	0.118665	0.173541	0.683785	0.4995
CASINO	**0.377530**	**0.165711**	**2.278239**	**0.0303**
DISCO	**−0.344748**	**0.191443**	**−1.800784**	**0.0821**
GOLF	−0.011932	0.171952	−0.069390	0.9452
SPA	0.063554	0.173147	0.367053	0.7162
TENNIS	0.314210	0.259461	1.211013	0.2357
GARBEVERY1	−0.487123	0.646453	−0.753533	0.4572
SMELL	**−1.154998**	**0.536406**	**−2.153216**	**0.0398**
SWASTEBEACH	−0.053327	0.168177.	−0.317088	0.7534
SEWTREAT	−0.142813	0.156840	−0.910568	0.3700
WATERMUN	0.288793	0.177625	1.625861	0.1148

R-squared	0.709708	Mean dependent var.		4.007057
Adjusted R-squared	0.509506	S.D. dependent var.		0.525759
S.E. of regression	0.368217	Akaike info. criterion		1.134984
Sum squared resid.	3.931929	Schwarz criterion		1.938034
Log likelihood	−7.374608	F-statistic		3.544963
Durbin–Watson stat.	2.157457	Prob. (F-statistic)		0.000996

Notes:
Sample (adjusted): 182.
Included observations: 50.
Excluded observations: 32 after adjusting endpoints.

new regression was run, where the hotel services variables were omitted. The coefficient for room density appears to be significant at the 5 per cent level. Notice that none of the coefficients for environmental variables is significant in this model. Moreover, the coefficients for the infrastructure variables have shown to be statistically zero for all models so far tested. Our next step is to perform separate regressions for Puerto Plata and Punta Cana.

Table 10.7   Regression-3 results

Variable	Coefficient	Std error	*t*-statistic	Prob.
C	−8.239528	17.70679	−0.465332	0.6446
ZONE1	0.348786	0.220880	1.579078	0.1233
ZONE2	**0.502640**	**0.285952**	**1.757779**	**0.0875**
AIRPORTKM	**−0.014581**	**0.004230**	**−3.447111**	**0.0015**
DISTKM	−0.000159	0.000157	−1.007828	0.3205
DISTURBANKM	0.001723	0.004225	0.407906	0.6858
POPDENSITY	−0.001003	0.001203	−0.834280	0.4098
ROOMDENSITY	**−0.002899**	**0.001415**	**−2.048305**	**0.0481**
STAR	**0.521037**	**0.118791**	**4.386160**	**0.0001**
YEAR	0.005807	0.009046	0.641897	0.5251
GARBEVERY1	−0.524424	0.564763	−0.928573	0.3595
SMELL	−0.564603	0.481281	−1.173127	0.2487
SWASTEBEACH	−0.199815	0.152997	−1.306008	0.2001
SEWTREAT	−0.159544	0.160184	−0.996000	0.3261
WATERMUN	0.238572	0.159300	1.497625	0.1432
R-squared	0.620521	Mean dependent var.		4.007057
Adjusted R-squared	0.468729	S.D. dependent var.		0.525759
S.E. of regression	0.383217	Akaike info. criterion		1.162895
Sum squared resid.	5.139937	Schwarz criterion		1.736502
Log likelihood	−14.07237	F-statistic		4.087980
Durbin–Watson stat.	2.381658	Prob. (F-statistic)		0.000355

Notes:
Sample (adjusted): 182.
Included observations: 50.
Excluded observations: 32 after adjusting endpoints.

6.2   Separate Regression for Zone 1 and Zone 2

Given that location appears to be an important characteristic, we performed individual regressions for Zone 1 (Puerto Plata) and Zone 2 (Punta Cana) (Tables 10.8 and 10.9). The common specification used is:

$$\text{LOGDOUBLELOW}_k = C(1) + C(2)_k * \text{AIRPORTKM}$$
$$+ C(3)_k * \text{DISTKM} + C(4)_k * \text{DISTURBANKM}$$
$$+ C(5)_k * \text{ROOMDENSITY} + C(6)_k * \text{STAR}$$
$$+ C(7)_k * \text{YEAR} + C(8)_k * \text{SWASTEBEACH}$$
$$+ C(9)_k * \text{SEWTREAT} + C(10)_k * \text{WATERMUN}$$
$$+ error\ term$$

where k = Zone 1 or Zone 2.

Table 10.8   Regression-4 results

Variable	Coefficient	Std error	t-statistic	Prob.
C	−46.50796	52.38828	−0.887755	0.3955
AIRPORTKM	**−0.023430**	**0.011496**	**−2.038090**	**0.0689**
DISTKM	−0.000920	0.001133	−0.811898	0.4358
DISTURBANKM	0.030954	0.031760	0.974602	0.3527
ROOMDENSITY	**−0.005410**	**0.002929**	**−1.847433**	**0.0944**
STAR	**0.898008**	**0.331915**	**2.705533**	**0.0221**
YEAR	0.024350	0.026166	0.930578	0.3740
SWASTEBEACH	0.132163	0.385286	0.343026	0.7387
SEWTREAT	−0.448172	0.324284	−1.382034	0.1971
WATERMUN	**0.852162**	**0.439903**	**1.937160**	**0.0815**
R-squared	0.651665	Mean dependent var.		3.903595
Adjusted R-squared	0.338163	S.D. dependent var.		0.568764
S.E. of regression	0.462709	Akaike info. criterion		1.603414
Sum squared resid.	2.140992	Schwarz criterion		2.101280
Log likelihood	−6.034140	F-statistic		2.078664
Durbin–Watson stat.	0.975373	Prob. (F-statistic)		0.134879

Notes:
Sample (adjusted): 431 IF ZONE = 1.
Included observations: 20 after adjusting endpoints.

The difference between the parameters in Zone 1 (north coast) and Zone 2 (east coast) is very large. In particular, such differences highlight the distinct nature of development challenges in each zone.

Model 4   Sample consists of Zone 1 (Puerto Plata) only
Room density matters on the north coast, characterized by out of control 'secondary development'[4] in the last decade. Due to this lack of planning, infrastructure services have lagged behind. This is supported by our regression. It seems that hotels with municipal water connection can command a higher price per room. Notice that WATERMUN[5] has a positive coefficient, which is significant at the 10 per cent level (Table 10.8).

Model 5   Sample consists of Zone 2 (Punta Cana) only
On the east coast, a lower number of rooms per square kilometre of beach (ROOMDENSITY) does not command a higher price per room. However, distance from the airport matters because this is an area poorly connected to major urban centres. The presence of a sewage treatment plant (SEWTREAT) in the hotel has a positive and statistically significant

Table 10.9   Regression-5 results

Variable	Coefficient	Std. error	*t*-statistic	Prob.
C	−8.718624	16.46573	−0.529501	0.6042
AIRPORTKM	**−0.013579**	**0.003529**	**−3.848069**	**0.0016**
DISTKM	**−0.000303**	**0.000121**	**−2.502030**	**0.0244**
DISTURBANKM	−0.000844	0.002958	−0.285201	0.7794
ROOMDENSITY	−0.002668	0.003263	−0.817663	0.4263
STAR	**0.395662**	**0.117038**	**3.380625**	**0.0041**
YEAR	0.006050	0.008548	0.707712	0.4900
SWASTEBEACH	−0.144699	0.153213	−0.944430	0.3599
SEWTREAT	**0.427943**	**0.192091**	**2.227811**	**0.0416**
WATERMUN	0.147627	0.140577	1.050152	0.3103
R-squared	0.778254	Mean dependent var.		4.200196
Adjusted R-squared	0.645206	S.D. dependent var.		0.435723
S.E. of regression	0.259537	Akaike info. criterion		0.429336
Sum squared resid.	1.010389	Schwarz criterion		0.916886
Log likelihood	4.633298	F-statistic		5.849425
Durbin–Watson stat.	1.881096	Prob. (F-statistic)		0.001422

Notes:
Sample (adjusted): 3270 IF ZONE = 2.
Included observations: 25 after adjusting endpoints.

impact on hotel room price (at the 5 per cent level), as shown in Table 10.9. The variable SEWTREAT may be associated with higher environmental quality (i.e. better water quality). However, one has to exercise care in the interpretation of this variable. Water pollution may not be easily perceived by tourists, so it may not be reflected in room price.

7. SUMMARY AND CONCLUSIONS

Room prices on the east coast (Punta Cana) are on average higher than prices on the north coast (Puerto Plata). These differences may be explained by quality of service, but also by environmental variables and natural resource endowments. Our analysis did not include site-specific information on environmental quality but factors such as beach congestion, the availability of treatment plant and water connection are important predictors of room price.

It cannot be concluded that environmental quality is higher on the east coast. What our analysis suggests is that the nature of environmental challenges is different and calls for specific policy interventions. Puerto Plata has traditionally depended on the municipal infrastructure for the provision of water services and waste collection. The hotel industry in Punta Cana on the other hand could not claim a 'right' to publicly provided services, having arrived there before urban development took place. The tourism sector in the east financed the construction of residences for tourism employees and the construction of the international airport, and a private firm is in charge of solid waste collection. Note, however, that environmental pressures in Punta Cana are not absent. The geological nature of the soil is such that underground wastewater disposal may in the long run cause serious damage to the aquifer which is the main source of drinking water in the area. Hence the importance of an adequate wastewater treatment facility.

Table 10.10 summarizes the information obtained. It identifies the variables whose coefficients are significant at the 5 per cent level for each site-specific regression. Availability of municipal water is positively linked to room price in Puerto Plata. Availability of sewage treatment plant is positively linked to room price in Punta Cana. The results mirror current thinking on development challenges in the DR, in which water resources management issues are becoming important in the development agenda. Room density is negatively linked with price on the already congested north coast.

These results are of particular relevance for the current plans for tourism development over the next 10 to 15 years. The Samaná peninsula and the south-east are currently undeveloped (<2500 rooms) and in 2010 the number of rooms is expected to grow to 20 000 (20 per cent of the national offer). If the government is to be successful in the new wave of development, it has to safeguard the 'golden egg hen'. The new areas have very high potential for nature-based tourism, an alternative which offers the possibility of protecting the environment while capturing the benefits of conservation.

Sustainable infrastructure supply calls for coordination with the private sector. Hotel rents can be successfully employed to provide basic infra-

Table 10.10   Variables whose coefficients are significant at 5 per cent level

Variables	Zone 1	Zone 2
Characteristic of the hotel	Star	Star
Location	Distance to airport	Distance to airport
	Room density	Distance from urban centre
Infrastructure characteristics	Municipal water connection	Sewage treatment plant

structure, but in the long term it is necessary to protect public commons such as underground resources and landscape beauty.

Finally, most of the environmental problems encountered in tourism areas can be linked to institutional factors. Management of environmental problems and the incentives structure should take into account the geographical as well as the demographic differences among tourism poles.

NOTES

*   The authors are with the World Bank. We are grateful to Horwath Sotero Peralta & Assoc. Consulting for conducting the survey and for providing helpful insights of the tourism sector in Dominican Republic. We are grateful to Anil Markandya for useful guidance on the methodology. The opinions expressed are those of the authors and not necessarily those of the World Bank.
1.   The chapter will specifically focus on the north (Puerto Plata, Sosua, Cabarete) referred to in this analysis simply as 'Puerto Plata' or Zone 1, and the east (Bávaro, Punta Cana), referred to here as 'Punta Cana' or Zone 2.
2.   Where treatment plants are located on site, smell from the treatment facilities can reach the visitors. This has been observed on the north coast of the Samaná peninsula.
3.   This is a dummy variable, where garbage collected every day = 1; garbage collected less frequently = 0.
4.   Secondary development refers to the growth of both urban areas and hotels around the areas that had been previously subject to government-led development. The fact that government investment acts as a catalytic for further private investment is a positive factor in development. But if the resource is finite (such as coastal area spaces), uncontrolled growth can also cause stress, which may lead to crisis.
5.   A dummy variable that takes the value of 1 if the hotel has a municipal water connection and 0 otherwise.

REFERENCES

Banco Central de la Republica Dominicana, Banco Interamericano de Desarrollo, Secretaria de Estado de Turismo (2002), *Directorio de Establecimientos de Alojamiento: Metodología y Resultados*, Santo Domingo, DN: Banco Central de la Republica Dominicana.

Brookshire, David et al. (1982), 'Valuing Public Goods: A Comparison of Survey and Hedonic Approaches', *The American Economic Review*, **72**(1), 165–77.

Freeman, Myrick (1992), *The Measurement of Environmental and Resource Values*, Washington, DC: Resources for the Future.

Horwath, Sotero Peralta (2003), 'Results of the telephone survey to hotel administrators', mimeo.

Kanemoto, Yoshitsugu (1988), 'Hedonic Prices and the Benefits of Public Projects', *Econometrica*, **56**(4), 981–9.

Rosen S. (1974), 'Hedonic Prices and Implicit Markets: Product Differentiation in Perfect Competition', *Journal of Political Economy*, **82**(1), 34–55.

11. A choice experiment study to plan tourism expansion in Luang Prabang, Laos

Sanae Morimoto

1. INTRODUCTION

Tourism development is often a very important strategy for fostering economic growth in developing countries. Tourism generates a variety of economic benefits such as foreign exchange earnings, employment, income and government revenues.[1] However, the budget and human resources for tourism development are usually very limited in these countries, and efficient planning is required. Planners of tourism development need to understand tourists' demand for the destination and activity and mode of transport in order to plan effective expansion.

This chapter presents the potential use of choice experiment (CE), one of the stated preference (SP) approaches, in planning effective tourism expansion. The advantage of the approach is that it makes it possible to analyse tourists' preference for the bundle of attributes of tourism separately. For example, tourists may make their choice based on what to see, mode of transport and cost.

Another advantage of this approach is that it allows analysts to investigate tourists' preference beyond the existing set of alternatives, which cannot be done in revealed preference (RP) approaches. This chapter, therefore, applies the CE approach and also tries to plan the most preferable tour from the estimation results. As a case study, this chapter deals with the tourism development in Luang Prabang, Lao P.D.R. (Laos).

Section 2 explains why this study uses the CE approach rather than other environmental valuation approaches by reviewing other studies. Section 3 contains a brief description of tourism in Laos. Section 4 sets out the methodology of our analysis. Economic and econometric models are described in section 5. Estimation results are reported in section 6. Section 7 shows the simulation results of tourism development, and section 8 provides concluding remarks.

2. CHOICE EXPERIMENT APPROACH

In the field of recreational demand modelling, a variety of studies have widely used travel cost (TC) or contingent valuation (CV) (Font, 2000; Fredman and Emmelin, 2001; Lockwood et al., 1996; Pruckner, 1995). Some studies have used a combination of TC and CV approaches (Fix and Loomis, 1998; Herath, 1999). These approaches are well known for estimating recreational benefit and price elasticity in the demand for tourism. However, these approaches are suitable for estimating benefit from visiting only a single destination, not multiple destinations.

Despite its potential, the CE approach has not been applied to tourism development except in the case of hotel amenities (Goldberg et al., 1984; Bauer et al., 1999), ski resorts (Carmichael, 1992), hunting (Gan and Luzar, 1993; Boxall et al., 1996; Adamowicz et al., 1997), and climbing (Hanley et al., 2002). These studies have estimated the preference for one type of resource, which was composed of multiple attributes. This study regards various types of factors for site choice as attributes, and investigates the preference for each factor. It enables us to predict which attribute should be strengthened most in order to achieve effective tourism expansion.

A variety of studies on the environmental valuation of recreation have been undertaken in developed countries, and fewer applied to developing countries. Most of the literature uses the TC and/or CV approach, for example the recreational value of wildlife in Kenya (Navrud and Mungatana, 1994), price elasticity in the demand for ecotourism in Costa Rica (Chase et al., 1998) and the recreational value of a reserve in China (Xue et al., 2000). This study is the first to use the CE approach for tourism in a developing country.

3. TOURISM DEVELOPMENT IN LUANG PRABANG, LAOS

3.1 Overview of Laos

Laos, one of the world's least developed countries, has recognized tourism as one of the most significant sectors for economic development (UNDP and WTO, 1998). The number of tourists and the revenue have increased since Luang Prabang was classified as a World Heritage site by UNESCO in 1995 (Table 11.1). In 2000, for example, there were about 737 000 tourists, and the revenue was approximately US$113 million, which implies that the average expenditure per person per night was US$28.

The tourism authority classified tourists into three categories: (1) international tourists, (2) regional tourists and (3) tourists for visa exten-

Table 11.1   Number of tourists, average length of stay, and revenue

Year	No. of tourists	Ave. length of stay (days)	Revenue from tourism (US$000s)
1991	37 613	N.A.	2 250
1992	87 571	N.A.	4 510
1993	102 946	3.50	6 280
1994	146 155	5.07	7 558
1995	346 460	4.25	24 738
1996	403 000	4.12	43 592
1997	463 200	5.00	73 277
1998	500 200	5.00	79 960
1999	614 278	5.50	97 265
2000	737 208	5.50	113 878

Note: N.A. = not available.

Source: National Tourism Authority (2001).

sion. International tourists are those who have valid passports and visas. Although the share of international tourists was only 25 per cent in 2000, their average expenditure per person per night was the highest (US$75). Of these tourists, the majority were from the USA (17 per cent), France (13 per cent), Japan (10 per cent), and the UK (8 per cent). Regional tourists are those from neighbouring countries such as Thailand, China, Vietnam and Myanmar. Seventy-three per cent of foreign tourists are classified as regional tourists. Of these, the majority are from Thailand (82 per cent) and Vietnam (13 per cent). Tourists for visa extension are the temporary international workers in Thailand who visited Laos to extend their visas in Thailand. These tourists are mainly from India (74 per cent), Bangladesh (11 per cent), and Pakistan (7 per cent) (see Table 11.2).

3.2   Overview of the Case of Luang Prabang

Luang Prabang is the best-known historic site in Laos. It was the capital of the first Lao kingdom, Lang Xang, from the middle of the fourteenth to the end of the sixteenth century and the home of the former Luang Prabang monarchy. At the end of the nineteenth century, the monarchy accepted French protection. It was finally abolished in 1975 when the communist Lao took over.

Many historic temples and Lao–French buildings, relics of this historical background, can be found in the town of Luang Prabang. UNESCO

Table 11.2   Revenue from tourism by category, 2000

	No. of tourists (persons)	Average length of stay (days)	Average expenditure per person per day (US$)
Total	737 208	N.A.	N.A.
International tourists	191 455	5.5	75.00
Regional tourists	541 616	N.A.	N.A.
Thai (border pass)	379 157	1.0	30.00
Thai (passport)	63 407	4.0	70.00
China (passport)	9 787	4.0	50.00
China (day tripper)	18 428	1.0	12.00
Vietnam (passport)	21 233	3.0	40.00
Vietnam (day tripper)	47 518	1.0	12.00
Myanmar	2 086	3.0	26.66
Tourists for visa extension	4 137	3.0	26.66

Note: N.A. = not available.

Source: National Tourism Authority (2001).

describes this World Heritage site as the best-preserved old capital in Southeast Asia.

UNDP and WTO (1998) proposes tourism centred on historic and religious sites, river and village tours, and natural scenic areas, as well as ecotourism at Phu Lori in Luang Prabang. They also suggest completing improvements at Kwangsi Falls, setting up management and ecotourism for Phu Lori, and expanding countryside and village tours.

Apart from the World Heritage site of Luang Prabang, tourists can also visit the surrounding areas, which offer various attractions such as scenic mountains, caves, waterfalls, and villages of a variety of ethnicities. However, well-organized ecotourism or village tours, originating from the town, are lacking. In order to plan tourism expansion in Luang Prabang, it is necessary not only to preserve the town but also to make more efficient use of existing tourism destinations and to establish new activities around the town.

4. METHODS

4.1 Design Details

Based on guidebooks and the results of a pre-survey, the well-known destinations are listed and the following six destinations are included as

Table 11.3   Description of tourism destinations

Destinations	Fee	Time/distance	Other features
Pak Ou Caves	8000 Kip	1.5 hours (boat), 25 km	More than 4000 Buddha images in the caves
Kwangsi Falls	8000 Kip	1 hour (*tuk tuk*), 32 km	Natural swimming pool and a public park for picnicking
Sae Falls	8000 Kip	25 min. (*tuk tuk*), 20 km	Not as high, but more pools than Kwangsi
Ban Phanom	0 Kip	20 min. (*tuk tuk*)	Cotton- and silk-weaving village; tourists can buy handicrafts
Ban Sang Hai	0 Kip	1 hour (*tuk tuk*)	Rice whisky village; tourists can buy handicrafts
Ban Chang	0 Kip	15 min. (boat)	Pottery village

Table 11.4   List of attributes

Attributes	Level
Tour price	$3, $5, $10, $30
Mode of transport	*tuk tuk*, mini-bus, bus, car
Pak Ou Caves	Visit, not visit
Kwangsi Falls	Visit, not visit
Sae Falls	Visit, not visit
Ban Phanom	Visit, not visit
Ban Sang Hai	Visit, not visit
Ban Chang	Visit, not visit
Trekking	Included, not included
Visiting an ethnic village	Visit, not visit

attributes for planning site choice: Pak Ou Caves, Kwangsi Falls, Sae Falls, Ban Phanom Village, Ban Sang Hai Village, and Ban Chang Village.[2] In this survey, subjects are given the basic information of these destinations, for example location and time required to reach and view them (Table 11.3).[3]

Table 11.4 lists all the attributes used in this survey. In the pre-survey, most tourists did not join any package tour and they had difficulty in finding transport to visit around Luang Prabang. To appropriately address this problem, that is, to recognize the tourists' preference for transport, transport is included as an attribute. Three levels are *tuk tuk*, mini-bus and car, which tourists usually use to travel to their destinations.[4] In order to examine the potential of alternative modes of transport, 'bus' is also included, as it is more comfortable and faster than travelling by *tuk tuk* or mini-bus and cheaper than by car.

The tourism development policy has proposed the expansion of tourism, which is based on natural scenic areas and ecotourism, and recommended the expansion of countryside and village tours (UNDP and WTO, 1998). In order to investigate these tourism potentials, 'trekking' and 'visiting an ethnic village' are also included as attributes. These activities are not provided but would be worth considering in any expansion of tourism.

There are $2^8 \times 4^2 = 4096$ possible profiles in total.[5] It is, however, hard to establish and use up all 4096 profiles in an experiment.[6] This chapter uses an orthogonal main effect design, in which attribute levels across alternatives are uncorrelated. This has the advantage of avoiding multicollinearity but, at the same time, it creates unrealistic profiles such as no destination and activity provided but at some cost. It is possible to delete these, but it is at the expense of losing the orthogonality of the attributes; this results in reduced statistical efficiency in estimating the preference for each attribute independently. In this study, therefore, statistical efficiency is prioritized and 64 profiles are created from an orthogonal main effect design.

4.2 Survey Details

Sampling was undertaken between 14 and 19 August 2001. A total of 159 questionnaire interviews were completed, and of these 153 were valid. The survey was undertaken at an airport, a bus station, a slow-boat pier, and a speedboat pier. In the questionnaire, first, subjects were asked about their demographic and socioeconomic characteristics, for example sex, age, nationality and annual income. The six well-known destinations around Luang Prabang were described in a colour photo panel. Then the problems in visiting these destinations were explained – limited provision of package tours and difficulty of finding a mode of transport. Finally, the six CE questions were asked. Three profiles were presented in each choice experiment, two of which were one-day package tours and the other was to stay in town without joining any tour, and subjects were asked to choose the best alternative among them (Figure 11.1).

Table 11.5 shows sample characteristics. Most subjects had already visited Luang Prabang (82 per cent).[7] More than 60 per cent were younger generation – in their twenties. It was in August, the summer holiday period,

Suppose local travel agencies provide several 'One-day tours around Luang Prabang'. Some tours will take you to a number of the main sightseeing destinations, and some will provide other activities. Tours run from 9 a.m. to 4 p.m. and include transport costs and entrance fees.

Which tour would you most like to join?

	Tour A	Tour B	No participation
Tour price	$5	$10	Do not join
Transport	*tuk tuk*	Mini-bus	either tour and only go
Main destinations	Kwangsi Falls Pak Ou Caves	Pak Ou Caves Ban Sang Hai Ban Phanom Ban Chan	sightseeing in the town
Other activities	Short trek Visiting an ethnic village		

Tour you would most like to join (check one): ☐ ☐ ☐

Figure 11.1 An example of choice experiment

and many students may have visited. Most of the subjects were international tourists; the majority were from France (17.0 per cent), the UK (14.4 per cent), and Japan (12.4 per cent). Luang Prabang is a well-known international destination, and WTO and UNDP (1998) reported that the majority of visitors to Luang Prabang in 1997 were French (22.2 per cent) German (12.6 per cent), Japanese (8.7 per cent), US (14.4 per cent), and Thai (5.8 per cent). It seems that more international tourists visited Luang Prabang than regional tourists.

5. MODEL

In the choice experiment approach, the utility function for an alternative *j* of each respondent *i* (U_{ij}) can be described as

$$U_{ij} = V_{ij} + \varepsilon_{ij}, \tag{11.1}$$

where V_{ij} is a systematic component, or observable utility, and ε_{ij} is a random component, or the unobserved idiosyncrasies of tastes.

Table 11.5 Sample characteristics

	No. of subjects	Share (%)
Valid sample	158	100.00
Leaving Luang Prabang	126	82.35
Arrived Luang Prabang	18	11.76
No answer	9	5.80
Sex		
Male	83	54.24
Female	69	45.09
No answer	1	1.30
Age		
Under 20	3	1.96
21–29	92	60.13
30–39	18	11.76
40–49	11	7.18
50–59	22	14.37
Over 60	5	3.26
No answer	2	1.30
Nationality		
Europe	73	47.47
Asia	31	20.26
Oceania	11	7.19
North America	29	18.95
Middle East	8	5.22
No answer	1	0.65

If individual i chooses alternative j from a set of alternatives, $J(1, 2, \ldots, m)$, when the utility for j is greater than the utility for others, k, we can present the probability of individual i choosing alternative j as follows:

$$P_{ij} = \Pr\{U_{ij} \geq U_{ik}\}$$
$$= \{V_{ij} - V_{ik} \geq \varepsilon_{ik} - \varepsilon_{ij}, j \neq k, j, k \in J_i\}. \quad (11.2)$$

McFadden (1974) demonstrated that if we assume that these random components in the utility function, ε_{ij} and ε_{ik}, are independent across alternatives and are identically distributed with an extreme-value (Weibull) distribution, then the choice probability, P_{ij}, is

$$P_{ij} = \frac{e^{\lambda V_{ij}}}{\sum\limits_{j=1}^{m} e^{\lambda V_{ij}}}, \quad (11.3)$$

where λ is the scale parameter. For this study, it is normalized to unity. This model is called the conditional logit model.

Parameters are estimated using maximum likelihood estimation. The log likelihood function is as follows:

$$\ln L = \sum_{i=1}^{n}\sum_{j=1}^{m}\delta_{ij}\ln P_{ij}, \tag{11.4}$$

where δ_{ij} is a dummy variable such that $\delta_{ij}=1$ if alternative j is chosen and $\delta_{ij}=0$ otherwise.

The observable utility (V_{ij}) is assumed to be defined by attribute vectors $(\mathbf{x})$ and tour price (p), or

$$V_{ij}(x,p) = \beta_p p + \sum_{j=1}^{m}\beta_x x_x. \tag{11.5}$$

The value of marginal change of the attribute j is expressed by

$$\frac{dp}{dx_j} = -\frac{\partial V_{ij}}{\partial x_j}\Big/\frac{\partial V_{ij}}{\partial p} = -\frac{\beta_j}{\beta_p}. \tag{11.6}$$

This is also known as implicit prices (Hanley et al., 2002).

6.   RESULTS

Since each of the 153 subjects answered six choice questions, the total sample size was 918. Table 11.6 presents the four estimation results using the conditional logit model: (1) the model including all attributes (Model 1); (2) the model removing some insignificant attributes, $p<0.1$, (Model 2); (3) the model including the number of destinations in an alternative with significant attributes (Model 3); (4) the model including alternative specific constants (ASC) for non-joining (Model 4).

The parameter for tour price measures the utility changes associated with increased expenditure. The parameter estimates show the expected negative sign and are significant ($p<0.01$) in the all models.

The parameter estimates of destination and mode of transport attributes indicate how utility changes when an attribute changes. All parameter estimates for existing destinations take the expected positive sign and are statistically significant ($p<0.1$). This implies that tourists preferred to visit any destination except for Ban Chang in Model 1. Since some guidebooks and web sites do not introduce Ban Chang, and the actual number of visits there is the lowest of all in the pre-survey, this destination may be less desired by tourists.

Table 11.6   Estimation results

	Model 1	Model 2	Model 3	Model 4
	Coefficient (*p*-value)	Coefficient (*p*-value)	Coefficient (*p*-value)	Coefficient (*p*-value)
Tour price	−0.051*** (0.000)	−0.050*** (0.000)	−0.050*** (0.000)	−0.052*** (0.000)
tuk tuk	0.188 (0.262)			
Mini-bus	−0.047 (0.738)			
Car	0.180 (0.295)			
Pak Ou Caves	0.541*** (0.000)	0.587*** (0.000)	0.601*** (0.000)	0.496*** (0.000)
Kwangsi Falls	0.313*** (0.003)	0.301*** (0.004)	0.315** (0.035)	0.210** (0.061)
Sae Falls	0.533*** (0.000)	0.558*** (0.000)	0.574*** (0.000)	0.497*** (0.000)
Ban Phanom	0.289*** (0.001)	0.280*** (0.001)	0.291** (0.011)	0.254** (0.002)
Ban Sang Hai	0.342*** (0.001)	0.342*** (0.000)	0.359** (0.020)	0.243** (0.021)
Ban Chang	−0.020 (0.859)			
Trekking	0.217** (0.045)	0.259** (0.012)	0.274* (0.059)	0.203* (0.053)
Visiting an ethnic village	0.170* (0.094)	0.199** (0.038)	0.216 (0.171)	0.100 (0.347)
The number of destinations			−0.013 (0.891)	
ASC (no participation)				0.399** (0.018)
Sample	918	918	918	918
Log likelihood	−866.232	−868.239	−868.230	−865.131
Corrected ρ^2	0.141	0.139	0.134	0.137
Prediction success (%)	55.7	56.1	56.1	55.8
BIC	907.165	895.528	898.929	895.830

Note: ***, ** and * indicate significance at 1%, 5% and 10%.

The mode of transport was included a dummy variable coded 1 for either *tuk tuk*, mini-bus, or car, and 0 for bus in order to investigate to what extent the potential transport, bus, is preferable to the other transport. None of the transport parameter estimates is significant ($p > 0.1$) in Model 1. This suggests that the mode of transport is not the most important concern for tourists, although this is normally an important factor in destination choice. Rather, their most important consideration is which site they can visit on their one-day tour. Tourists would choose a tour based on destinations rather than on mode of transport. It is also possible that subjects would not exactly recognize the difference among modes of transport, because the information regarding travel time is limited and no visual aids are provided, while existing destinations are explained using colour pictures.[8]

The coefficient on 'trekking' and 'visiting an ethnic village', the two new tourism potential activities, take a positive sign in Models 1 and 2 ($p < 0.1$). Judging from these, tourists seem to be interested in these activities. However, the parameter estimates of an ethnic village are insignificant in Models 3 and 4 ($p > 0$). Because no visual aid to these activities is provided, as for mode of transportation, respondents would find it hard to understand what these involve.

The subjects may prefer to visit (join) as many destinations (activities) as they can during the tour, no matter which destination (activity) they will actually visit (join). The number of destinations in the CE questions is included in Model 3, coded 1 if there is only one destination or activity, and coded 2 for two destinations or activities. The parameter is statistically insignificant ($p > 0.1$), and indicates that the number of destinations or activities does not affect their choice; rather they make a choice based on where to visit or what to do.

In Model 4, ASC for non-joining are included in order to test the *status quo* bias, which is coded 0 for no participation and 1 for choosing any alternative. If the parameter estimates of ASC are negative and statistically significant, this implies that the subjects prefer the *status quo*, in this case not joining any tour and only visiting the town. The result is, however, positive and significant ($p < 0.5$), which implies that they prefer visiting only the town to joining any tour and visiting around Luang Prabang. It strongly supports the potential of tourism expansion in the study area, however, indicating which destinations are preferred most by tourists.

As a criterion of model selection, the Schwarz Bayes Information Criterion (BIC) is used. The BIC of Model 2 is the smallest of all the models. The implicit prices for visiting existing destinations and joining new activities are calculated from equation (11.6), using Model 2 (Table 11.7). The 95 per cent confidence intervals of the implicit prices are also calculated using the methods of Krinsky and Robb (1986).

Table 11.7   Implicit prices (US$)

Pak Ou Caves	11.74 [8.12–15.89]
Kwangsi Falls	6.02 [2.54–9.50]
Sae Falls	11.16 [7.78–14.68]
Ban Phanom	5.60 [2.86–8.43]
Ban Sang Hai	6.84 [3.44–10.45]
Trekking	5.18 [1.91–8.60]
Visiting an ethnic village	3.98 [0.88–7.06]

Note: The numbers in brackets are 95% confidence intervals, obtained using the methods of Krinsky and Robb (1986) and based on 1000 random draws.

Pak Ou Caves had the highest value among all the existing destinations ($11.74), followed by Sae Falls ($11.16), Ban Sang Hai ($6.84), Kwangsi Falls ($6.02) and Ban Phanom ($5.60). Although Kwangsi Falls is a better-known destination than Sae Falls, according to guidebooks and the results of our pre-survey, the implicit price for Kwangsi Falls was lower than that of a similar resource, Sae Falls. Many subjects had already visited Kwangsi Falls, so they may have preferred another resource, Sae Falls, which most of them had not seen.[9] Moreover, while Kwangsi Falls is located 32 km outside town and requires one hour in travel time, Sae Falls is located only 20 km outside town and takes only about 25 minutes to reach.

Regarding the implicit price for the potential activities, trekking was $5.18 and visiting an ethnic village $3.98. These are significantly different from $0, but are not higher than those for existing destinations. This may be explained by self-selection of the sample and the sample size.

7.   SIMULATION

Using simple simulations, this chapter now considers planning for tourism expansion. Once coefficients are estimated, one can predict the probability that tourists will choose an existing destination or a new activity (hereafter called 'choice probability') if they are given only one chance to either visit anywhere or join an activity outside of Luang Prabang.[10] It is assumed that the utility of visiting any destination or joining any activity is derived from (1) cost of transport, (2) entrance fees, and (3) benefits received that are parameter estimates.[11] For example, the utility of choosing Kwangsi Falls is derived from $5.87 for the cost of transport, $0.94 (8000 Kip) for the entrance fee and $11.74 for benefits. Similarly, the utility for each destination is defined and the choice probability for each destination calculated.

Three simulations are tested. The first case is to consider the cost of trekking if the trekking is provided as a new activity. To keep the choice probability of the activity the same as that of the other existing destinations, how much is the cost of trekking: the cost of transport plus entrance fee? The second case is, similarly, about the cost of visiting an ethnic village. The last case considers what is the most preferred package tour in order to plan effective tourism expansion.

Case 1: Cost of a New Trekking Route

The choice probability is simulated when the cost to participate in trekking changed from US$1 to US$10. As expected, the lower the cost, the higher the estimated choice probability of trekking (Figure 11.2). When the cost exceeds US$3.5, however, the choice probability is the lowest of all destinations. This implies that the cost of joining a trekking expedition must be

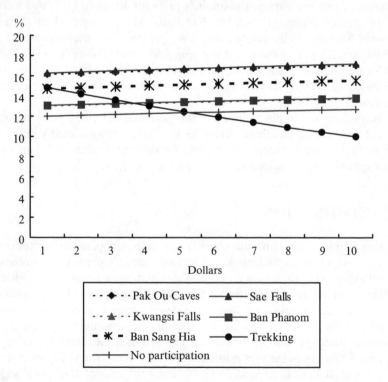

Figure 11.2   Choice probabilities of a trekking route

less than US$3.5 in order to keep its choice probability the same as that of other destinations.

Case 2: Cost of Visiting an Ethnic Village

Similarly, the choice probability of a village tour is estimated (Figure 11.3), and again, the lower the cost, the higher the estimated choice probability of the village tour. However, if the cost exceeds US$2.5, the estimated probability is the lowest of all destinations. This implies that in order to keep the choice probability for the village the same as for the others, the costs of visiting it must remain at US$2.5 or less.

Case 3: The Most Preferred Package Tour around Luang Prabang

Suppose that local travel agencies provide one-day package tours, and that tourists can visit two destinations during the tour. Since there were five

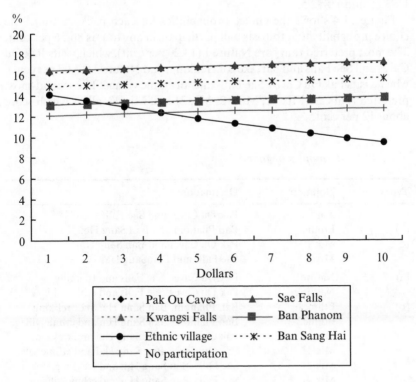

Figure 11.3   Choice probabilities of an ethnic village

existing destinations, ten possible tours can be provided. These are classified into three groups: (a) tours to enjoy natural environments ($n = 3$), (b) tours to enjoy ethnic culture ($n = 1$), and (c) tours to enjoy both ($n = 6$). We also considered another alternative, that is, no participation, which implied staying in the town of Luang Prabang.

The choice probabilities of tours in each category are calculated and the tours with the highest probability are regarded as representative of each category. Because there are relatively many tours of type (c), the highest two probabilities of tour (c) are chosen. Then, the choice probability is re-estimated when these four representative tours and no participation are given. The four out of the ten possible tours are shown in the upper portion of Table 11.8, which are labelled Nature, Ethnic, Mix 1 and Mix 2.[12]

The next step is to consider the most preferred package tour when the new activities, trekking and a village visit, are included. Based on the re-estimation results, the four tours are extended to eight package tours (the lower portion of Table 11.8). To represent the costs of trekking and visiting an ethnic village, we used the results from Case 1 and Case 2, which were US$3.5 and US$2.5.

Figure 11.4 shows the choice probabilities for each package tour. The choice probability that tourists will participate in any tour is 86.56 per cent. The most preferred tours are Nature 1 (13.20 per cent), which visits Pak Ou Caves and Sae Falls and partakes of trekking, and Nature 2 (13.07 per cent), which visits Pak Ou Caves, Sae Falls and an ethnic village. The second-most preferred tours are Mix 11, Mix 12, Mix 21 and Mix 22, all of which score about 12 per cent.

Table 11.8   Examples of tours

Types	Notation	Destinations
(a)	Nature	Pak Ou Caves and Sae Falls
(b)	Ethnic	Ban Phanom and Ban Sang Hai
(c)	Mix 1	Pak Ou Caves and Ban Sang Hai
	Mix 2	Sae Falls and Ban Sang Hai
(a)'	Nature1	Pak Ou Caves, Sae Falls and trekking
	Nature2	Pak Ou Caves, Sae Falls and ethnic village
(b)'	Ethnic1	Ban Phanom, Ban Sang Hai and trekking
	Ethnic2	Ban Phanom, Ban Sang Hai and ethnic village
(c)'	Mix 11	Pak Ou Caves, Ban Sang Hai and trekking
	Mix 12	Pak Ou Caves, Ban Sang Hai and ethnic village
	Mix 21	Sae Falls, Ban Sang Hai and trekking
	Mix 22	Sae Falls, Ban Sang Hai and ethnic village

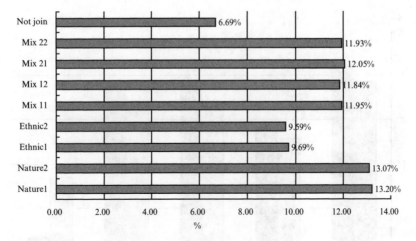

Figure 11.4   Choice probabilities of package tours

Finally, in order to show the potential of new tourism activities, the choice probabilities of these eight tours and no participation are compared to those of four package tours and no participation, which are described in Table 11.8. To show the result simply, eight package tours are re-integrated into four tours. For example, Nature 1 and Nature 2 are grouped into Nature. The comparison is shown in Figure 11.5. The choice probabilities of all tours increased, while the probability of no participation decreased by almost 50 per cent, from 13.44 per cent without new activities to 6.99 per cent with new activities. Thus tourism potentials such as trekking and village tours can be expected to expand tourism in Luang Prabang.

8.   CONCLUSIONS

This chapter applies the CE approach to planning tourism expansion in Luang Prabang, Laos, while most studies have used TC and CV approaches. The CE approach provides significant information about tourist preference, not only for existing destinations but also for non-existing activities. This kind of study is of benefit to policy makers, as it helps them to decide how to extend tourism development, what kinds of activities are expected to be established, and to determine the costs of participating.

The results of the survey indicate that Pak Ou Caves and Sae Falls have the highest values of all existing destinations. Regarding non-existing activities, the subjects are interested in trekking and visiting an ethnic village;

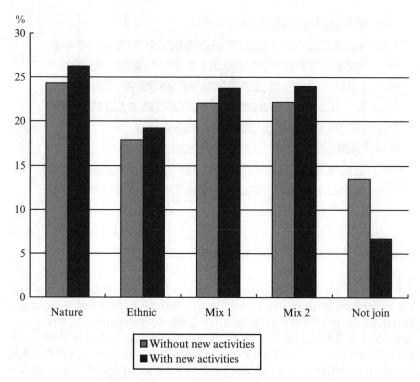

Figure 11.5   Comparison of choice probabilities of package tours

however, these do not score higher than existing destinations. The survey also finds that tourists are interested in visiting not only the World Heritage site, but also other destinations around Luang Prabang, which indicates the potential of tourism expansion.

The simple simulation investigates how the cost of participating in new activities, trekking and a village visit, changes the site choice. The most preferred package tour is also examined by the simulation. It shows that participation in any tours is increased by combining popular existing destinations with the new activities.

This study uses the conditional logit model, whose important property is independence from irrelevant attributes (IIA). This property implies that the introduction or removal of other alternatives does not affect the relative choice probabilities of the two main alternatives. If the IIA hypothesis is violated, more complex statistical models are necessary such as the random parameter logit model and the nested logit model (Train, 2002). Some literature (Hanley, 2002; Schwabe et al., 2001) has tested the

IIA assumption and found a violation. This chapter can also test this assumption in order to determine whether the conditional logit model is appropriate.

The framework of this study can be extended to consider seasonality and potential tourist effects. The value of natural resources like waterfalls would be flexible because of their seasonality in Laos. Because of the large amount of precipitation during the rainy season, it is expected that the landscape will vary with the seasons, and so will tourism values. Therefore further studies should consider the effect of seasonality on natural resources. This study can also be extended to consider the preferences of potential tourists. All respondents in this survey are tourists who have actually visited Laos and not people who have not been to Laos. These people could be potential tourists once new tourism activities are provided and well-organized tours are available.

NOTES

1. Tourism development can, however, also negatively affect natural environments and socio-cultural conditions. In cases where the natural environment is used as the tourism resource, that is, ecotourism, environmental conservation may be promoted. However, large-scale or mass tourism development may generate various environmental problems, such as soil erosion, water pollution and landscape degradation. Tourism also often drives the citizens to change traditional lifestyles and culture as a result of expanded income distribution due to increases in the number of tourists and capital flow. This chapter does not discuss these negative impacts but focuses on economic benefit; the former are beyond its aim.
2. Before the survey, the author interviewed some international tourists about site destinations which they had visited in Luang Prabang.
3. The exchange rate was US$ = 8500 Kip in August 2001.
4. A *tuk tuk* is a three-wheeled taxi, also called a *jambou*, which can hold six to eight passengers.
5. A profile is a set of attributes that includes tour price, main sites and other forms of recreation described in our survey.
6. The design using all profiles is called a 'complete factorial design'. As the number of attributes, levels, or both, increases, the design grows exponentially in size and complexity. For profile design, see Chapter 4 in Louviere et al. (2000).
7. Since the survey was undertaken at an airport, a bus station, and at piers, most of the tourists who were waiting for departure agreed to the interview. However, tourists who had just arrived did not agree to the interview because they were in a hurry to start their travel. Sampling bias, therefore, may exist, but it could not be tested because of too few arriving samples.
8. In the survey, subjects were only told the travel time to their destination by *tuk tuk*, except Pak Ou Caves (Table 11.3). No information was provided on other transport.
9. As another explanation for this result, a government officer commented that because the area around Kwangsi Falls is rather modernized it might be less attractive to tourists, who may prefer the natural environment of Luang Prabang.
10. The results in Model 2 are used in this section judging from BIC, therefore the choice probability of visiting Ban Chang is not considered.

11. For cost of transport, the mean cost of transport in the pre-survey is used.
12. The choice probabilities of these tours were 11.49 per cent (Nature), 8.43 per cent (Ethnic), 10.40 per cent (Mix 1) and 10.49 per cent (Mix 2).

REFERENCES

Adamowicz, W., Swait, J., Boxall, P., Louviere, J. and Williams, M. (1997), 'Perceptions versus Objective Measures of Environmental Quality in Combined Revealed and Stated Preference Models of Environmental Valuation', *Journal of Environmental Economics and Management*, **32** (1), 65–84.

Bauer, H.H., Huber, F. and Adam, R. (1999), 'Utility-Oriented Design of Service Bundles in the Hotel Industry, Based on the Conjoint Measurement Method', in R. Fuerderer, A. Herrman and G. Wuebker (eds), *Optional Bundling: Marketing Strategies for Improving Economic Performance*, Heidelberg and New York: Springer, pp. 269–95.

Boxall, P.C., Adamowicz, W.L., Swait, J., Williams, M. and Louviere, J. (1996), 'A Comparison of Stated Preference Methods for Environmental Valuation', *Ecological Economics*, **18** (3), 243–53.

Carmichael, B. (1992), 'Using Conjoint Modeling to Measure Tourist Image and Analyze Ski Resort Choice', in P. Johnson and B. Thomas (eds), *Choice and Demand in Tourism*, London and New York: Cassell Mansell, pp. 93–106.

Chase, L.C., Lee, D.R., Schulze, W.D. and Anderson, D.J. (1998), 'Ecotourism Demand and Differential Pricing of National Park Access in Costa Rica', *Land Economics*, **74** (4), 466–82.

Fix, P. and Loomis, J. (1998), 'Comparing the Economic Value of Mountain Biking Estimated Using Revealed and Stated Preference', *Journal of Environmental Planning and Management*, **41** (2), 227–36.

Font, A.R. (2000), 'Mass Tourism the Development for Protected Natural Areas: A Travel Cost Approach', *Journal of Environmental Economics and Management*, **39** (1), 97–116.

Fredman, P. and Emmelin, L. (2001), 'Wilderness Purism, Willingness to Pay and Management Preferences: A Study of Swedish Mountain Tourists', *Tourism Economics*, **7** (1), 5–20.

Gan, C. and Luzar, E.J. (1993), 'A Conjoint Analysis of Waterfowl Hunting in Louisiana', *Journal of Agricultural and Applied Economics*, **25** (2), 36–45.

Goldberg, S.M., Green, P.E. and Wind, Y. (1984), 'Conjoint Analysis of Price Premiums for Hotel Amenities', *Journal of Business*, **57** (1), Part 2, S111–S132.

Hanley, N., Wright, R.T. and Koop, G. (2002), 'Modelling Recreation Demand Using Choice Experiment: Climbing in Scotland', *Environmental and Resource Economics*, **22**, 449–66.

Herath, G. (1999), 'Estimation of Community Values of Lakes: A Study of Lake Mokoan in Victoria, Australia', *Economic Analysis and Policy*, **29** (1), 31–43.

Krinsky, I. and Robb, A.L. (1986), 'On Approximating the Statistical Properties of Elasticities', *The Review of Economics and Statistics*, **68** (4), 715–19.

Lockwood, M., Tracey, P. and Klomp, N. (1996), 'Analysing Conflict between Cultural Heritage and Nature Conservation in the Australian Alps: A CVM Approach', *Journal of Environmental Planning and Management*, **39** (3), 357–70.

Louviere, J.J., Hensher, D.A. and Swait, D.S. (2000), *Stated Choice Method: Analysis and Application*, Cambridge: Cambridge University Press.

McFadden, D. (1974), 'Conditional Logit Analysis of Qualitative Choice Behavior', in P. Zarembka (ed.), *Frontiers in Econometrics*, London: Academic Press, pp. 105–42.

National Tourism Authority of Lao PDR (2001), *2000 Statistical Report on Tourism in Laos*, Vientiane.

Navrud, S. and Mungatana, E.D. (1994), 'Environmental Valuation in Developing Countries: The Recreational Value of Wildlife Viewing', *Ecological Economics*, **11** (2), 135–51.

Pruckner, G.J. (1995), 'Agricultural Landscape Cultivation in Austria: An Application of the CVM', *European Review of Agricultural Economics*, **22**, 173–90.

Schwabe, K., Schumann, P., Boyed, R. and Doroodian, K. (2001), 'The Value of Changes in Deer Season Length: An Application of the Nested Multinominal Logit Model', *Environment and Resource Economics*, **19** (2), 131–47.

Train, K. (2002), *Discrete Choice Methods with Simulation*, Cambridge: Cambridge University Press.

UNDP and WTO (1998), *National Tourism Development Plan for Lao PDR: Final Report*, Vientiane.

Xue, D., Averil Cook, A. and Tisdell, C. (2000), 'Biodiversity and the Tourism Value of Chanbai Mountain Biosphere Reserve, China: A Travel Cost Approach', *Tourism Economics*, **6** (4), 335–57.

Index

The following abbreviations are used in the index:
SITE: Small Island Tourism Economics
TSA: Tourism Satellite Account